Colleen Pierce

TAG THE PRESENT:
A CHARIOT YEAR

By
Colleen Pierce

Tag the Present

Tag The Present: A Chariot Year

Copyright © 2022 Colleen Pierce

All rights reserved. No part of this book may be reproduced or transmitted in any form or by any means, electronic or mechanical, including photocopying, recording, or by any information storage and retrieval system without the written permission of the author or publisher, except where permitted by law.

ISBN: 979-8-218-00317-3 (paperback)
Library of Congress Number: 2022920497

Edited by: Colleen Pierce and Williams and Richardson Publishing

Cover Design by: Elizabeth Smith and Williams and Richardson Publishing

Author Photo by: Lauren Edinger

More information about the book and the author at *colleenpierce.com.*

Colleen Pierce

Most of life is spent waiting for the juice.
~ Marty Miller
This one is for you, Marty.
Juice. FINALLY!

PROLOGUE

My family has a crazy tradition of writing silly gift tags, something we call *"To-Froms"*. This wonderfully entertaining ritual began during my childhood in Wisconsin with my paternal grandmother, Thelma, who recycled the covers of old Christmas cards and used them for tagging her gifts. She would scribble our pet names in black marker across the glittery scenes, and it was equal shares of gaudy and endearing.

Over the years, content of the tags took precedence over presentation, as we elevated the creation of *To-Froms* into a hilarious, tattling artform. Every ridiculous, outlandish, funny, preposterous thing anyone said or did would find its way onto a gift tag. Wacky tagging was loads of fun and the *To-Froms* soon became the highlight of our gift exchanges, causing more fuss than the gifts themselves. Our gatherings would find us rolling with laughter recalling the sordid tales behind the tags, poking harmless fun at getting caught in ludicrous situations, the gifts beneath the *To-Froms* secondary to their tags and temporarily forgotten.

As is natural with all meaningful traditions, the giving of whimsical gift tags traveled with me from Wisconsin to Florida, becoming a ritual when I grew my own family, and eventually encompassing my entire village of friends, neighbors and even co-workers. Most of them in turn have started writing silly *To-Froms* in their own families. The practice is good, clean fun and wildly contagious.

As an author pining to write a book, one would have thought the idea of using the stories behind the nutty tags would have been a no-brainer. But, no, it took my sister-in-law to have the *"Aha Moment"* at one of our Christmas celebrations. My niece had just read aloud the comical *To-From* on a package from me, when my sister-in-law leapt out of her chair, grabbed me by the shoulders, looked me square in the eyes and shouted, "Colleen, the tags! Oh my God, the tags! It's perfect! You need to write about the tags! The tags!" Then, crazed with excitement, she ran over to the garbage and started ripping the tags off the discarded gift wrap, stuffed the wad of tattered *To-Froms* into my hand, and hovered over me with wide eyes.

Dumbfounded, I stared at the handful of scraps for a long moment before I understood. When the lightbulb came on, I realized she was absolutely correct. This off-the-wall tradition of contriving ludicrous tags held all our best stories. Hundreds upon hundreds of them. Our history. These sparsely worded quips scribbled on a gift tag encapsulated the hilarious and touching vignettes of our lives, the unexpected lessons, and the sometimes seemingly insignificant events that weren't insignificant at all. The stories behind the tags were the epicenter of memories we held dear, our laughter and our joy. Indeed, they begged to be in a book, lest our history be forgotten.

Unfortunately, crafting a book took more than just a great idea and a giant helping of desire. It required time, and time was a commodity I just didn't have as a house-poor wife and mother working full-time. And as the years marched on, I had even less. Soon my daughter went off to college and there was tuition to pay. I got divorced. The cost of living increased faster than my salary as an engineering document specialist, so I had to take a part-time waitressing gig on the weekends. I hardly had enough time for sleeping, much less writing, so sadly the book, which was never far from my mind, waiting and self-perpetuating with *To-Froms* multiplying with every passing year, became nothing but a pipe dream.

My daughter graduated, I went from an apartment into a house, I quit the part-time job, and life settled down. With a razor-thin modicum of time in my coffers, I excitedly took *Tag the Present* off the back burner and began writing with gusto. But, as the saying goes, we make plans and God laughs. For me, His laughter came in the form of a beautiful, perfect granddaughter. Without regret or a second thought, my book got reshelved and writing time was redirected into becoming a gloriously doting Gigi.

Being Gigi has been an incredible experience, ranking right up there with being Mom, these two titles tying me to an extraordinary, magnificent girl. Assuming these roles were my life's purpose, I made peace with the fact that I would never pen the book that I had longed to write for nearly two decades. I was good with it; I had an amazing little bundle of joy to chase around, and my life was happy and full. At least, that's what I thought. I didn't hear God laughing again.

His laughter this time came in the form of a number that began appearing about a year ago. Or at least that is when I first noticed something fishy was going on. When the madness began, every day for a week I found myself looking at the clock when it was 12:34. Sometimes it was 12:34 AM, sometimes it was 12:34 PM, but more often it was both. Then, as if that wasn't freaky enough, like rabbits, the 34s multiplied.

The following week, 34s no longer confined themselves to the 12 o'clock hour. Instead, thirty-fours appeared everywhere at every hour. During a meeting I would glance at the clock at 11:34 AM, return from lunch at 1:34 PM, pack up to go home at 5:34 PM, and leave the gym at 7:34 PM. I would wash up for bed at 9:34 PM, wake up to pee at 1:34 AM, or 2:34 AM, or 3:34 AM, and hit the snooze on the clock at 5:34 AM. I'd randomly open the door of the microwave and see the timer still had 34 seconds left. I'd get 34 cents back in change at the store. My Amazon order came to $34.34, and even the sticker on my granddaughter's toy phone said it was 12:34. I couldn't escape them or ignore them, and it was maddening!

When this continued for two more weeks, exasperated, I googled the phenomenon. I typed *What does it mean if I constantly see the number 34*, and seconds after I clicked the enter key, two pages of links popped up for *Angel Number 34*. I stared at the screen in disbelief. Angel Number 34? Intrigued, I began clicking the links, and as I read through each one, I became equal shares of excited and horrified. With little variation, all said the same thing: 1) my angels were trying desperately to send me a message, 2) the message was to finish my book, and 3) they would be kicking my ass until I got it done. Angel Number 34 was God's ball pein hammer for wordsmithing. Like some twisted version of Thor.

Angel Number 34 is a brutal taskmaster. Its 34s are unrelenting little suckers that will not be deterred and from which I cannot hide. They are like a genie I unknowingly let out of the bottle that refuses to go back in. They poke me like jolts from an electrified prod the minute I begin to slack. Throughout this writing project, I have seen 34s each and every day, several times a day, in a myriad of forms. And God help me when I don't get time to write. The 34s will haunt my every move and fighting back is futile. One week Angel Number 34 had me up checking the clock every single night at 34 minutes passed every hour. Every. Single. Night. By Sunday I was so exhausted I canceled everything on my schedule so I could spend the entire day writing and get some rest. This plan worked for the night, but at 8:34 AM Monday morning when I walked into work, Angel Number 34 was back in action.

If I'm being honest, I must admit that I am ever so grateful for the motivation from Angel Number 34. *Tag the Present* has been a long overdue fulfillment of a dream. I hope you will enjoy reading the result as much as I enjoyed writing it. It has been cathartic, a true labor of love.

So, let's get to it, shall we? If you are still confused about the *To-Froms*, soon you will not be. This book will allow you to follow me through a calendar year, as I create new tags or am reminded of the great ones of the past. You will see how everyday life provides everything needed to take up the *tag game* with your own family and friends. No special talent is required. However, I will offer some notes of advice and a word of caution: 1) so as not to forget one precious moment, scribble down epic quotes and events as they happen, or make notes in your phone or capture them in pictures, 2) be prepared to get addicted, as the *To-From* game is completely irresistible, and 3) remember that tags are meant to be playful and fun, never hurtful or mean-spirited.

There! That's everything you need. Come, let's appease Angel Number 34 and tag the present. Let the journey begin!

Chapter 1: JANUARY

It was a new year. Time to dust off resolutions, create new goals, freshen up closets and get things done. My friend Clark, who was like a brother to me, was all about the New Year's restart. This year, since the weather in Florida was particularly warm, Clark decided he would begin with gusto by replacing the screens on his back porch, which had suffered irreparable damage during the previous year's *Great Unsuccessful Squirrel Assassination Attempt in Underpants*, a brutal skirmish that Clark had unfortunately lost. The squirrel had been a formidable foe and Clark's screens had been reduced to fringe in the ensuing battle. Hard fought, as it was.

Having already purchased materials for the screen repairs in anticipation of his New Year's project, Clark went about assembling everything in his matter-of-fact way on the front lawn. When satisfied, he headed to the back porch with a roll of screening and his favorite measuring tape. Clark was a measurer—"measure twice, cut once," were words he lived by.

When he arrived at the back porch's side screen, Clark laid down the roll of screening and surveyed the job that awaited him, feeling a tinge of excitement for all the measuring it would entail. Stretching out a length of metal measuring tape and about to place it against the porch's metal post is where we find him, frozen and glaring unhappily at the upper corner of the porch's eave. With a harrumph and a grimace, Clark breaks his stare, throws down his measuring tape, and heads back to the garage in a huff. He has gone to gather a cleaning arsenal: ladder, broom, Mr. Clean, bucket, sponge, rags, hose, trash can, the works, because he has noticed the eaves are infested with spiders. Clark hates spiders.

After several minutes spent crisscrossing the garage and marching in and out of the kitchen, Clark returns to the back of the house, arms straining under a mountain of supplies, which he unceremoniously throws in a pile on the lawn and scowls. His war face. Gathering his resolve, Clark takes up the broom and, holding it as far from his body as possible, he swipes at the webs in the corner of the eave. He is immediately seized by a fit of willies and drops the broom with a display of jazz hands, writhing and wiggling in arachnophobia disgust. Not one of his prouder moments. But colorful.

Sucking up his manhood, Clark tries again, swiping aggressively at the webs and then shaking the daylights out of the straw broom on the lawn. He reasons a good pounding will pitch out clingers-on, and he is careful to choose a patch of grass far enough away to ward off any crawl-back attempts. For additional insurance against survivors, Clark stomps the hell out of the grass with his tennie-flips. A very impressive display.

When Clark reaches the end of the first eave, where it intersects with the house, he opts to use the bedroom window ledge for his broom-beating, certain the bristles are loaded with the enemy. He immediately regrets this decision, as a slight breeze kicks up and wafts the cloud of dust and web debris back into his face. Horrified, Clark throws down the broom, swats imaginary creepy things out of the air and doubles over to rake his fingers violently through his half-inch of brown hair. This is accompanied by a piercing, off-pitched squeal in High C. His war call.

As Clark contemplates retrieving the broom to continue, he spots a large wasp nest in the corner of the window. Relieved to have a diversion, he once again strikes off to the garage to get the bug spray. Wasps were far more his wheelhouse.

He locates the can of Raid and strides confidently back to the porch to unleash a poisonous fog. Clark is back in *The Zone*. He is The Man.

Returning to the bedroom window, Clark shakes the Raid can violently and snaps off the lid. He lifts the can into the air and points it at the dangling hive. He takes aim and is just about to fire, when a dark, moving shadow on Clark's right shoulder catches his attention. He freezes with foreboding terror, and droplets of sweat gather on his brow. As slowly as possible, he turns to look at his raised shoulder and comes eyeball to eyeball with a giant black widow spider. It is the size of a Volkswagen!

Clark leaps into the air, launches the spray can onto the roof, pirouettes across the yard and swipes madly at both shoulders. Not satisfied the purification is complete, he whips off his shirt, throws it on the ground, stomps it with both feet and runs wildly for the house, waving his jazz hands and screaming like a girl. Clark doesn't stop until he is under a scalding hot shower and nearly kills himself when he mistakes a stray dollop of purple body wash for another eight-legged foe. Poor Clark. He is wrecked.

About an hour later, when he meets me at a local sports bar to watch the Green Bay Packer v. Miami Dolphins football game, Clark is still a mess. His face is flushed, he has a twitch and when I ask him what the matter is, the story comes spilling out with more passion and flourish than I'd ever seen him garner. Truthfully, I found it a little sexy. Although it might have been the pheromones from all the body spray and three showers. It was a heady mix.

At the sports bar we settle in with some chicken wings and beer, and Clark begins to feel better. My Packers score a touchdown, and I hoot and holler with delight. I excuse myself to the ladies' room as VISA's newest commercial comes on, poking fun at the latest touchdown dance. I watch the sports bar's giant screen enthralled, as clips are shown of various people performing a *Porch Spider Shuffle*: shoulder wipe, shoulder wipe, chicken dance, repeat.

I look at Clark, who knows where this is going.

"We shall not speak of it!" he shouts at me with a warning finger.

Returning his smirk, I do a backwards *Porch Spider Shuffle* all the way to the loo, and when the door shut behind me, I whipped out my phone and typed on the notepad under "CLARK":

> *To: Dances with Spiders*
>
> *FROM: Would love to have been a spider on the wall*

I was stoked. The *To-From* would be perfect on the back of a VISA gift card for Clark's birthday. Just a week into the new year and I already had my first tag!

****

At home the following evening, I contemplated my own desires for the new year. Slowly finishing the last spoonful of Cheerios that was my dinner, I stared at my laptop bag in the corner and sighed. I felt like I hadn't been on a real date since Reagan was in office, and if I had to listen to my girlfriend Stephanie nag me once more about getting back out there, my ears were going to bleed. It was time. The moment had come to attempt online dating. Eichhhhh. I felt nauseous.

Convincing myself this was for research purposes only, I began to peruse the online dating sites. How hard could this be, right? Hours passed. Eyestrain set in. Finally, unable to stomach one more shirtless bathroom mirror selfie, I congratulated myself on being single, slammed my laptop shut and went to bed.

The next day, after a trouncing from Stephanie, I tried again. This time, thankfully, I stumbled across the fun and interesting profile of a guy named Phillip. Gathering my courage, I held my breath, and with one eye closed, I clicked the icon to contact him. Instantly, a firewall popped up notifying me I could not continue until I registered and created a profile.

"Seriously?" I shouted at the screen as I pounded my foot on the floor like a toddler. Then I grumped off to the kitchen for a snack.

After much deliberation and two calls to Stephanie (one just to bellyache and the other for some direction), I entered the required information and fashioned a profile that was both charming and delightful, despite some nonsense about enjoying first date breakfasts (Stephanie's idea). Allowed to move forward after completing my profile, I composed an enchanting email to my new man, Phillip, pushed the send button, and began planning my future wedding.

Phillip never replied.

A week passed with my laptop gathering dust on the sidebar in my kitchen. Then on Saturday night, I booted up the dating site and began another surfing expedition. That's when I stumbled upon Jack. His bio was simple but witty, his picture wasn't hideous, and he could capitalize and punctuate. This was a rarity. The only drawback was that he was a New York Jets football fan. This was a problem. Brett Favre had years ago gone to the Jets, and as a lifelong Packers fan, I found that whole situation deplorable.

I wrote Jack a message that said as much, figuring I might as well be honest from the start. I doubted I'd hear back from him. And I didn't.

Flash ahead two Sundays. I had just watched the Packers get knocked out of the NFL playoffs and was washing up for bed when my computer lit up with an email message.

JACK: Hey, Cheesehead...did you see that debacle? We both went down in flames!

I looked at the message and the email address with confusion. Who was Jack? Obviously, he was someone I knew from home (even though I had lived in Florida for over twenty years I still thought of Wisconsin as "home"), because he had called me Cheesehead. But I couldn't recall knowing anyone from Wisconsin named Jack. Annoyed, thinking it was some weirdo or stalker, I went to sign out just as the lightbulb came on: Jack was that online dating guy! Yep, that was him, Jets fan Jack. I was both excited and pissed. Two weeks to reply? Really? I contemplated waiting two weeks to write him back, if I even wrote back at all, but then caved.

COLLEEN: Really...that's your opening line? Wow, you're quite a Casanova, Jack. Smooth.

There, I thought. That ought to get rid of him. But, as I again went to close my laptop, another message came in.

JACK: Right?! Okay, so your Packers are out. Favre is out. My Jets are out. When are we going out for breakfast?

Interesting. A sense of humor and snarky. I loved snarky. Game on.

COLLEEN: *Whoa, slow down, cowboy! I must find something redeeming for you being a Jets fan. Punctuation will only get you so far.*

JACK: *Cowboy? Don't ever call me a Cowboy! I loathe Dallas! Now my feelings are hurt. I'm very sensitive.*

Okay, that had me outright laughing. It had been a long time since I'd enjoyed this kind of playful banter with a man. My ex-husband and I used to carry on like this before we allowed life to suck the fun flirtation out of our marriage, and I didn't realize how much I'd missed it. Jack was intriguing and I wanted to meet him. But I needed to be safe, too. There were far too many nut jobs out there.

Recalling some parameters about dates with men one met online, I did a mental review: meet them in public during the day, let someone know where you're going, and have an escape plan. Okay, I could do this. I took a deep breath and plunged ahead. Stupid Stephanie. This was so outside my comfort zone.

COLLEEN: *Lucky for you your Dallas comment won me over. How about breakfast Saturday? Time? Place?*

JACK: *I get to pick the place and time? This is a setup, isn't it? You're hooking me in. Then, if we match up, it'll be the last decision I ever make.*

COLLEEN: *So, do you want to go to breakfast, or don't you, Jack? Seriously, your courting skills need work.*

JACK: *I do want to have breakfast! Really, I do! But I have to be in North Carolina for my brother-in-law's 50th birthday party Saturday night. I am trying to get sick or wreck my car before that. If I manage to do either one, I'll get with you.*

Ah, there it was. Stephanie had warned me about being duped, like on that *Catfish* show, where the handsome guy was in reality a 13-year-old hormonal teenager corresponding with you on his laptop from the basement while his parents were asleep. I was definitely being catfished. I prided myself on being astute, signed off and went to bed.

The next day I signed onto my email after dinner to find a new message waiting from Jack. I decided I would open it for the sheer purpose of acquiring enough information to report him to the authorities. Doing my civil duty, and all.

JACK: I know you're upset that I'm busy this weekend, but please, can't we do it another time? Another time soon?

COLLEEN (with a sigh): I suppose. Lucky for you I have a thing for pancakes.

JACK: I love pancakes! It's decided: I'll crash my car and get out of the trip. So, where's your favorite place for pancakes?

COLLEEN: There you go again rushing me, Jack.

JACK: Oh, sorry, m'lady. Ok, I'll ask slower: Where's…your…favorite…place…for…pancakes?

Wow, this guy was good: trying to figure out where I hung out. Nope, I wasn't taking the bait. I'd flush him out!

COLLEEN: Guess.

JACK: Hmmm, I don't want to blow it. I'll guess The Blueberry Muffin.

Whew, that was a relief. I hadn't been to The Blueberry Muffin for years. If he was a stalker, he wasn't a very good one.

COLLEEN: Sorry, you blew it.

JACK: See, I knew it! Let me try again. Good thing you kinda like me. I've grown on you, like a fungus.

COLLEEN: Don't be fresh, Jack – it's so unbecoming.

JACK: LOL, I wasn't being fresh. Ok, back to pancakes. Where should we go?

COLLEEN: Guess.

JACK: Last time I guessed, I was wrong. If I keep getting it wrong, my chances diminish. How about a hint?

COLLEEN: Hint. Sigh. Go back and read my profile, Jack. I'll give you three minutes only because I'm feeling generous. On your mark, get set, go.

Silence ensued as Jack must have gone back to review my profile, which said, "…don't ask me to make the plans. Step to the plate and take some initiative!" And while he was busy doing that, I called Stephanie and filled her in. In reply I got an unexpected earful: "If he's willing to actually meet you, he's not catfishing! Meet the man!"

"Fine!" I retorted. "If I wind up floating in the ocean with a belly full of pancakes, it's going to be all your fault!" But she'd already ended the call. Pouting, I saw the next message from Jack come in with 20 seconds to spare.

JACK: Got it! Okay, so there's a place over here called Sun on the Beach. We'll go there. Sound good?

COLLEEN: *There you go. Finally. Geesh, that was about as easy as herding cats. P.S. Sun on the Beach is my favorite.*

JACK: *Great! So, it's pancakes at Sun on the Beach, Saturday morning, not too, too early, 10:00-10:30AM?*

COLLEEN: *What, you're not a morning person, Jack? How sad. Strike two.*

JACK: *Aww, c'mon! I work Friday night till 3AM.*

Till 3 AM? Oh, hell no. His profile said he was retired. The catfish flag went up again. Stephanie was going to get a big, fat, "I told you so!" Provided I lived to tell about it.

COLLEEN: *3 AM?! Sorry, Jack, I don't date hookers.*

JACK: *I'm not a hooker, but I'm flattered. Hotel security. So, what do you say: 10 AM on Saturday? Pretty please?*

Ugh, a respectable late-night job. Foiled again! Not only was stupid Stephanie beginning to sound right, but I was going to have to meet this guy and the thought was terrifying!

COLLEEN: *Fine. If I must.*

I logged off and went to bed. My dreams were filled with hookers in hotel security uniforms fishing for catfish using pancakes for bait.

The next day I came home for lunch. I worked just a few blocks from where I lived, so I did this quite often. This day, as I sat down with a salad, I logged onto my laptop to see if I had a new message from Jack. I did.

JACK: *So, how's your day going? I'm trapped at home, waiting for a furniture delivery. They said between 1:30 and*

4 PM. That means it will show up tomorrow sometime. Other than that, I cleaned some chairs, mopped the floor, gonna clean my bathroom, and I sit here eating animal crackers looking up stuff to pass the time.

It was harder and harder to find a flaw with this guy. He did housework, had enough scratch for new furniture and took interest in my day. How annoying.

COLLEEN: Day is busy. Trying to keep my engineers from burning the place to the ground. I love my job, I love my job.

JACK: You're not one of those engineers who have that thing in their shirt pocket with the 15 pens and pencils are you?

COLLEEN: Absolutely. I love those things!

JACK: Great. At least I know what to get you for Valentine's Day.

COLLEEN: and, I wear one of those cool blue lab jackets with my name embroidered over the pocket, safety glasses, and steel-toed boots. Shall I wear them to breakfast on Saturday?

JACK: Sure. I'm certain that will get us a table right away (eyeroll). Just as long as you don't wear one of those cheese hats you Packer people wear.

Again, I was outright laughing at our snarky exchange. This was too easy.

COLLEEN: Oh, that's a spectacular idea! I have three cheese hats – one just for formal events. I shall wear it, too.

JACK: I believe you.

COLLEEN: Did I mention I've gained a couple dozen pounds since that picture on my profile was taken?

JACK: Did I mention my picture was taken right before I got out of jail?

What? A piece of lettuce fell from my open mouth as I read and reread the words on the screen. He had been in prison? For what?! My mind went down every shady lane imaginable.

JACK: I was kidding!

Was he, though? Was he?

COLLEEN: No worries – my brother's a cop and my cousin has ties to the mob. What's your shoe size?

JACK: No comment. And FYI, hint: the only time I was ever in a jail, I was dropping people off.

COLLEEN: OMG! Are you a cop?

Though I was relieved he wasn't an axe murderer, nonetheless my heart fell. I'd married a cop, did not enjoy being the wife of a cop, and had subsequently vowed to never get involved with a cop again.

JACK: Chill, my sweetest. Retired cop.

Well, now what to do? My fingers hovered over the keyboard as I contemplated. I guess there were worse alternatives.

COLLEEN: Lord, what I won't do for good pancakes.

JACK: Let's analyze this: You wear a pocket protector, walk around with goggles on all day, on Sundays during the Fall you wear a triangle of cheese on your head, while I, being the upstanding citizen I am, was a cop, and you say, "What I won't do for pancakes?"

COLLEEN: *Yeah, you're right. You don't deserve me.*

As I chuckled proudly at my witty comeback, the clock on the microwave caught my eye. It read 12:34 PM, meaning I was already late getting back to work. I bolted to the sink with my dishes, rinsed my hands, grabbed my purse, and bolted out the door without being able to type another word to Jack. And after work I went right to dinner with friends, didn't get home until late, and headed right to bed without checking emails.

Early the next morning I had to rush to make a 7:30 AM meeting, so I didn't get a chance to check my home email then, either. After my meeting I was horrifically busy, wound up working straight through lunch, and didn't get home until after 7 PM. When I finally sat down with my dinner and booted up my laptop, there was an email marked URGENT from Jack.

JACK: *What happened, did they confiscate your computer? I haven't heard from you ALL day.*

COLLEEN: *Is that your way of saying you missed me, Jack? How sweet.*

JACK: *You busted me.*

COLLEEN: *By the way, I thought you were going to North Carolina this weekend?*

JACK: *I said I was looking for an excuse not to go. You are it!*

COLLEEN: So, let me get this straight...you gave up going to your brother's 50th birthday to have pancakes with some strange, no, let me rephrase that, "delightful" woman you met online, who weighs 987 pounds, wears a pocket protector, and runs around in goggles and a cheese hat? Maybe I've been watching too many documentaries on serial killers, but your last name isn't "Ripper" is it?

I paused to congratulate myself on my ingenious reply. Nothing so appealed to the writer in me as having a crafty comeback. It was like creating a perfect *To-From* that had a play-on-words feature. I was a word addict, and puns were my addiction.

JACK: No, Jack is just a nickname. My real name is Bond, James Bond.

Oh, snap, Jack's comeback game was strong! I didn't know whether to applaud him or be pissed. My wounded ego won out.

COLLEEN: Great, a comedian. Strike three. Okay, I'm out. Goodnight, Bond.

And with that, knowing full well I wasn't out, nor was he, I signed off for the night in mock exasperation, betting there'd be a message from Jack waiting in the morning. I wasn't wrong.

JACK: Good morning! I knew you couldn't resist me. Ummm, in your profile, you mentioned a banana split with a cherry on top. Well, why wait till Saturday? How about that banana split later tonight?

Tonight?? I panicked. I hadn't washed my hair, or shaved my legs, or done any of the girly things one does for a date. Don't men know these things? It's a whole process. I couldn't meet my future husband with hairy legs and greasy hair! I had to think fast.

COLLEEN: *Sorry, now serving number 386. You'll have to wait till Saturday unless I have a cancellation.*

JACK: *What? I got skipped – I'm number 385! How did that happen???*

COLLEEN: *You snooze, you lose, Jack.*

JACK: *No, someone cut in line!*

COLLEEN: *Jack, stop whining. Did you really think a witty, pancake-eatin', cheese-hat-wearin', smack-talkin', football-lovin', looks-like-she-should-be-sumo-wrestlin', fine piece of woman such as myself would stay on the market for long? Be real, Jack.*

JACK: *I know. I pinch myself every day wondering if this is just a dream.*

COLLEEN: *As well you should.*

JACK: *So, to recap, we are meeting Saturday at 10 AM at Sun on the Beach, right? But…wouldn't IHOP be better for pancakes?*

COLLEEN: *Oh, for Pete's sake, Jack, no! I have my heart set on Sun on the Beach. I'll be there at 10.*

JACK: *Oh, alright. See 'ya there. But who's Pete?*

COLLEEN: *He's Number 386.*

I finished out my week, got primped for my pancake breakfast, and on Saturday morning an hour before we were to meet, I took one last opportunity to mess with Jack. I couldn't help myself.

COLLEEN: Hey, Jack...I changed my mind.

JACK: You changed your mind? No pancakes? Why? What'd I do?

Then, I unexpectedly lost my internet connection and couldn't get it back. For ten minutes there was no signal at the house. When I finally did regain reception, there were three desperate messages from Jack.

JACK (#1): Ok, I gotta ask again, Why?

JACK (#2): I kinda thought we had a fun banter going on here. What happened?

JACK (#3): Sorry you changed your mind. All I can do is wonder why. Why? Well, whatever. Have a good day. Mr. Sad Face.

Oh, geeez, now I felt bad. I would have to do some quick damage control. I typed as fast as my fingers would fly.

COLLEEN: Calm down, Bond, my internet peaced out for a sec. And just because I'm in the mood for eggs, doesn't mean you have to be so melodramatic! Geeez Louise, Jack, can't a lady change her mind?

JACK: Honey, darling, dear... are we going or not? I haven't even met you yet and you're driving me crazy!

COLLEEN: Yes, of course we're going. Or at least I am. A lady of my profound stature doesn't miss a free meal (you are paying, aren't you?). I'll be there shortly. If you're a no-

show, I'll have them bill you. Now, please, Jack, stop whining.

JACK: I'll be there. And I don't whine!

I met Jack at the appointed place and time and presented him with an envelope containing a gift certificate for a banana split with this *To-From*:

> *TO: Jumpin' FlapJack*
>
> *FROM: The Dairy Queen*

Jack was delighted and chuckled mightily over the witty tag. We settled into easy conversation but knew before the syrup hit our hotcakes that the certificate would go unused. The internet can't account for whether there will be chemistry or not, and alas, for us there just wasn't any. Story of my life. I offered to split the bill, but Jack insisted on treating, and so we said our "was nice to meet ya's" and that was the end of it.

****

The evening after my breakfast with Jack, I threw myself down on the white leather couch in my best friend Phyllis's apartment. Her couch was an oddly shaped thing, long and curved up on the ends, reminding me of the banana seat on my first Schwinn bicycle. While Phyllis went to the kitchen to fetch us some wine, I dished on my failed breakfast date with Jack.

"So, Phyllis, I'm zero for one already. Not the way I wanted to start the year," I said, sliding down the leather seat and talking to the ceiling.

"Cheer up! Whatever's in store for you this year, it's guaranteed not to be boring," Phyllis exclaimed with a giggle. True that. My life was many things, but boring was not one of them.

Phyllis set the bottle of Pearl and Stone on the coffee table and went to retrieve two glasses while I grabbed the remote and switched on her TV to find a music channel. As I remotely flipped through the selections, I was struck with an idea. I sat bolt upright in my seat.

"Phyllis! You know what we forgot to do on New Year's? We forgot to check on what tarot year we're having!"

Phyllis is my very own personal astrologer. She is an expert on anything new-age, like tarot or numerology. Back in the day when she lived in New York, Phyllis had attended workshops taught by some of the greats like Deepak Chopra and Brian White. Her depth of knowledge on the metaphysical realm seemed endless, and we often teased her about having a book, a workbook, and a cassette tape on every holistic subject imaginable. "We" consisted of me and our other two besties, Beth and Sinjin, at whose house we would gather every New Year's Eve. For six years running, the four of us would ring in the new year by enjoying belly laughs over delicious fondue as Phyllis read our tarot cards and computed what tarot "year" we were headed into. By plugging our birth date and the upcoming year into a formula, Phyllis could determine the tarot card that corresponded to our new year. She would then read the prediction of what that year beheld from a book she had purchased at one of her infamous workshops. We would "oooo" and "ahhhh" at each other's horoscopes like a bunch of kids. This past New Year's, however, we had been joined by several other friends and calculating our tarot year had slipped our minds. Until now.

"You're right! How could we have forgotten to do our tarot years?" Phyllis cried, already heading down the hallway to retrieve her signed copy of *Tarot Constellations; patterns of personal destiny* by Mary K. Greer, otherwise known to us as "The Book".

I had known The Book even longer than I had known Beth and Sinjin. Nearly two decades had passed since Phyllis and I had first met and became friends while moonlighting as servers at a local country club. After we had finished working the New Year's party for the country club members that first year, Phyllis had pulled The Book out of her bag and placed it on the stainless-steel worktable in the club's kitchen, so she could "do my numbers". That year she had calculated I'd be having a Hangman's Year, which according to The Book would be fraught with challenges and obstacles. And true to form, it had been 365 days of just that. A total nightmare.

Barely able to contain herself, Phyllis came running back into the living room, hands full, asking breathlessly, "Now when's your birthday again?" She donned her readers and peered at me over the top. This is exactly how it played out every year. You had to love Phyllis!

I gave her my dates and waited while she scratched away on a scrap of napkin, muttering quietly for what seemed an eternity before finally declaring, "Seven! You're in a Chariot Year!"

"Fabulous!" I declared ecstatically. "What's a Chariot Year?"

Chuckling, Phyllis flipped to "Chariot Year" in her Greer reference, glasses perched low on her nose, looking like a schoolmarm ready to give a lesson. She was in her element. She held up the book and began reciting:

"THE CHARIOT YEAR: In the Chariot Year you act and move ahead on the decisions made in the Lovers Year...," she began.

"Wait, last year was my Lovers Year? Crap, I totally squandered that one!" I blurted, making us snort with laughter and have to recompose. I topped off our wine as Phyllis continued.

"This year you will need to work on self-control and self-discipline. If you give free rein to your instincts and emotions, they may tear you apart causing you to lose your temper or worse, like experiencing an accident possibly literally acted out in your automobile/chariot."

"What?" I cried, as she momentarily paused to meet my open-mouthed accentuated gasp with her own before jumping back in.

"You act as a warrior in a Chariot Year, with a need to serve and protect others, or to champion a cause, but if you drive too hard, you could become belligerent and egotistical, running roughshod over everyone else."

Again, we exchanged an exaggerated gape.

"People often travel or relocate in a Chariot Year, you must retain your sense of roots to feel secure in a possibly turbulent year. Being near water this year can help you relax those touchy emotions and calm your jangled nerves."

After the last sentence, Phyllis whipped off her readers and looked at me with her mouth agog. "Wow," she gasped.

I sat in stunned silence trying to digest the words. Self-control and self-discipline? Instincts and emotions tearing me apart? Turbulence? Running roughshod? Breakdown? Car accident? Good Lord!

I shot Phyllis the stink eye, and she shrugged in apology. "Well, at least we live near the beach, so 'being near water can help you relax'," she conceded, making air quotations as she said the words. Phyllis always looked for the bright side. Kindness was her nature.

"If I don't kill myself getting there," I said with a harrumph. "You know how crappy my driving is!" To this she just nodded. I'd nearly killed us both several times.

"Now is not the time to agree with me!" I chided.

"Oh, c'mon, there's a lot of good stuff in here. It's gonna be a great year! Now, let's do my numbers," she went on, scribbling numbers on the same scrap of napkin, anxious to change the subject. "Oh, my goodness, I'm in a Lovers Year!" she cried. Lucky dog.

"Of course, you are," I replied in mock disgust. "To think I pissed away my Lovers Year really chaps my hide. I demand a do-over! Does The Book say anything about a Mulligan Year?" To that, Phyllis just chuckled. I made a mental note for her birthday tag:

> *TO: Lovers Year*
>
> *FROM: I demand a Mulligan Year!*

Then I headed home in my chariot: an aging red Chevy Cobalt, which I not-so-lovingly called The Blood Clot. I patted the dashboard and spoke to her as I drove, "Well, it looks like we were going to have one heck of a year, old girl." Nothing new. For either of us.

Tag the Present

****

The following Sunday I rose early, showered, dressed, and attended breakfast at the corner diner with Phyllis and a handful of our other friends. We did this every Sunday. Called ourselves the *Breakfast Club*. We had been meeting for Sunday morning breakfast for so long I couldn't remember what I did with myself on Sunday mornings before I knew them all. Must have been terribly boring for them.

I arrived late, as was typical, and they gave me grief for it, also typical. Over omelets and pancakes we chatted, laughed, and I filled them in on my upcoming project.

"So, this being my Chariot Year, today I'm going to wax my chariot," I announced gaily. Everyone at the table was momentarily silent, then all erupted in loud guffaws of laughter. My friend Arthur choked on his mimosa, which threatened to come out his nose.

"I need new friends," I cried with a scowl, another Sunday morning tradition. More chortles of laughter ensued from the ungrateful lot.

After breakfast, in keeping with my vow to wax my car, I stopped at Auto Zone to pick up cleaning supplies and a buffer. I had always wanted a buffer. This had been a staple on my Christmas list every year since 1985, but nobody ever purchased me one because they said they were afraid of what I might accidentally do with it. Well, that ended today. Today I was buying a buffer. If I inadvertently hung myself with the cord and the mailman found me rotting in my carport on Monday, it would be nobody's fault but my own.

Walking through the aisles of Auto Zone gave me the same thrill as I felt while perusing the long rows of Home Depot.

"Guy stuff" was fascinating. All those shelves of boldly colored labels fighting for my attention and endless containers of goop and goo with technical sounding names. It was like being in a science lab. I loved science labs. Well, except for that one time in Chem II when I accidently poured a beaker full of chemicals down the sink thinking it was water, causing a reaction that flushed every toilet in the school and called out the fire department in the middle of a frigid Wisconsin ice storm. The ladies' room on the second floor never did work right again. And the poor school secretary who was in there at the time probably didn't either.

I grabbed a cart and made my way to the auto detailing section, scanning the colorful shelves of products. Orderly lines of bottles and jars, tall and short, large and small, skinny and fat all puffed out their little chests to present their labels. *Pick me! Pick me!* they all seemed to shout. A tall crimson bottle caught my eye and I bent to get a better look. *Mothers California Gold Brazilian Carnauba Wax.* Brazilian? For my car? I snorted out a laugh and was seized by a wave of the church giggles. With one hand on my belly and the other still gripping the handle of the cart, I held back great waves of laughter. I had no idea what "carnauba" meant, but just the thought of announcing to the Breakfast Club that I had given my car a Brazilian was worth the money. Into the cart went the Mothers, a bottle of Rain-X, some tire spray and a bundle of microfiber cloths.

When I got to the floor mat section, it was not so fun. Back and forth I went with my cart, finally abandoning the buggy in the middle of the aisle. There were too many choices. Carpet or rubber? Or carpet with rubber? Preformed or cut your own? Charcoal or black? Clear? Logo or plain? Expensive or cheap? Ribbed or smooth? (Ribbed or smooth? Was I buying car mats or condoms?) After ten minutes of indecision, I slogged empty-handed back out to my car, pulled up one of my old foot mats, carted it back into the store and found the closest match: a carpet/rubber combo in charcoal grey with a reinforced patch by the accelerator pedal so the stiletto heels I wore to work wouldn't easily rip a hole (I guess it was rather like picking out condoms). Pleased with my selection, I moved on. It was buffer time!

I doubt anyone had ever been more excited about purchasing an electric buffer. I was seized by the same feeling I had when Mom took me to Treasure Island to pick out my first nap mat. I ogled the multitude of handled discs, half-exposed in their peekaboo cardboard boxes and was astounded at the selection. Oh, just look at them! Did I want 8" or 10"? Handle on side or handle on top? Craftsman, Black & Decker, or an off brand? All, please. I wanted them all! In the end I settled on a 10" ROB (Random Orbital Buffer) with a top handle. Go big or go home. This was gonna be great!

Back home in my carport I assembled my purchases, got out my bucket, unwound my hose, and waved over my neighbor Don to show him my new toy. He meandered over with his big German shepherd, Duke.

"What 'cha got there, Blondie?" Don asked, looking over the array of car products.

"I finally bought a buffer! Look," I said, hoisting the contraption up to his face, "isn't she a beauty?"

Don took the buffer from me and turned it over appreciatively, making me feel like a proud mother, then handed it back to my waiting grasp. I was grinning like a fool.

"Yep, that'll do a nice job! So, when did you get the boat?" Don asked.

"A boat? I don't have a boat," I said, confused.

"You mean to tell me you're planning to use that buffer on that tiny car of yours? Colleen, that one there is meant for boats! Big ones!" And with that he let out a mighty roar of laughter.

"Well, I guess I'll just get done all that much quicker, then. Move aside now, I have work to do. Gotta give The Blood Clot its first Brazilian!" I exclaimed proudly, holding up the bottle of wax in one hand and swiping the fingers of my other hand under the label, like I was modeling it for the *Price is Right* showcase. Don looked up with tears in his eyes and was crippled with another wave of belly laughter.

"Girl...," was all he could get out before being seized by a fit of smoker's cough. He gave me a half-wave as he headed back down the driveway to his house, only getting to the curb before having to catch his breath, unable to stop an onslaught of cough-laced laughter and head shakes. No respect.

A half-hour later, I stood before my squeaky-clean car, reading the instructions on the buffer package, which stated to sit the buffer levelly on its handle and fit the terry cloth bonnet over the top of the foam pad, ensuring the outer edge of the bonnet's elastic fit securely over the edges. Okay, easy enough. I sat down cross-legged in the carport and got started.

Placing the buffer as instructed, foam side up, I laid the bonnet, which looked like a shower cap, in the center of the foam pad and fitted one end over the edge. I then turned the buffer around to stretch the bonnet over the opposite edge, but the elastic only gave enough to make it halfway. Pulling the buffer closer to me, I secured the handle between my knees and yanked and pulled with all my might, but the bonnet elastic would not stretch. I needed more leverage.

Standing and planting my butt squarely against the trunk of my car, I secured the buffer handle between my feet with the bonnet-covered end against the ground this time. Taking a power-lifting stance, I grabbed hold of the bonnet's free end and began wrestling it over the top of the foam. Only marginally successful, I had to regroup and try again. And again. And again. By the time I was done, I was on all fours, sweat streaming down my nose into a mascara-streaked puddle on my carport floor while I panted and wheezed like Don's dog, old Duke. From across the street came a peel of laughter from Don, who was watching me from the shade of his oak tree where he had pulled up a lawn chair and gotten a beer. I hoisted the bonneted buffer in the air and jabbed it towards Don.

"I am victorious!" I cried. Don laughed so hard I feared he might cough up a lung.

Filled with breathless anticipation, I smeared a dollop of Mothers Brazilian wax on the car's hood and plugged in the extension cord for the buffer while I waited for the wax to dry. Finally, the moment had arrived. Excited as Clark Griswold when he threw the switch on his Christmas lights, I pressed the button on the buffer. The contraption sprang to life with a deafening *BWAHHHHH* and vibrated so violently it nearly shook every tooth out of my head. Holy cats!

Trying to control the mighty beast, I grabbed tight to the handle as I placed it as gently as possible on the dried patch of Mothers Brazilian. The buffer immediately took hold and away we went: up over the length of the hood, across the top of the quarter panel and straight into the carport wall. Watching the whole spectacle, Don began laughing so hard he nearly fell out of his chair. My only consolation was that I couldn't hear him over the buffer.

Opting to try it again rather than hear Don's *I told you so*, I assumed a firmer stance and attacked the remaining spot of dried Mothers with more determination. That worked better, but this was not how I had envisioned this scenario playing out. This was way too taxing and not at all fun. Stupid Chariot Year.

An hour and two Don beers later, I was spent and sore, but The Blood Clot had a shine worthy of an ocean liner, and I had a *To-From* for Don's Christmas banana bread:

> *TO: Who needs cable when your neighbor is giving her car a Brazilian?*
>
> *FROM: Wielder of a big 10-inch*

Never again, though. I retired the buffer to my shed, and that's where it has been ever since.

****

I read an interesting article online just recently about siblings. Apparently, new research suggests that siblings have as much influence on a child's development as the parents. When my daughter reads this, I will take another ration about how I deprived her of a well-rounded childhood by not giving her a little brother or sister. In reality I am not the one to blame; she can blame her Uncle Sean for her unfortunate fate.

I have only one sibling, a younger brother, Sean. His birthday is the end of January and this year I got him a long overdue gift: a new Winnie the Pooh bear. I wrapped the bear in a letter of apology with this *To-From*:

> *To: Baby Brat*
>
> *From: Driven Pooh-icidal*

Five years apart, Sean and I fought tooth and nail, 24/7, 365 days a year from the moment my parents brought him home. Prior to his arrival, I was blissfully happy basking in my parents' undivided attention. That ended the second he crossed the threshold, and I spent the entirety of my childhood letting him know my displeasure. And he spent the entirety of his letting me know he was my parents' favorite.

Anybody with a sibling must agree that no other person on the face of the earth, except for perhaps a spouse, has the innate ability to irritate the snot out of you by simply breathing, nor can effortlessly work you into such a frothing, venomous frenzy over absolutely nothing. This was certainly true with Sean and me. We had our sibling arsenal honed to perfection, he was always running in tears to Mom brandishing the Baby Card, and me retaliating with "Baby Brat, Baby Brat" in that special tone that can only be heard by younger brothers and dogs.

Our loathing went on fairly harmlessly for many years until there came a day that Sean pushed me clean over my kid edge. I cannot recall at this time what crime of his I found so heinous as to commit Pooh-icide, but it would be over 50 years before I would feel guilty enough to seek atonement by buying him a new Pooh bear and proffering my sympathies.

Okay, I'll admit in advance my sibling retaliation on that day was harsh and a wee bit much, but I was only about 10, so I wasn't strong enough to hoist him over the toilet for a swirly, and a wedgie just wouldn't cover it. Therefore, I did what I thought to be the next best thing: I seized his coveted Winnie the Pooh bear, chopped it into sizable bits, and flushed it out to sea in the manner of its namesake. I was delightfully successful, except for the head, which clogged the commode and nearly caused a flood.

I probably would have gotten away with the dirty deed had I left it at that, but I got greedy. I fished the dripping Pooh head out of the toilet and was deciding upon my next move (good thing I hadn't yet seen *The Godfather*), when Mom came along and caught me red-handed.

Unfortunately, corporal punishment wasn't frowned upon back then, so I got my backside tanned but good. And thereupon was the defining moment I made a mental note to never, ever give my child a sibling. Hell hath no fury like a female scorned, no matter the age.

So, reflecting upon our younger days, I would have to say the sibling influence article holds a modicum of truth. The Pooh-icide incident alone may have been what set my brother on the path to becoming a cop and seeking justice for victims of heinous crimes. Either that, or he knew he could extract retribution for decades by relishing in pulling me over. Which he does. Every chance he gets.

Chapter 2: FEBRUARY

This morning in Florida I woke up to frost forming on my bedroom window. For real. It was awful.

Everyone that lives in cold country, such as my home state of Wisconsin, thinks Florida never gets chilly and has no seasons. Well, you cold country people are full of bean dip. Our Florida winters might not have snow, but the temps dip low enough that snowflakes could form and because of Florida's high humidity, the wind bites just as deeply as it does in the Midwest. Thankfully, though, the Florida cold doesn't last but a handful of days, reverting back to balmy breezes after less than a month, so I'm cool with it. (*Like what I did there?*)

Now, as for whether your blood gets thinner when you move to warmer climates, I cannot say, but after 35 years in the Sunshine State, I am completely acclimated. Up North friends and family say I am a disgrace to my Wisconsin heritage, as evidenced by finding me carrying a jacket even during the dog days of summer, running for a sweater and mittens when it gets below 70°F, and when the temps dip into the 40's, forget about it; I'm miserable!

So, this morning when I awoke, teeth chattering as our Florida weatherman excitedly blathered about it being 36°F, I seriously contemplated calling in sick to work. Just the thought of stepping out of a hot shower onto the cold bathroom tile brought on a wave of Wisconsin Winter post-traumatic stress. I mentally calculated how many remaining vacation days I had banked as I reached for my phone, already deciding that however low the number was, staying warm in bed buried beneath the covers would be worth burning a sick day. My boss was probably even expecting the call. I'd done it before.

Then, mid-dial, I remembered I had a fabulous new sweater in the most gorgeous shade of tiffany blue stashed in my closet. I'd found the beautiful pullover misplaced among the summer clearance at ROSS the past August and hadn't yet had a chance to show it off. Fishing it from the hanger and holding it up to me in the mirror, I felt its velvety softness and beheld its lovely color, causing me to hang up the phone. Donning the spectacular garment would be worth venturing out into the arctic blast. What can I say, I am a slave to fashion.

Another thought that crossed my mind was the fun of seeing what my engineering compadres would be wearing. Their cold weather clothes from days of yore did not ever disappoint. As a documentation specialist working almost entirely with men for over 15 years, I had seen it all. Though brilliant of mind, these guys had fashion sense that would give Tim Gunn from *Project Runway* a coronary. Clothes so ugly even the moths wouldn't eat them.

Resolute now in my decision, I braved the cold after-shower bathroom floor tile, slipped into my lovely new blue sweater, bundled up like a sausage, and headed out. I was already late, but doubted anyone would notice, so I stopped to grab a coffee. I am late for work so often I think if I was on time three consecutive days in a row, the planets would align, the four horsemen of the Apocalypse would mount up, God would float down on a pink fluffy cloud, and the world would end. My birth was the only thing for which I can recall being early, and even then, I made my mother wait 27 hours for my arrival. She has resented my tardiness ever since.

At work I share an office space with Doug, a young, witty, up-and-coming industrial engineer that I bonded with at hello. With his shock of blonde hair and mischievous smile, Doug could pass for a grown-up version of Dennis the

Menace. He has a magnificent, dry sense of humor, and we trade barbs and pot-shots throughout the day. Our endless badgering and belly laughter has gotten us in trouble so often that our killjoy *There Will Be No Fun at Work* boss gave up trying to silence us. Instead, the boss moved his desk to a closed-door office in the farthest corner of the department, leaving Doug and me in our shared cubicle to pester each other at will, which we are delighted to do. Fortunately, we are both masterful at our jobs, which is undoubtedly the only reason we are allowed to keep them.

Scurrying down the hallway of work, heels clicking on the terrazzo tile below me, I burst through the double doors of my office trying to juggle my coffee while simultaneously wriggling out of a wool jacket, mittens, and scarf. When I reached my desk, I unceremoniously threw my pile of outerwear atop it and turned to greet my mate. The sight of him stopped me in my tracks. He had on the most ridiculous hat I had ever seen. I couldn't decide whether to laugh or take flight.

"Douglas, what on earth is on your head?" I blurted, aghast, reaching out cautiously to inspect his peculiar headwear.

Doug batted my hand away with a wide sweeping gesture without taking his gaze from his computer screen. "What? It's from Nepal. It's yak," he said, like everyone owned one. Or should.

"Nepal yak? Or should I say Nepalese? Nepalean?" I laughed so hard I choked on my own spit and began to cough and hiccup.

Doug's hat was truly a sight. It was a wool knitted cap, crocheted perhaps, black with big white snowflakes, lined in powder blue satin, ill-fitting with two oddly shaped ear flaps, each flap with its own long black and white braid for use as a chin tie, and a third braid that came straight off the top. I'm thinking the last braid was for decoration rather than function, but I was afraid to ask. Every time I looked at Doug in his technicolor headdress, I broke into giggles, which threatened to send coffee spewing out my nose.

Undaunted by my stares, Doug sat at his desk typing away in his ridiculous hat, resembling some twisted version of Heidi. When I felt composed enough to contain my fluids, I ventured back into the fire.

"So, Doug," I asked, "When were you in Nepal?"

"I wasn't," he replied while continuing to tap on his keyboard. "I bought this off a street vendor in New York when I was visiting, and the weather turned ugly. Only cost me 10 bucks!" Pride in the last statement made him break his concentration to look at me with a wide grin.

I gave him two thumbs up, unsure how else to respond, as I was quite sure genuine Nepalese yak must be far more expensive than a ten spot. My brain danced with visions of its actual roots, which was far more likely to be a shady operation in New York City's back alley, where half-naked black and white tabby cats roamed about yowling in the cold. And about that time, I sneezed a dozen times in succession and my eyes began to itch, confirming my suspicions. I was deathly allergic to cats. No way this hat wasn't cat.

Later in the day, the headdress abandoned on our shared office file cabinet, I got a text from Doug. He had gone across town to work in our sister building in Palm Bay and needed a list of information he insisted I had, which I didn't.

DOUG: Dude! C'mon! You really don't have the list?

COLLEEN: *No, Doug, I do not have your list. You had it last, not me.*

Just to confirm I wouldn't get caught in an *I Told You So*, which was the worst with Doug, I took a quick sweep of our office looking for the list and came up empty.

DOUG: *I don't believe you. Work wife, you're holding out on me! I hate it when you do that. Fork over my list!*

COLLEEN: *Douglas, darling, I do not have your list. Truly do not have. Sorry, my sweet.*

DOUG: *I know you have it, wife! You gave it to someone else, didn't you? That's it, you're cheating on me. I want a divorce!*

COLLEEN: *Oh, please, you know you can't live without me; I'm delightful!*

DOUG: *So, are you asking me to stay with you?*

COLLEEN: *That depends. If we break up, do I get the Nepalese yak?*

Curious and alone now with the yak hat, I picked it up to have a closer look and was immediately seized by another sneezing fit. Yep, definitely cat.

DOUG: *Yeah, no! You should have read the fine print – the hat's in the pre-nup, which is probably stapled to the back of the list. And for the record, it's Nepalonean!*

That did it. In the manner only Doug could manage, he hit my funny bone, crippling me with giggles. I had just refilled my coffee, which went cascading down the front of my beautiful new blue sweater as I let out a chuckle at the same time as I was gripped by another sneezing fit. Stupid hat! I reached for paper towels to dob up the mess, only to discover the list Doug had been looking for. It had been on top of the file cabinet under his silly hat. I emailed Doug and told him I'd leave the list on his desk, which I did with this *To-From*:

> *To: The Yak in the Hat*
>
> *From: Get rid of the hat or I want a divorce!*

****

The following evening at a birthday dinner for my fabulous friend Beth, I regaled everyone with the tale of Doug and his yak hat. They loved it!

"Seriously, you should have seen this thing," I told them. "The ear flaps with those braids! Who knew it was so windy in Nepal?" I joked. Another round of laughter and head shakes ensued.

The birthday gathering, an intimate group of my closest pals, gathers every New Year's Eve. We are the Fab Four: Phyllis, Beth, Sinjin and me. We differed in personality, physical appearance, and background, yet complemented one another perfectly. We drew on each other's strengths, appreciated rather than envied our friends for their superpowers, and had become tight as family. We were each other's cheerleaders, besties, and safety nets.

Phyllis, the same Phyllis who determined I was in a tarot Chariot Year, was our Fab Four Matriarch. She was a New York Italian, complete with accent and hand gestures. She'd tried countless times to teach me how to do the renowned New York "forget about it" expression with the palms up hand motion but was forced to finally forget about it for real. It just wasn't part of this Midwest girl's DNA. Every time I attempted the movement, my hands would gravitate to chest level and look as though I was performing the derogatory motion for big breasts. Something everyone found endlessly entertaining.

Phyllis had never met a cat she didn't like and had several with whom she shared an apartment. She relished all things Medieval and had furnishings and decorations that one would envision King Arthur had possessed. Her flowing black curls fell to her waist and would have looked perfect under one of those tall, conical Renaissance hats with the veil that flowed out of the point.

Phyllis was an herbalist, a quality that served her well as an aesthetician. She gave the world's best facials, always knowing what combination of serums, moisturizers, masks, and rejuvenators was needed for her clients' lackluster skin. After an hour with Phyllis, one walked away with the blush and softness of a newborn.

But of all her many qualities, it was Phyllis's gentle kindness for which we loved her most. Phyllis had a heart of gold. She put others before herself to a fault, was the first to call and bring soup if someone was sick and made everyone a homemade cake for their birthday in their favorite flavor. The only reason I can figure she never married was there was never a man that thought himself worthy. I do believe they were right. Phyllis is a rare gem.

Sinjin and Beth were the Fab Four's Marrieds. Married to each other, this was a second marriage for them both, and the second time around was definitely the charm. They were that golden couple from high school that everybody envied, and even at 50 they still looked the part.

Sinjin was a muscular hulk of a dude with massive, broad shoulders and a penchant for plants. He could grow anything. One night after we four had enjoyed lychee fruit for dessert at our favorite sushi restaurant, Sinjin took the pits home and grew lychee tree seedlings for Phyllis and me. Sinjin presented them to us at our next get-together, a potted plant each, with detailed care instructions to guarantee we could enjoy lychee fruit from our own tree for years to come. Phyllis's cats ate hers and mine suffered death by dryer vent after I chose an unfortunate spot for transplanting. I am apparently as good at growing things as I am at New York hand gestures.

Besides having a green thumb, as a gifted engineer, Sinjin can talk quantum theory and all manner of science jazz the rest of us merely pretend to understand. He works on secret projects in his in-home lab and humors us by asking our opinion on simple stuff, like which fluorescent paint color on an LED bulb looks most like a firefly when lit. That's about all we can handle, and he knows it.

But as imposing as Sinjin is, he is just a big ole' softie. He gets cold when the weather drops below 70°F, has a passion for anything Polynesian, dances hula, makes us girls fresh leis from homegrown plumerias and orchids, and can pack a storage shed like nobody's business. He's great to have around for lifting heavy stuff and loves to be our protector. He gives me hope that chivalry is not dead.

On the flip side, his beloved bride Beth is as tiny as Sinjin is big. Petite, blonde, and light-footed, Beth also dances hula, which is where she met Phyllis. When Beth came to Florida from Pennsylvania several years ago, Phyllis was in the hula group she joined, and just like when Phyllis and I met at the country club, it was friends at first sight for them, too. Beth then introduced Phyllis to Sinjin, and Phyllis introduced them both to me, and the rest, as they say, is history.

Beth is the Fab Four's Martha Stewart. She's a gifted interior designer, incredible cook, accomplished seamstress and delightful hostess. She's one of those people I really want to dislike because she's so bloody stinkin' perfect, but she's as sweet as she is talented, so I just can't help but adore her. It's so annoying.

Beth's gentle, loving demeanor is irresistible. She laughs easily and spreads kindness like fairy dust. She's Tinkerbell in the flesh, and we swear she was transported to us straight from the 1950s. Everything about the 50s is Beth. She gravitates to that era of design and fashion, and I could totally see her in a poodle skirt and saddle shoes, ponytail swinging. Whenever I need a shot of wholesome enthusiasm, it's Beth that I call. She can find the upside of anything and has the patience of a saint.

That leaves me. What do I bring to the Fab Four table? I've often wondered that myself. To the best of my knowledge they rely on me for entertainment. The Fab Four *Fool*. I am the bull in their china shop, blowing in and out of our gatherings like a fart in the wind, always armed with a new outrageous story to tell. Stories they seem to thoroughly enjoy, as my anecdotes make their lives seem calm and peaceful in comparison.

Beth's eyes landed on the birthday gift bag sitting next to me on the table, which I now forked over. She went right for the *To-From*, which read:

> *To: Seagrass and Silk* (the name of Beth's interior design company)
>
> *From: Flames and Destruction*

She twittered with approval, shooting me a grin filled with mock trepidation as she fished through the tissue and located the gift. The package contained a jar candle from the Malicious Women Candle Company with a label that said: "Mermaids Don't Have a Thigh Gap: Infused with a Nice Tail". I had selected it not only because Beth adored mermaids, but because it was a candle. My candle stories were our group's most retold and treasured of all my tales. And there were many.

I had so many stories involving fire that the Fab Four had a best hits list. Each member had their favorite. The story Beth liked best was the one when I attempted to put good mojo into a new apartment using a Happy Home Quick Blessing Kit and nearly burnt the place to the ground before I even unpacked.

My intentions had been pure, so I have no idea why the mojo went awry. I had purchased the Happy Home Quick Blessing Kit from the new age shop thinking it would bring me some good luck. Having just extracted myself from yet another bad post-divorce relationship, I needed all the good vibes I could get, so I gave it a shot

Following the candle kit's instructions, I sat the candle in the middle of my apartment's foyer floor before I unpacked a single box, lit the enclosed white votive candle, meditated on good thoughts, and repeated the prescribed poem three times. Reading that good luck was sure to follow, I rejoiced.

Rising from the floor to find somewhere safe to put the burning candle, I stepped on a cone of incense. Re-reading the kit instructions, I discovered I'd forgotten to incorporate the incense in my ceremony. Unsure whether to start over, I opted instead to light the incense cone and travel with it from room to room pinched between my fingers, muttering a little wish for good things while wafting the smoke about like they used to do with the incense at Catholic high mass on the holidays. I regretted I didn't have one of those nifty decanters on the end of a chain that I could swing about like the priests did. Had I unpacked my tea ball at the time, you can bet I would have used it.

When I felt the infusion was complete, I returned to the burning votive, placed it on a plastic lid from a can of roasted almonds, which was the only thing I could find to use as a base, and left it on the linoleum by the front door. I thought blowing out the candle would negate the infusion process, and I didn't want anything to screw it up, so I decided to let the candle burn itself out while I unpacked. In hindsight I know how stupid this was, but it seemed to make sense at the time.

Cranking up my boom box, for an hour went back and forth between the rooms of the little apartment finding a place for everything and putting everything in its place. I was in my element. In a jiffy I was done with the bedroom and ready to start on the kitchen. Gathering a load of empty boxes, I came out of the bedroom and immediately a flash of flame caught my eye. The Happy Home votive candle had burnt down to the nub and was on its way to becoming one with my linoleum floor.

"Holy crap!" I hollered, running in a circle with the empty boxes, my mind devoid of any rational ways to extinguish the flame. Quick thinking in these situations was not my forte. In the end I threw the boxes into the kitchen, bolted over to the foyer, crouched down on all fours, and blew out the inferno. In the process I singed the tip of my bangs and burnt my finger. Thankfully, those were the only casualties, as the fire hadn't had a chance to create a permanent burn mark in the linoleum. In hindsight, perhaps the Happy Home incantation had worked after all in that all I got was a blister.

Unfortunately, I hadn't fared as well in Phyllis's favorite fire story. That one I'm still bitter about, having suffered a nasty burn from a healing candle. A healing candle!

This story begins with an innocent trip to a street fair, where I was drawn to a slender violet pillar candle with a heavenly lavender scent. The candle had a beautiful parchment wrapper with an embossed prayer, touted to help heal the soul and restore the peace. Perfect, I thought when I read it. I had just broken up with a cheater who moved his secret girlfriend into his house while I was on vacation in Ireland. If there was anyone that needed some soul healing after all that, it was me. I debated on whether or not to buy two.

When I got home with the lavender candle that day, I set it on a little glass trivet, no plastic lids this time, and carefully read the instructions beneath the prayer on the wrapper. The directions said to find a quiet spot and "infuse your candle with healing energy by repeating the prayer three times". Doing exactly as told, I found a comfy spot on my apartment floor and repeated the words. Infusion complete, I was feeling instantly lighter. I lit the wick and decided to scrub my floors. Cleaning is what I did when feeling energized. I'd be healed and cleansed. A double bonus!

I picked up my throw rugs, dug out a pail, snatched up the Mr. Clean and turned up the ceiling fans. Getting my Cinderella on, I went about my floors on my hands and knees. Soon, the bathroom, hallway, and kitchen floors were clean as a whistle, and I was delighted. Marveling at how such a little thing could make such a huge difference, everything looking so fresh and new, I shot an appreciative glance at my lavender candle and noticed that the entire top third of the 6-inch cylinder was engulfed in flame!

At first, stunned, I was frozen in place and could only stare at the towering inferno in the middle of my dining room table. I should have stayed catatonic, because when I snapped out of it, I completely freaked out. I ran back and forth across the carpeting and then scurried on tippy toes across my freshly scrubbed kitchen to the cupboards. I randomly opened and shut cabinets and drawers looking for Lord knows what. Then I bolted over to the candle and started blowing furiously. A futile attempt nothing short of ridiculous. Served only to piss it off. The brilliant orange flames licked at the air and threatened to ignite my hair. I pulled back and reevaluated, frantic. Damn thing was going to start my whole apartment on fire!

In hindsight, you'd think I would have grabbed the fire extinguisher under the sink. Or sprinkled the flames with baking soda. Or suffocated the fire with a pot. Nope. Instead, I seized hold of the trivet at the candle's base, intending to usher the whole works to the sink, and immediately regretted my decision. The first touch disrupted the balance, causing the burned wrapper holding the melted wax to fall away, sending scalding wax cascading in a flow that covered the back of my right hand. Hot! Omg, hot! HOT! HOT! HOT! HOT!!! I did the dance of the pain fairies all the way to the kitchen sink, mouth frozen in a blood curdling scream with no volume.

In pain the likes of which I hadn't felt since childbirth, I threw the tap on cold full blast and thrust my hand under it. Water sprayed me in the face and showered down my front onto my still wet floor. Then, blinded by pain and not thinking, I did the worst thing imaginable. I grabbed my scrubbie sponge and started scouring the wax off my hand. The skin came off with it. "Owwwwww," I screamed, letting out the pain. "What the Hell are you doing?!" I shouted at myself, chucking the sponge into the sink. I scowled at the sponge horrified, as if it was a character in *Fantasia* with a mind of its own.

Gathering my wits, I picked up my cell phone and dialed my daughter, an ER nurse. If I ever needed an ER nurse, it was now. Unfortunately, she was on vacation with no cell coverage.

"Dammit!" I cried, holding my burnt hand under the cold water, which felt good, while my mind raced for an alternate. It settled on Phyllis. An herbalist should know what to do! She answered my call on the first ring.

"Hey, Colleen! I'm at the hula show about to go onstage. Wha'sup?"

"Ummmm, well, I kinda did something really stupid…" and I went about explaining the summarized version of what had brought me to that point. "So, what can I do for myself?!"

"Oh my God! Okay, do you still have some of the herbal poultice I gave you the last time you burned yourself?"

Rolling my eyes, I answered through a pucker, giving a monotone "Yes."

"Good. Schmear a layer of that on there, then put the hand back in a bowl of cool water and hightail it to Glenn and Paul's (good friends of ours that lived nearby). I'll call Glenn and give him a heads-up on what to do when you get there and check on you later. We're being called, so I gotta run. Good luck!" And with that, the call clicked off and she was gone.

Following Phyllis' directives, I attended to the wound, which was very angry and already blistering. After ever so gently applying the herbal mixture, I plunged my right hand into a mixing bowl of ice water, snatched up my keys and raced across town. In minutes, I was at our friends' house, which I had lovingly nicknamed the IHOP (Illustrious House of Paul and Glenn), where Paul met me standing in the threshold of an open door.

"Come in, Blondie. What on earth did you do to yourself now?" Paul asked, chuckling.

"Get in here and talk later," Glenn hollered from the kitchen. He was fussing about assembling a triage area. "Lemme see what you did...oh, good Lord! Nice job, Blonde One. We need to get the heat out of that. Go wash it gently with soap and water. Gently!"

Doing as told, I felt like a 5-year-old with a boo-boo, especially when Glenn sprayed my hand with Bactine, the stand-by of my youth. The familiar smell brought back every cut, scrape and owie I'd gotten as a kid. And I'd had a lot of them. Some things never changed.

Glenn followed up the Bactine – which incidentally drew out all the burn and pain on contact, God bless the lovely people at Bayer – with an herbal concoction mixed from Paul's garden, as instructed by Phyllis. The burn was then topped with a non-stick pad and wrapped in soft gauze, the end secured with medical tape. When finished, Glenn looked over his work like Van Gogh after the final brush stroke, and I wondered if he was going to lop off an ear. Instead, he stalked over to the freezer, drew out a frozen compress, grabbed a clean kitchen towel and ordered me to sit on the couch and chill my hand.

"Paul, please get the princess here a drink; she's gonna be here awhile," Glenn instructed, wielding all the command of Hawkeye in the MASH unit. "Movie?" he asked.

So went the next four hours – applying cool, watching movies, and hydrating with liquid pain reliever – till I was dismissed to my home barracks with a goody bag and the new nickname of Flame Dame, which Paul and Glenn used on their Christmas gift to me: a flameless, electric candle heater.

It took many months to heal that nasty burn, which left a scar on both my hand and my ego. Upset that I wasn't warned to remove the wrapper from the candle before lighting it, I was about to write a strongly worded letter to the manufacturer when I discovered the instructions clearly stated to do so. It had all been my own damn fault. Lesson learned.

I'd love to say that this is the end of my burn stories, because I did stop using open flame candles and made good use of the electric candle heater from Paul and Glenn. Unfortunately, I found my talents extended far beyond flaming candles. This brings us to Sinjin's favorite burn story: when I ceviched myself with lime juice, proving I didn't even need fire to get 2nd degree burns. Never underestimate a Flame Dame's creativity and resourcefulness.

This gem of a tale happened the Sunday before I left on a summer trip to Wisconsin. I was making Margaritas for the Breakfast Club over at the IHOP (Paul and Glenn's). Paul had picked me some fresh limes off his tree, and I had rolled one on the counter Emeril-style to make it juicy before cutting into it. The rolled lime emitted wonderful-smelling oil onto my hands, which I rubbed into my skin, basking in the heavenly fragrance.

Hours later, back at my apartment, I changed into my swimsuit, put on sunscreen, and went about washing my car. Every so often I would get a whiff of lime. It made me happy. It shouldn't have.

Flash ahead two days, and I'm on the plane to Wisconsin. The flight attendant is handing me my cup of coffee and I notice the back of my left hand is splattered with sunburn. I held my hand up and looked at the rouged skin in wonder, contemplating how I could have missed a spot so big with my sunscreen. I've had half my back and face carved up by dermatologists mining for basil cells, so I am always diligent with the SPF.

My hand seemed to become increasingly inflamed and angry with every passing mile. I couldn't for the life of me figure out what was going on. Then, the gentleman sitting in the window seat next to me noticed my hand and said, "Wow, I haven't seen anything that looked like that since I got lime burn from climbing citrus trees when I was a kid!"

"Lime burn? What's lime burn?" I asked, trying to hide the beginnings of mild hysteria.

I proceeded to get educated. The gentleman informed me the oil in the peel of the lime makes the skin hypersensitive to the sun. It intensifies the UV rays and causes severe burns. He had gotten lime burn all over his body as a kid, causing his elementary school teacher to quarantine him, thinking he had some horrible disease and was contagious. Looking at my hand, I could understand her alarm. One might have thought I'd tried to fish something out of a vat of acid. The skin on the back of my hand looked hideous.

"Well, that's interesting and all, but I haven't come in contact with any liiiiii…" Oh. Crap. Sunday morning Margaritaville replayed in my head. Doggonit, I hated when I did stupid stuff!

When I returned to town and recounted the tale to the Fab Four, Sinjin, intrigued and delighted with the new information, had done extensive internet research on it. The more he shared with me, the dumber I felt. Just as you could cook raw fish by simply marinating the flesh in lime juice to make ceviche, citrus oil when combined with the sun could cook your skin clean off the bone. Though they gave the result cute little names like Margarita Burn or Mexican Beer Dermatitis, lime burn was no joke and would take six months to heal. Six months!

Thankfully, after about a month, Phyllis's concoction of aloe, calendula, chamomile, and eye of newt had the skin calmed down to a mild dusty rose rather than Three Mile Island red, and the cashiers at Publix, the local grocery store, would take payment from me without recoiling. I healed with a minimum amount of scarring and vowed to be more fastidious when going near my little green friends, no matter how alluring their smell may be.

As for me, I have no favorite burn stories, because it is no fun being the one who always gets burned. I wish I could say the lime burn saga was the end of it, but alas, the heat's still hot and I'm still in the fire. I went to lunch with Glenn the other day and nearly set the whole restaurant ablaze. We were at our favorite Chinese place where I accidentally tipped over a lit hibachi pot, sending a tidal wave of flaming liquid across our food and table.

"Really?" Glenn shouted at me in exasperation, trying to flee the booth without getting burned.

What can I say? Blondie's just a hot mess.

****

Valentine's Day. Hearts and flowers and all that jazz. Ugh. Not a fan.

One of my newly single coworkers sat a cheek on the corner of my desk today and kvetched about Valentine's Day being right around the corner. She'd just broken up with her longtime boyfriend, so she was dreading it. I listened and nodded, searching the recesses of my mind for something positive to say. I came up with nothing.

Nothing good has ever happened to me on this one day of the year when we are supposed to celebrate romance. In my defense, it is certainly not for lack of trying. I have put in the effort and done everything in my power to fall in line with the utopian sentimentalists. But each time I have failed. I'm simply romantically challenged.

When I was a newlywed, while my husband was on shift, I spent all day cooking a beautiful Valentine's dinner, set the table with candles, and adorned myself in a microscopic black lace baby doll. When our Doberman, Winkles, announced that Daddy was home, I dashed to the threshold of our 3rd story apartment, gave my hair a last fluff, threw open the door, and scared the beejeebus out of the neighbor lady. Preoccupied reading her mail, she had taken the wrong flight of stairs and wound up on our doorstep. I startled her so badly she shrieked loud enough to wake the dead, launched her handful of mail into the air, and envelopes showered down around me like confetti. She was so embarrassed that she turned tail without uttering another sound and ran all the way back to her apartment, leaving me to pick up the mess, throw on my sweats, and sheepishly deliver the post back to her. My husband arrived home while I was out, neglected to see the beautifully set table, and by the time I got home he was sound asleep in bed, exhausted from his day. Some romantic February 14th.

There was also the year I nearly set the house afire by igniting the kitchen curtain with candlelight (another flame story), or the year I scalded my right boob draining boiling water off spaghetti for another surprise Valentine's dinner, or the year I met the UPS man at the door wearing nothing but a red bow… the list goes on and on ad infinitum.

So now, I've come to accept my circumstances. I won't be the one called down to the receptionist's desk at work to pick up the gargantuan spray of fresh flowers, like the cute little 20-something girl over in accounting with the long, flowing ponytail, flawless skin, and waistline tiny enough to wrap a bread tie around (like she needs another shot of self-confidence). I am, however, a strong, independent woman that can do that anytime for myself. And I do.

Pondering this, I felt the need to spread a little humor and love to my like-minded gal pals this Valentine's Day. I sat down with pen and paper and crafted a "gal-entine" for those who might be feeling a little puny on the year's most romantic day. I wrapped each copy of my poem around a square of chocolate, inserted a lotto ticket, and tied each little packet with a bow. The poem read:

HAPPY INFERIORITY COMPLEX DAY!

If you're an Insta-perfect couple,
I love you just the same,
But till I find my laddy,
Valentine's is lame.

Pairs, enjoy your perfect meals,
Dress up in heels and tux,
I'm good with wine in hand,
Cheering "Valentine's Day sucks!"

Singles, say this with me,
While we highly hoist a glass,
"The sun will rise tomorrow,
Love will never kick our ass!"

> Now, let's gorge on chocolate,
> At least it gives us that,
> And we have no one to tell us,
> "Hun, you're getting fat!"
>
> Also, here's a lotto ticket,
> May you win a couple bucks,
> A reason to proclaim,
> "This day no longer sucks!"
>
> My mood seems to be lifting,
> A smile upon my face,
> Happy V-Day to you all,
> May it not be a disgrace!

Then, I made *To-Froms* for each little parcel using funny quotes I had caught them saying. There was:

> *To: It'll harden up*
> *From: That's what she said!*
>
> *To: I'm a couple finials short of a dauber*
> *From: Are you speaking in tongues?*
>
> *To: If this teaching gig goes bad, I can always count marshmallows*
> *From: Or test weed*
>
> *To: I'm in the Fitness Protection Program*
> *From: I have a dropped set*
>
> *To: I lactate wine*
> *From: I have walking farts*
>
> *To: My shaker is always ready to go*
> *From: I gave mine to Goodwill*

To: My thighs aren't ready yet
From: I brine mine first

To: Squeezing my box of wine for every last drop
From: Girl, here's $6 for a box of the fancy stuff

I delivered or sent each one and received the desired result: smiles all around. Chin up, ladies. I got you!

Chapter 3: MARCH

March blew in like a lamb, and with a job interview. Because of the unstable economic market, I entertained all potential employment prospects even when I was not actively looking. Such was the case this balmy March morning, which found me taking advantage of an opportunity that had come out of the blue. Just days before, a former coworker phoned me with intel about a position with her company that sounded perfect, so I had thrown my hat in the ring. Nothing ventured, nothing gained. And sure enough, the company's Human Resource department had called two days later to set a meeting for me to meet with the position's supervisor, a company director. As among the rare 8% of the population who loved to interview, I was excited about the one-on-one.

Sadly, though, this morning, the day of my meet-and-greet with my potential new boss, I had routinely hit the snooze on my alarm, overslept, and was subsequently running behind. Hurriedly throwing on the navy interview suit I had set out the night before, I stormed into the bathroom to frantically slap on some makeup basics, brush my teeth, and pull my hair into presentable order.

"That's gonna have to do," I said hurriedly to my reflection in the mirror after giving my hair a quick spray. I switched off the bathroom light on the run and scurried down the ceramic hallway, hopping on alternate feet trying to get on my navy pumps as I went. I slipped and nearly face-planted.

"Shit!" I cried, one hand on the wall steadying myself as I jammed my toes into the shoe, holding it behind me by the heel. Then off I clacked through the kitchen, grabbing my kid leather satchel and car keys in one motion. I tore out the back door, listened for the click of the lock behind me, jumped in the car and was off.

Stopped at a red light a few miles from my interview destination, much calmer now that I was going to make it on time, I tilted the car's rear-view mirror toward my face to give my makeup a quick check. Presentation was everything and given how hastily I had gotten ready, I feared I might have forgotten to put on lipstick or only mascaraed one eye. Deeming my reflection acceptable after securing a loose strand of hair, I hit the gas pedal as the light turned green. Returning the mirror to its normal position, I was checking the view behind me when I spotted a huge bee buzzing angrily in the back window. I had been terrified of bees ever since getting stung in the thigh as a kid. Watching the insect bounce repeatedly against the glass in an attempt to break free, I tried not to panic, reasoning that so long as the bee stayed back there, everything would be fine. But, then, as if my eyes had been magnets, the enraged bee headed right for me, its giant stinger dragging down its hind end, looking lethal.

Terrified as the insect closed in, I screeched in horror and hit the down button for every window in the car. A tornado blew in from every direction, tousling my beautifully coiffed hair into a rat's nest. Doing nothing to free the bee, but everything to annoy it further, the bee began dive-bombing my head, intermittently banging against the front windshield. The terror-stricken side of my brain screamed that I should open the door and bale out of the moving car into the street, while the rational side fought with me to keep one eyeball on my foe and the other on the road until the opportunity came to pull over. When there was a break in traffic, allowing me to lurch onto the road's unpaved shoulder, I pulled over, the bee buzzing in my left ear. Barely waiting for the car to stop, I catapulted out the door onto the hot gravel, screaming and tearing my hands through my shoulder-length blonde hair.

For the next minute or so, I wiggy danced all over the side of the road and can just imagine what it must have looked like to passing traffic. I know I would have been delighted to witness such a spectacle, but when you're the one dancing, it's not nearly as fun. But my efforts were rewarded. The hornet, bee, wasp, or whatever the little demon was, seemed to be gone.

Regaining my composure, I straightened my suit jacket, tucked the loose tail of my white blouse into my skirt, hopped back into the car, and checked the damage to my makeup in the rearview mirror. Mother of all creatures, I looked like Alice Cooper after a week-long bender! Frenzied, I pulled out my emergency car makeup kit and did what I could with a 4-inch comb, some mascara, and a lipstick before hightailing it the short distance to the interview. Stupid bee!

Still looking a wreck, I checked in at the company's reception desk. Late, flushed, and rattled, I knew the situation was hopeless, but I was already there, so I plastered on a happy face and resolved to do my best. The director with whom I was interviewing came out to greet me and introduced himself as Ed. He was a clean-shaven, pleasant looking guy of moderate build in his mid-forties with perfectly gelled spiky blonde hair beginning to show silver, and kind hazel eyes. His crisp, white oxford shirt looked freshly pressed, his expensive grey trousers were impeccably creased, and he smelled divine – the perfect mix of morning shower and smallest hint of Versace cologne. I liked him immediately. After exchanging pleasantries, I followed him down a carpeted corridor to his office. Deciding to break the ice, I entertained him with my bee story while we walked.

"...so there I was on US1, flailing away at the blasted thing. People driving by must have thought I was a crazy woman!" I said, laughing.

Ed stopped dead in his tracks and gazed at me. He had a huge smile on his face and was trying very hard not to laugh. "So how long have you had that Chevy; Cobalt, is it?" he asked. My jaw dropped open in horror. He must have seen me doing my jig on the shoulder!

I blushed the color of a ripe tomato and threw my hands over my face. Peeking through my fingers, I saw Ed struggling to apologize while trying to stifle the chortles of laughter he could no longer contain. Hazel eyes dancing, he waved a hand toward the open door of his office and the two burgundy cushioned chairs that sat in front of a huge mahogany desk. He stood before one of the chairs and motioned for me to sit in the other. Regaining his composure but still smiling with an air of compassion, he said, "Please, I didn't mean to embarrass you. Was it a bee? My wife had one in her car last week and called me screaming from the freeway. Florida Highway Patrol had pulled her over thinking she was a drunk driver!"

Still tomato red, I answered in the affirmative—yes, a hitchhiking bee had been responsible for me running about US1 like a fool. A simple admission that would transform the meeting from awkward to enjoyable. The bee disaster launched us into tangents of small talk and chuckles, allowing us both to relax and recover. By the time we got down to the business of discussing my qualifications, past work experience, and education, we were chatting like old friends.

Fate had played her hand, and by the end of the hour, I was certain I had landed the position. And sure enough, Human Resources called me shortly after lunch with an offer that I accepted. My flailing about like a psychopath had done the trick. Who knew getting a bee in the car could have been such a boon? But as I have since learned from talking with friends and family, no other unfortunate situation seems to possess a common thread that is so far reaching. Everyone that drives, no matter the gender, age, race, or demographic, seems to have a bee-in-the-car story that they will share with great enthusiasm.

Stopping by my mother's house the evening of the interview to share the day's events, I learned that even my mother had a bee-in-the car tale. A real doozy at that. After I recounted my saga, which had Mom laughing with more abandon than I had witnessed in ages, she told me of a similar thing that happened to her back in Wisconsin when I was just a toddler. Mom drove a pea green Oldsmobile sedan back then. I remembered that car after she mentioned it. The thing was like a freaking tank with vinyl seats that would get as hot as a stovetop in the summer. A wavy torrent of hot air would escape out of the door if it had been sitting in the sun, and even if we cranked down all the windows, the inside never seemed to get cool. You didn't dare wear shorts in that thing lest you burn your bottom clean off.

While driving around in her pea green "Olds" running errands with all the windows rolled down one hot summer day, Mom, like me, had heard a buzzing coming from the back window. Glancing in the car rearview mirror, she spied a huge, furious bee that must have flown in while she was stopped at a red light. Sensing her horror, the insect headed for the front, and again like me, Mom freaked. The apple doesn't fall far from the bee infested tree.

Mom said she let out a blood-curdling scream and pulled to the curb, weaving across two lanes of traffic. Not even bothering to shut off the ignition, she bolted out of the car, swatting at the air, and ruining her heavily shellacked "beehive" updo (the irony of that had us in stitches). In her pale-yellow pedal pushers and white Keds, Mom ran around the car shrieking, opened all the doors, and did everything she could think of to urge the pesky bug to freedom. But the bee would have none of her nonsense. It continued returning to the back window to resume its fight, only becoming more and more angry.

Dissolving into tears, Mom didn't know what to do. Then, she spied the bus stop down the block and checked her watch. To her relief the bus was due down the route any minute. She steeled her nerves, lunged inside the car to shut off the ignition, retrieve her purse, roll up the windows, and lock the doors, before making a dash down the street to catch the arriving bus home.

When Mom got to the house, she called my father at work. "Ummm, honey," she said, "I have a little problem…" and she came clean about the bee.

"You did whaaaat?" my father shouted on the other end of the receiver. Oh dear. Mom said he sounded even more furious than the bee.

Deciding in hindsight maybe her plan hadn't been the best, Mom told my father never mind, she'd take care of the situation herself, and hung up. Then Mom phoned her dad, my beloved, sweet grandpa, who had been babysitting for me while Mom was out. Grandpa packed me up in his black 1956 Ford Fairlane (the "Batman car"), and the two of us picked up Mom before heading downtown to de-bee and retrieve the "Olds." But by the time we arrived at her car, no action was needed. The bee was dead. It had incinerated to a crispy crunch from the heat of the vinyl interior.

Delighted by Mom's story, I bought her a white cotton top embroidered with little bees for her birthday and crafted this *To-From* for on the box:

> *To:* Took the bus and left the car bee-hind
>
> *From:* Got out and wiggy danced with my new boss watching

She loved the gift, twittering with laughter as she retold her bee tale to our family over corned beef and cabbage and green iced cake, her birthday falling on St. Patrick's Day, March 17th. Since she loves corned beef and cabbage and the color green, she opts to keep the theme traditionally Irish, even though she is 100% German and has not a drop of Irish blood in her.

****

Making tags for my mother has always been easy. All I need to do is keep it real. I can play on our similarities, like I did with the bee tag, or I can craft one from our many, many differences. As with most mothers and daughters, what we don't have in common far outweighs what we do. We differ so dramatically that if Mom and I were spheres of a Venn Diagram, one would need a magnifying glass to see where the two intersect. Mom is a brunette, while I am blonde. Mom is olive-complected, while my skin is so fair, I can get sunburned walking to the mailbox. Mom's a lefty, and I'm right-handed. Mom's barely over 5 feet tall and can never find pants she doesn't need to hem. I tower over her at 5'5" and can never find pants long enough for my legs.

Our physical differences are just the tip of our disparity iceberg. Mom is a shy, quiet, dainty introvert, who is forever concerned about what everybody else thinks. I am the opposite of all those things. Everyone knows where I am in the room, I have no filter, and if I had a nickel for each time I heard my mother say "Co-lleen!" in that *You Did Not Just Say That* tone, I'd have a nickel mint named in my honor.

And then there's the matter of our organizational styles, the widest chasm of our mother-daughter divide. I'm a Virgo, the most meticulous sign of the zodiac. Orderliness is my jam. Give me that junk drawer and I will gleefully arrange the contents by color, shape, size, and function in neat teak containers fitted together like a Tetris game before you can say "…kiss my biscuits." As a Pisces, Mom, not so much. One time while I was staying overnight at her house, I went into the pantry to get a tea bag and nearly had a stroke. Everything was stuffed onto shelves willy-nilly, and I couldn't find anything. Unable to stand the disorder, I pulled everything out, weeded through it, threw out expired items, and arranged the contents back on the shelves in an orderly fashion before I even put sheets on my bed.

The next day, assuming my pantry tidying had been a good deed, I found my efforts to have been in vain. Separating canned goods by category, making sure all labels faced the front, aligning boxed goods by height and putting all baking products on their own shelf is apparently only a Virgo thing and doesn't work for those born under the sign of Pisces. Mom couldn't find anything. Every day she'd be rooting around behind the louvered pantry door and I would hear, "Colleen, have you seen the (*fill in the blank*)? It was right here before you moved everything around!"

Then I'd walk up behind her, pick out whatever it was she was looking for, and reorganize the mess she'd made in the process. It was like playing the world's longest shell game.

In Mom's defense, when asked about her system of organization, her explanations were so creative they almost made sense. Here is a sample:

Tag the Present

"Hey, Mom, why isn't the bread in the bread box?"

"Because that's where I keep the Saran and tin foil."

"Mom, are we all out of sugar? There are tea bags in the sugar canister."

"No, there's a full bag of sugar in the fridge. Look in the vegetable drawer."

"Colleen, did you move my glasses? They're not on the back of the couch where I always put them."

"Did you check on top of your head? In the bathroom? On the newspaper pile? In your purse? On the hood of the car? In the bushes? Under the rug in the kitchen? In the refrigerator?" (All places they had been known to be…and more…)

"Mom, do you have any wrap for this birthday gift?"

"Yes, go in the plastic container under my bed and then there's bows and ribbons in my nightstand."

"Colleen, could you please bring me the crock pot from the garage? …a battery from the freezer? …the vodka from the entertainment center? …a tablecloth from the guest room?"

This lively exchange resulted in a fun tag for Mom's birthday present that year, too:

> *To: She who keeps Saran Wrap in the bread box*
>
> *From: She who alphabetizes the soup*

Like I said, for Mom, I just keep it real.

All joking aside, I have learned through the years to accept these multitude of differences between Mom and me as more endearing than irritating. Moms will be moms and daughters will be daughters, and as often as we daughters wonder if we could have been switched at birth because we just don't fit together with our moms, we know in our hearts we really do. Or at least this is the case for me. And whenever my life has hit crisis mode and I needed a place to flee, where did I go? Home to Mom.

I have zero regrets about those times when I dragged my defeated backside home to the one person I disagreed with most. On the contrary, it was during those times, when I ran back to Mom's to roost and recover, that we both came to know and appreciate both our similarities and our differences. Mom was my safe harbor, where I could vent and rail at the world, sometimes directing my frustration and anger directly at her, knowing that no matter what, that little German woman would still love me unconditionally, warts and all. She allowed me the space to come back to myself, apologize when needed, and get recentered. That's not to say I agreed with everything she did, or her me. Instead, we came to understand our differences. In the vulnerable moments while I healed, Mom told me she admired my strength and independence, and I told her how much I appreciated her considerate ways and the sacrifices she'd made for me. And there had been many.

My mother's life had not been easy. Though to the outsider her youth may have appeared envious because she was spoiled, the circumstances were far from fortunate. In 1931, ten years prior to conceiving my mother, my grandparents lost their eldest son, Gerald, whom they called Jerry. He died of pneumonia on Christmas Eve at nine years old. My grandparents were shrouded in grief and became overprotective to guard against any more pain. They could not bear the loss of another child.

In 1941, when my grandparents' second child Vernon was seventeen, my mother was born. Mom was a preemie, exacerbating their worries. She struggled to survive and then she struggled to put on weight. Anxious about her being so thin, my grandparents let her eat whatever she wanted whenever she wanted. They indulged her every request. As a result, her teeth went bad from too many sweets. To correct the dental issues from a poor diet and complications of being premature, my grandfather drew from his fireman's pension to have braces put on Mom's teeth when she turned ten. She complained so bitterly about the pain the braces caused, she had my grandparents take her back to the orthodontist to have them removed the next day. Subsequently, Mom suffers from painful dental issues to this day.

Only after my mother became a young adult did my grandparents finally put their foot down about anything, which was probably the worst possible time for them to start. Mom had come to them for permission to become a flight attendant with Pan American Airways. Becoming a stewardess had been my mother's dream for as long as she could remember, and Pan Am had accepted her application. The position required her to move to Arizona, a bonus for her because she hated the cold Wisconsin winters, but a dealbreaker for my grandparents. They would not hear of her moving so far from them, so they denied her for the first time in her life, crushing her. Too depressed, defeated, and angry to entertain attending college as a consolation, she took a low-paying entry job working for Liberty Mutual Insurance Company as a clerk.

Not long after she started with Liberty Mutual, my mother was set up on a blind date by her friends. Mom's friends were worried about her and felt it was time she stopped moping and got out of the house. Their shenanigans worked. Mom met my dad and was unable to resist his James Dean look in cuffed jeans, white t-shirt, black leather jacket and greased blonde ducktail. In turn, Dad was smitten by Mom's soft brown curls, miniscule waist, and Sandra Dee cardigan with saddle shoes. They were the yins to each other's yangs. He was the life of the party; she was a wallflower. He loved adventure; she played it safe. He was opinionated; she was diplomatic. It was an attraction of opposites, and a whirlwind romance.

If I was to guess, I believe things would have fizzled pretty soon thereafter, had it not been for one fated steamy night in a borrowed '57 Chevy. Having always been a good swimmer and rule breaker, I proved the Pull-out Method didn't work and bada-bing, bada-boom, Mom was pregnant. The year was 1961 and Mom was only 19 years old. Under pressure from both sets of furious parents, Dad "did the right thing" and a hasty, high mass Catholic wedding was arranged. Not exactly the Cinderella story any of them had envisioned.

The freezing winter wedding, though beautiful in a pastel rainbow theme, was a fiasco. Dad came down with the chickenpox and had to quarantine until the very last moment, hiding his healing blisters under cake makeup. Meanwhile, Mom, over three months pregnant and suffering from vicious morning sickness, had to make a mad dash to the church's sacristy in the middle of the ceremony to vomit in the garbage can. All foreshadowing the six tumultuous years to come.

Vague, fuzzy memories are all I have of the days when we all lived together, and not many are good. Most are recollections of bitter, loud arguments that I revisit when I hear shouting coming from the houses in my neighborhood.

How Sean came into being is a miracle. They say he was a souvenir from our last family trip to Florida when I was four. The only thing I can remember from that vacation is that we drove down from Wisconsin with my aunt, uncle, and two cousins. Four adults and three toddlers in one Chevy. Many stories have been told about that trip, and all are colorful. In one, my Uncle Steve mistakenly left the trunk open at a rest area, unbeknownst to my dad, who was driving, because the Chevy's open blue trunk cover was the same color as the sky. When clothes started flying onto the highway, Dad couldn't figure out where they were coming from because all he saw in the rearview mirror was a cloudless blue sky. Except he was really looking at the open trunk cover. I don't personally remember that one, but I do recall a goat sticking its head out of the window of the car driving next to us, something I will forever associate with Alabama.

Mom divorced my father in 1967. Sean was just over a year old at the time, and I was turning six. That era did not take kindly to divorced, working women as heads of households, especially ones with two young children. Mom may as well have been a leper. My father paid child support and saw me on weekends, but were it not for my mother's dad, my grandpa, who cared for me when I was sick and Mom had to work, I don't know how we would have survived. As an asthma sufferer, I was sick a lot.

Two years after they divorced, my father left on a trip to travel the world, leaving money with his lawyer to fulfill his monthly financial obligation, while Mom was left to work without respite and raise two young kids. She borrowed money from her folks to move the three of us into a two-bedroom apartment in Whitefish Bay, the Queen Mother of wealthy Wisconsin suburbs, to ensure Sean and I got a decent education. The "Bay", with its lakefront mansions and guest houses larger than hotels, was known for its impressive public school system. As a divorcee's kid, the Bay was not a welcoming place for me and my brother, but I imagine the scorn was infinitely worse for Mom. A sacrifice she always said was worth making.

To Mom's credit, I did get a noteworthy education, and I have thanked her for that. It has served me well. I sailed through college and have never wanted for a good job. The difficulties I faced living as a latchkey kid in a June Cleaver world developed the inner strength my mother so admired. I became a survivor.

Mom met my stepfather Ron at work in 1976 and they married a year later when I was 16. Mom always wanted to live in a warm climate, so Ron made that happen two years later when I graduated high school. I went off to the University of Wisconsin in La Crosse while they packed all they owned into a 20-ft U-Haul van, loaded up my 13-year-old brother and hit the road to Melbourne, Florida. I thought they were insane to move to a place with such oppressive heat, but that would change when I came down from Wisconsin after college for a visit and met the man that I would marry on our fourth date (but that is a story for another time).

Mom and Ron stayed in Melbourne happy as clams until Ron passed away of a massive heart attack in 1994. Mom and Ron had been living in the home of their dreams for just four months. The house had a pool, which Ron loved and put to good use. The day he died was a Saturday, and he had just come back from the pool store with an inflatable island to blow up as a surprise for my mother, who was in the shower at the time. She came out to find him floating in the pool. He had passed in the blink of an eye.

Though Mom was 53 years old, she had never lived alone until the day she became a widow. Adjusting was difficult for her; she was afraid of being by herself at night in their new house yet couldn't bring herself to sell it. She and Ron had sacrificed and scrimped 17 years to buy that place. So, for months, while she grieved and got her footing, I would go over and sleep in her guest room after putting my daughter, Dani to bed. Slowly, Mom was able to overcome her fears and adjust to living by herself, eventually downsizing to a smaller townhouse. She, too, is a survivor.

That brings us to the present, as I sit at my kitchen table with a pretty green blouse I've wrapped to take to my mother on her 81st birthday. These days Mom lives in a memory care facility. She has dementia, likely Alzheimer's, a disease doctors cannot determine until after death. Sean and I are her guardians. He and I are a united front in getting Mom the best possible care and making her life as comfortable as possible. We are very, very lucky to have each other.

Mom's battle with dementia has been a long, tough, heartbreaking road. The disease is cruel and robs its host of the most important possessions they have–their memories. It dissolves each one into dust from the present day backwards, hopping and skipping in an arbitrary way, leaving its inhabitant confused, angry, and scared.

Everything about dealing with Mom's dementia has been difficult. As she has declined, my normally quiet mother has become paranoid, irritable, and sometimes violent, taking her fears and frustration out on whomever is closest. That person is usually me; I am her safe harbor now. I have had to watch her struggle for normalcy when nothing around her is normal or familiar. Simple things like going to the grocery store became confusing. In the early stages of her decline while she was still able to drive, she went on a quick trip to the store for milk and halfway there didn't recognize any of her surroundings. She didn't even know what city she was in. Thankfully, she had a moment of clarity and somehow found her way to where I worked, showing up at the front desk of my office building. The angels were looking out for her that day.

There has been the never-ending, exhausting, battle getting her the care she needs. Her denial of needing assistance and refusal of allowing in-home healthcare in the early days of the disease is a common problem I never anticipated. None of my efforts resembled what is shown on those happy, cheerful, hunky-dory in-home care commercials. Mom called the police on every in-home caregiver I tried to hire. Then she would accuse me of all sorts of ill will for inviting a stranger into her home to spy on her, insisting I was gaslighting her into thinking she was losing her mind. Any prescribed medications were met with equal resistance and accusations of poisoning. My once mild-mannered, sweet mom would rage in my face with crazed eyes. It was terrifying. I learned to deal with these outbursts sympathetically by envisioning the scenario through her eyes, although that was even scarier. Mom 100% believed I was going to have men in white coats come to drag her away, gagged and straitjacketed, to throw her into a dungeon with snakes. This was her reality for nearly two years and nothing I could say or do could convince her otherwise. I can't imagine living with that kind of fear and paranoia, the world a living nightmare.

At the same time as we dealt with the dilemma of in-home care, Sean and I were dealing with the bureaucracy of the elder care system. And what an effed-up system it is. To add insult to injury, a couple of family members started preying on her financially, forcing Sean and me to begin the process of obtaining guardianship to protect her. We had to hire a good attorney who specializes in elder law. This is a necessity for all the court orders and whatnot involved in this very complex process, but extraordinarily expensive. Going on the recommendation of a coworker in a similar situation, I found a great lawyer. By the time the guardianship was all said and done the bill came to just under $10,000.

The process of obtaining guardianship was exhausting. We first had to get Mom formally deemed "incompetent". To do this, three formal medical assessments had to be made, involving a battery of invasive questions and tests to determine Mom's mental ability. Or inability, as it were. But guess where, by law, the assessors are required to leave a copy of the assessment outlining the state of incompetency? With the patient! The same patient that is in denial of having anything wrong with them and is convinced the ones seeking guardianship are trying to get them locked up in a place they have no desire to go. Nothing, to me, could be more asinine. After receiving these reports, which all agreed about her incompetency, Mom would stew in her own juice, reading them over and over, underlining the words "incompetency" and "Ward", until she finally erupted like a powder keg, spitting the words in my face. I find no justification for the law requiring this automatic distribution of these reports if incompetency is determined, unless, at the very least, the report is requested by the patient. Handing these over simply for the sake of doing so only causes undue pain and duress for all parties involved.

Regrettably, getting the incompetency determination was only the beginning. The next step was the court hearings. Plural. For these, Mom was assigned legal representation, a woman who knew nothing about her and was therefore prone to believe anything Mom said. And believe me when I tell you, dementia patients can be very convincing about their perceived reality. Because they fully believe the deceptions they are hawking, it is their reality. Add to this their uncanny sense of knowing when to be on their best behavior, and the wool is easily pulled over any unsuspecting person's eyes. Mom was a master of all these things. For years she had every member of the family except for me convinced she was fine, saying she was just getting a little old. She knew what to say, what to ask, or when to be quiet to make you believe she was following a conversation. Even Sean believed I was exaggerating the extent of her mental slip. She was that good.

True to form, when Mom's assigned legal representative visited her for the first time, she saw a sweet little old lady, who seemed mentally acute and utterly sincere about claims that her daughter was trying to commit her to a "home" in order to get her hands on the bank account and belongings. When I arrived at the end of their meeting for my daily visit and met the woman, her gaze was cold and critical. I am certain she would have fallen for Mom's story had my mother not had a momentary angry lapse when she saw me, resulting in a nasty accusatory outburst. The woman looked utterly shocked by my mother's sudden change, and as embarrassed as I was for Mom, I was never so thankful for one of her Dr. Jekyll and Mr. Hyde moments.

At the first court hearing, the dementia patient and their legal representative face off against the guardian seeker(s) and their attorney in front of the judge and the case is argued. Prior to this hearing, I had never been in a judge's chambers, and I found the place intimidating as hell. When asked to state my name, I was so nervous I momentarily forgot it. The judge's massive walnut desk sat on a platform behind which hung a huge Florida State Seal, flanked by state and national flags. The judge was a refined looking woman in her late sixties, tall with short dark hair, impeccably dressed in a cobalt blue suit, wearing glasses. Before she said the first word, I could tell she was brilliant. There was something about the way she carried herself and the air of respect she evoked from everyone around her, even the attending guard, that gave her unquestionable presence. When little girls dream of becoming a judge, they dream of being like this woman.

Normally the patient is supposed to attend this hearing, for what purpose I can't understand, since everything the court needs to know can be gleaned from the doctors' reports. Blessedly, Mom's attorney had agreed to excuse her. I can't imagine how painful and confusing this hearing would have been for her. Sean and I were forced to air Mom's dirty laundry and drag her dignity through the dirt to drive home the incompetency point and her mental decline. A hollow victory was won with temporary guardianship granted, rubbing salt in an already open wound. The day was painful and left me nauseous.

A second and final hearing was held several weeks later to grant Sean and me permanent guardian status. Same scenario, different day. Dual guardianship was granted to us, overriding our Power of Attorney. I would have thought that would have made things easier for us, but it didn't. Explaining guardianship to the financial institutions, insurance companies, medical and assisted living facilities has been a losing, frustrating battle. None of them understands that being the legal guardian for an adult is no different than being the legal guardian of a child. The order entitles me to act as my mother's representative of person and property, all inclusive, with access to all her financial statements, which I'm required by law to file annually with the courts in a ninety-page document outlining the expenditure of every penny.

Obtaining these financial statements is supposed to be as easy as providing these institutions copies of the guardianship grant from the court, but nothing has been as easy as it was supposed to be. I have spent whole days on the phone just trying to get the address changed. And failed. To this day there is still one annuity company that will not change the address on the statement, nor will they forward a copy of it to me, claiming they don't honor the guardianship court order, nor the power of attorney. They want my mother to go online and put in her password. The absurdity of this is mind numbing. Fortunately, I found a work-around. Every year I place a call to my mother's former financial consultant, the one who sold her the annuity, and he draws down the form using some mysterious password on some mysterious website. He then admonishes me for not updating the address, but will not help me do so, claiming he has no authority to assist. I have some choice words for all of them that do not bear repeating.

Since we knew Mom would not easily transition into any type of an assisted living facility, perceiving them all to be "homes" where every manner of torture was carried out, Sean and his wife Rosa decided to take her into their home and care for her. We set up their guest room with all Mom's furnishings and comforts, making everything look as close to what she was used to as possible, and gave the new living situation a trial run. After only one week it became clear this plan wasn't going to work. Mom hit her hip on the bedpost when getting up to use the bathroom in the middle of the night, and then freaked out when she saw the bruise the next day, accusing Rosa of beating her. Mom then repeated this lie to everyone that called or stopped in to see her. My brother was terrified he was going to lose his job in law enforcement, should someone believe Mom and file a complaint against them.

Before my brother or sister-in-law got incarcerated for things they didn't do, we decided Mom would be better off in assisted living where she could be cared for by trained professionals. We went on an intensive search to find the best assisted living facility for Mom in our area. Unbeknownst to us, we were about to embark on the most troubling learning experience of our lives.

****

If you have a loved one with dementia and need to go through this process, this is where you need to start taking notes.

Sean and I first enlisted the help of an agency that assists families with location and placement of dementia patients in care facilities. These services are free because the placement companies get paid directly from the facilities (Remember the last part of that sentence. They. Get. Paid. By. The. Facilities.). The placement agency representative, usually a former nurse, sets up appointments for you to tour each location, ensuring when you arrive everything is hunky dory, then hands you off to the facility's marketing person, who will paint you a rosy picture that includes everything you want to hear. If you have not done your homework, you are a sitting duck and they will get you. They got us.

Polished marble floors. A lovely dining room with white tablecloths. A baby grand piano and crystal chandelier in the foyer. A cozy self-serve snack café. An inviting bar with happy hour. All sounds wonderful, right? Wrong. Unless all those pretty trappings come with top notch, compassionate, qualified care, run for your life. Care is what you're looking for. All the rest is just lipstick, rouge, and nothing more than a pretty façade to impress the family. The patient could care less about all that garbage. What they need is comfort, compassion, and competent care.

Taking the bait not knowing any better, Sean and I chose the facility with the gleaming marble floors and baby grand piano in the foyer. We stroked a hefty check to place a hold on a junior suite for Mom. With a large bedroom, bathroom, and separate sitting room, the layout looked perfect for her furniture and there was to be an opening the following week. Except there wasn't. The following week we found out we had been bumped down the list, the junior suite had gone to someone else, and they had no idea when another would become available. We were given the option of taking an efficiency room until a junior suite opened up, or we would have to wait. We chose to wait, not wanting to move Mom any more than necessary. If there is one thing dementia patients don't do well, it is move.

Home at Sean's, Mom's outbursts got worse. She downright refused to shower. This was nothing new. Not showering had been one of the first red flags for me years before her dementia diagnosis. This little woman who had always been one to have her hair, makeup, outfit, and accessories just so, started to go a week or more without bathing and never brushed her teeth. At Sean and Rosa's, she became adamant, digging her feet in like a kid, absolutely refusing to get in the shower. She could not be cajoled, bribed, or convinced, and everyone was afraid to push the subject, fearing she'd call the police and make accusations of us doing something horrible.

Besides the hygiene issues and beating delusions, Mom began a whole litany of accusations involving food. When she got an upset stomach from overeating, she would accuse Rosa of poisoning her food. Overeating became as common as not showering. Mom would forget she had eaten a full meal within a half-hour of finishing and be looking for food, saying she was hungry. If there were sweets in the house, forget about it. In a day they'd be gone. And if we explained to Mom that she had just eaten, she would call us liars and accuse us of trying to starve her. There is no explaining or reasoning with dementia patients. Like very young children, they are mentally unable to do the cognitive math. We, unfortunately, were not aware of that fact at this stage of our learning experience.

Utterly exhausted by the day-to-day challenges of dealing with her disease and seeing no other option, we decided to take the efficiency offer at the assisted living facility. We moved in Mom's things, hung pictures and drapes trying to make the room feel homey, got counseled on how to leave her there, and did as we were instructed. I felt exactly like I had after dropping Dani off on her first day of kindergarten. Guilt. Horrible, awful guilt, bringing back unresolved abandonment issues from my childhood. Making things even worse was the harsh, unsolicited judgment from family members that had no business judging. These were the same family members that had done nothing but play on Mom's sympathies when they realized she was vulnerable, robbing her of thousands and thousands of dollars before I could stop them.

Which brings me to critical lessons learned about planning for the future of an aging adult:

> *Immediately after deciding upon the beneficiary of any liquid assets, go to the bank, and have the beneficiary assigned as the POD (Payable on Death) on all accounts. By doing this, all cash will transfer to the beneficiary after your death without any red tape. Also, the minute guardianship is obtained, lock those bank accounts down by taking away the loved one's signatory rights. I know it sounds mean. I know it's hard. I know you will feel like you are violating them. But you are not. You are protecting them and*

their assets. Assets you will need to provide for their care. And as their guardian, keeping your loved one safe and looking out for their best interests is your responsibility and duty.

Before I leave this tangent, a couple more things. Make sure you have a formalized will and think about establishing a trust. Keep it easy and make sure your designations are clear. Have a power of attorney. Let your beneficiary know where they can find a list of your holdings, statements, account numbers, and passwords. Ensure designees can get a hold of your annual statements. Have a living will and appoint a healthcare surrogate in writing. Be sure the person you designate will be able to carry out their duties. If you have wishes for how you want to be handled after death, including any ceremony or celebration of life, let them be known. Lastly, clean out your stuff! Shred the paperwork you don't need, get rid of the clothes that don't fit, donate things you no longer use, and earmark the particulars you want to keep for specific family and friends. Leaving this for your family to handle is a burden they don't want or need and handling your business in advance will greatly ease the suffering of those you leave behind, either in death or later stage dementia.

These were all lessons we had to learn the hard way.

Back at the assisted living facility, it took months before a junior suite was available. Mom was cramped in the tiny efficiency, which barely fit her queen bed and a dresser.

Though she had adjusted, I was elated when the suite came open. She desperately needed more room. Sean and I arranged for movers to bring over the furniture and accouterments we had placed in storage, and we took the day off to make the switch.

> *Speaking of which, if you have a full-time job, be sure to apply for FMLA (Family and Medical Leave Act). The paperwork is a pain, but acceptance ensures safety of your job with all the time off you will burn for court, attorney consults, patient care meetings, medical appointments, and miscellany. And there's a lot of miscellany.*

After the movers had packed up Mom's things from storage, I met them at the facility to set up Mom's new space. Meanwhile, Sean and Rosa took Mom out for the day so I could get everything situated. I obtained the keys to the junior suite from the front desk, opened the door, and found it wasn't a junior suite at all. The only difference with this new room and the efficiency was that the bedroom area was larger. Furious, with movers holding Clampett-looking dollies of Mom's belongings behind me, I called down to the marketing woman, who insisted I had the right room. Not believing my claims, she finally met me upstairs, saw that the room was a single bedroom open layout without a sitting area, and apologized for her mistake. Not knowing what else to do, stuck there in the hall between a rock and a hard place, I moved Mom into the smaller one-bedroom and called it a day. There was no way I was putting Mom through yet another move, so I leveraged the massive inconvenience for a discounted rent and made the best of it.

Mom grew accustomed to her new apartment, but Sean and I never grew accustomed to the lack of promised care.

Laundry, which was to be done twice a week, was never done unless I physically put the overflowing laundry basket on the floor attendant's desk. Mom's twice a week shower never happened, so she began to smell and got chronic urinary tract infections, which are notoriously dangerous for seniors and cause extreme moodiness and irritability. Sheets that were to be changed once a week, never once got changed unless I did it. Reminders to go down to the dining room and eat were rarely given, so meals were sent up to Mom's room for an additional charge. Medication was improperly dispensed, handed to her in a cup, which she would stash in her cupboard or throw away. And because she wasn't getting her meds, her paranoia quadrupled, and she began phoning everyone on her contacts list to come rescue her.

Don't for a moment think Sean and I didn't take any action. We installed canary cameras and either he or I was up their ass every single day. We scheduled meeting after meeting, at which our complaints were met with every excuse in the book. They said her laundry wasn't done because she would insist there wasn't any when they asked. I gave them permission to just go in and get the laundry basket. They still didn't do it. They said she didn't heed reminders to shower, so there was nothing more they could do. To address this, I had to go to her apartment several times a week to get her into the shower, an effort that exhausted the both of us. The ironic thing was that once she was under the water, she'd say how nice it felt, and after I'd blow dry and style her hair, she'd be happy as a clam and thank me. When I brought up the medication issue to the executive director, a violation that could have shut the place down, at one meeting he accused me of planting the pills and at another meeting he said staff told him Mom had spit the pills back into the cup after the nurse left. The pills were so tiny she would have had to be a magician for that to happen. It went on and on and on. Excuse after excuse, no positive outcomes, no changes, only charges for care my mother was not receiving.

A couple months in, the Executive Director and head of Nursing told us that in order to get the level of care we desired (the care for which Mom was paying but not receiving), we would need to either hire private care, or move Mom into the memory care section of the facility. This is where we began to get clarity. The lack of care for my mother and the disregard of our concern was all about money! The facility was trying to squeeze us by forcing Mom into the more expensive part of the facility, which offered the exact same level of "care" and fewer accommodations. Our response was a firm "no thank you!"

After a battle over them increasing the price for Mom's care without actually increasing the care itself, something that sounds insane, but they tried to pull constantly and have to be challenged on, we sought out private care. In this quest, we for once got lucky. So very, very lucky. A male nurse I trusted gave me the name of a private healthcare worker named Sharon, and she turned out to be a godsend.

In a matter of days Sharon had Mom freshly showered and dressed, sheets and laundry done on schedule, ensured medication was taken, had introduced Mom to a new friend in independent care who sat with her in the dining room, and texted us pictures and shift reports to record Mom's progress and any issues. Sharon would take Mom on outings to the grocery store or to her favorite restaurants for lunch, make sure her nails and hair got done when I couldn't get away from work, and spoke to her with warmth, compassion, and kindness. I was in awe and Mom loved her. Immediately Mom's demeanor brightened, and she looked and sounded more like the mother I remembered. Sharon had brought her back to us.

Two years passed and Mom continued to decline. She became incontinent and had to be transitioned into adult diapers. That was a hard one. Mom fought against it tooth and nail, but with the help of Sharon and my friend Phyllis, who had begun working in patient care when not doing facials, she eventually got used to it. During this time the COVID 19 pandemic hit and for a year and a half Sharon and Phyllis stepped in as Mom's advocates and our only lifeline when family was not allowed to visit. I don't know what we would have done without them, and shudder when I am left to wonder what happens to patients who do not have family or caring people to look out for them.

At the end of that second year in assisted living, Mom's doctor agreed that the time had come to move her into memory care. She needed more help than private part-time care could provide, needing full-time assistance managing mealtimes, adult diapers, hygiene, and other common daily tasks like dental care. Sean and I both agreed to begin a more in-depth search of memory care facilities in the area. We toured each one recommended by friends. We looked at reviews online. We queried our medical friends. Then we sat down and poured over each facility, choosing the one we hated least. On a rainy December morning, we moved her into the new place and followed the misguided advice of the nursing staff, who told us not to visit for the first week or two so she could adjust. This advice was seconded by Mom's doctor. My gut screamed that I shouldn't listen, and I shouldn't have! Moving her there and leaving her there unattended would be the worst thing I could have done, and a decision that will haunt me for a very long time.

After a week had passed with Mom in the new facility, I stopped in for a quick visit before leaving town on a week-long trip. Staff buzzed me in, and I saw Mom sitting in the Activities Room. She seemed to be engaging in an art project, so I had the CNA let me into her room to put away the clean laundry I had washed after the move. When the CNA opened the door, the rancid smell of urine hit me like a punch in the face. The floor, which had been clean at move-in, was sticky and disgusting. Through the apartment window, I could see Mom in the Activities Room and she looked unwashed and was not wearing her glasses, which had been left on her nightstand. I brought all of this to the attention of the CNA accompanying me and her response was, "Well, this room doesn't smell as bad as most." That should have been my cue to get Mom the hell out of there!

As I looked around Mom's room, in her bathroom I noticed several pairs of Mom's soiled pants in the laundry basket, so I began asking questions. When was the last time Mom's laundry had been done? When was the last time she had showered? How was she adjusting? When would her room be mopped and cleaned?

The CNA accompanying me took a defensive stance and said she could answer none of my questions because she was new. I asked her who I could talk to that wasn't new and could give me some answers. She told me she would get the nurse. I waited an hour, visited with Mom when she came back from crafting, never saw the nurse or CNA again, and had to leave to catch my plane. On the way out I asked the CNA sitting at the desk talking on her cellphone to please schedule a UTI test for my mother, make sure her laundry was done, that her floors got mopped and that she got in the shower. The CNA, with a dismissive attitude, said she would "tell the nurse." Before I left town I put in calls and left phone messages at the nursing station, with the facility manager, and with the executive director. None gave me a call back.

Five days later when I touched down from my trip, I went directly from the airport to visit my mother. The urine smell in her room was now even stronger and she looked equally worse for the wear. In the bathroom I collected eight pair of urine-soaked pants and one dirty blouse that had been scattered from the toilet to the unused shower stall. I had set the shower nozzle to face the wall on my last visit so it would have to be moved to be used, and it hadn't budged. I also found two feces-stained towels on her lazy boy, which I added to my dirty laundry heap. All this I collected while trying to be nonchalant and ascertain the state of my mother's emotional and mental condition, which were not well. She was down, unhappy, irritable, and grumpy, so I stayed with her until she went for dinner trying to bolster her spirits. I really wanted to get her in the shower, but I knew that would be impossible in her frame of mind and only further upset us both. I promised her I would return the next day and stopped at the nurses' station to demand some answers. The same CNA that had let me into her room on my prior visit, the one claiming she was new, was the only one there. She claimed again to have no knowledge of why my mother had not had a shower, why her laundry had not been done, why her floor had not been mopped, or if the UTI test had been ordered. I left my phone number on a sticky note and asked that "the nurse" call me immediately. I never got a call.

At home I washed Mom's laundry three times in hot water with bleach and borax to get the urine smell out. I took the laundry over the next day on a mission to get the situation rectified. This time when I arrived, there were five pairs of soiled pants in the laundry basket since I had been there the day before. I soon discovered why. After talking Mom into taking a shower and washing her hair, I found she was not wearing a pull-up and the pants she was wearing were urine-soaked. That made six pairs of soiled pants in 24-hours, and her shoes and socks were also soaking wet with urine. She had been wearing the same socks and shoes for the thirteen days that she had been there.

Below her bathroom sink, I found the still unopened package of adult pull-ups that had been placed there on the day she moved in. Pull-ups that they had told us would be checked every two hours for changing. This explained the putrid smell, the multiple soiled pants, the wet shoes, the soiled bed clothes, the sticky floor, and the red sores on her buttocks. Swallowing the tears, the guilt, the anger, and the frustration, I lovingly bathed and dressed my mother in clean clothes. I put her in clean socks and dry shoes. I did her hair. We did a word search. We watched a Hallmark movie. And I thanked God that by the time I left, Mom's dementia had evaporated the memory of ever having been dirty.

Leaving her, I hunted down "the nurse" and spoke to her through anger so thinly veiled I was uncontrollably shaking from head to foot. The nurse said she had no knowledge of a UTI test being ordered, nor had she received any calls, messages, or notes from me. She informed me Mom's shower days were Mondays, Wednesdays, and Fridays, and that Mom had been showered on those days. She said Mom's laundry had been done that morning, and her floors had been mopped on Friday. These lies made me furious.

I went out to the car and phoned my brother and his wife, who had just returned from a trip to take care of Rosa's dad, who was also suffering from dementia. I filled them in on what had been happening and asked Sean to come over and immediately install the canary cameras. We had not installed the camera earlier because we were waiting to get a copy of the contract to see the exact camera stipulations. The director at the new facility told us during our initial visit that cameras were permitted, and Sean remembered signing an authorization for it. Though we had asked for a copy of the contract, none had yet been provided.

Note to readers: Always get a copy of the contract on the day of signing.

What happened next left us infuriated. Immediately after camera installation we witnessed staff interacting aggressively with Mom. They stood over her menacingly barking orders "Change into your pajamas!" and using my name as a threat "Your daughter says you need to change!". Aides startled Mom out of a sound sleep several times during the night by letting the door slam loudly behind them after wellness checks. At 5:17 AM the "new" CNA came into Mom's room, threw off her covers waking her from sleep and shouted at her to "Go pee!" When Mom was done, the aide ordered her to dress and took her to a lazy boy in the TV room to wait for breakfast, which wasn't served for two more hours at 7:40 AM. We got our answer as to why she looked so exhausted after being there for only a few days. This was their idea of compassionate care. And it got worse.

The afternoon of the following day, Sean, Rosa and I met with the executive director, the facility manager, and a healthcare representative friend of ours, to discuss what we had witnessed. Excuses and denials were made for all of it, and we were told it was all one big misunderstanding. They assured us Mom's room would be sanitized, her UTI test would be ordered, her pull-ups would be regularly checked, and shower/laundry schedules would be followed. We were told that aides would not weaponize my name, they would watch their tone, and no one would wake my mother while she slept. We left the meeting apprehensive that all would be fine. We told them we would give them one last chance and that we'd be watching. Good thing, because they retaliated.

That evening, not five hours after we left that meeting, one aide badgered mom to get into her pajamas. Another hovered over her and tormented her by saying things such as "Your daughter is getting us in trouble because she says you are sleeping in your dirty clothes!" and "Your daughter says you must change into your pajamas!" When Mom balked and didn't comply, another aide came in and ordered Mom to "Go pee!" When Mom still didn't comply, the second aide threw a pull-up onto Mom's bed in frustration and left.

A short time later the second aide came back. Mom greeted her in a friendly manner but was ignored. The aide stalked over to stand in front of Mom sitting quietly in her chair and ordered her again to "Go pee!" Presumably this aide was trying to get a urine sample for the UTI test, though she never explained that. The aide was dressed in street clothes and had no visible identification. For all my mother knew, she was some nefarious stranger who wandered into her room. When Mom did not comply with the order, the woman threw herself onto my mother's bed and for forty minutes talked on her iPad device, flashing Mom dirty looks whenever Mom glanced over at her. Mom became more and more visibly upset, clutching her purse to her body and appearing confused. Finally, Mom got up, went over to the bed and demanded the woman leave. The aide refused and continued to order Mom to pee. Mom declined, opened her room door and motioned for the woman to get out. The woman ducked from Mom's hand motion and an altercation took place just out of view of the camera. Next thing we saw was Mom holding the door open in the hallway while ordering the woman to leave, the woman refusing, and the video skipping to Mom clearly upset in her chair, clutching her purse, muttering "that bitch" and biting the air.

Sean and Rosa were at dinner when this video was happening, but thankfully Sean happened to check his feed and caught the altercation taking place. I was playing with my granddaughter without my phone but got in my car to go home just as the whole thing ended and Sean called me. We all raced over to the facility as fast as we could get there. Sean and Rosa contacted the executive director on the way. He was more concerned that we had a video camera in the room than he was about the event. Sean reminded him the contract specifically stated we could have a video camera in the room and asked him again for the contract copy we never received. He said he would get the contract to us and have his facility director address the situation with the aide. Sean told him the aide was to have no contact whatsoever with my mother.

While Sean spoke to the executive director, I arrived at the facility and went directly to Mom's room. It took me over an hour to get her calmed down. She was so upset she was feverish. Sean and Rosa arrived soon after with a hot fudge sundae and with all of us there Mom finally relaxed. I got her changed into her pajamas and once we were sure she was okay, we went out to Sean's car and called the Department of Child and Family Services to file an elderly abuse report. Nobody from the facility ever contacted us or came to the location.

We kept watch on the video through the night. It notified us whenever anyone entered the room. Aides checked on Mom several times throughout the night, slamming the door behind them when they left, waking her each time. At 6:08 AM an aide woke Mom for breakfast by ordering her to "Go pee!", and that was it for me. I had seen enough. At 7:15 AM I arrived to spend the day, fearing for Mom's safety and unable to sleep. I spent the next 24 hours in the room with her, afraid to leave her alone for fear of further retaliation. Sean and Rosa, meanwhile, called and toured other memory care facilities desperate for a safe place to relocate her.

In the afternoon, the executive director and facility director arrived in the room to deliver a copy of the contract. The executive director said because we had reported the incident, he had been in contact with his corporate office, and they had informed him the contract was incorrect because the memory care unit was not allowed to have video cameras, so I would have to remove them. I told him to get the eff out.

Minutes after the executive director left, Sean called with great news. He and Rosa had found the perfect facility for Mom. It was clean, small, homey, developed by Alzheimer researchers, run by dementia care doctors, and the staff seemed excellent. Their visit had been unannounced, but they could find nothing amiss or lacking. They had even spoken to a family member leaving from a visit, and he had raved about the care his father was receiving there. Seemingly meant to be, they had an opening that morning for immediate move-in, and the cost was $2,000 a month cheaper than the horrible place we were moving her out of. Ecstatic, I told Sean to jump on it and I began quietly packing up Mom's room as she napped in her chair. I continued packing through the night while she slept peacefully and had her ready to go by morning.

By the end of the following day, Mom was relocated. Her adjustment was a breeze thanks to a skilled, brilliant staff, and she is happier than I've seen her in many years. A lovely, wonderful woman named Jackie, whom they all call the shower whisperer, gets Mom to shower willingly. I don't know how she does it, but she has the magic touch. Jackie also alerts medical staff if Mom is having an "off day" so they can check her for a UTI. Mom has only had one since she's been there, caught early and treated immediately.

Mom's nurse Peggy calls me with frequent updates or any concerns no matter how small, and I am never wanting for information. Claire and Antoinette at the front desk greet me by name and know exactly who my mother is and what she's been up to. Their executive director, the incredible Joy, also knows every resident and their families on a first name basis. Everyone from the top down is hands on.

Mom eats at a dining room table that looks very much like one she would have in her own home and sits in the same seat with the same people. Joey, the facility's amazing activities director, engages her in creative, fun activities that keep her entertained and moving. I have caught Mom playing volleyball in the kitchen area using a pool noodle and beach ball, decorating giant Mardi Gras masks for a wagon float, and fishing in the front pond (which has no fish). She is sometimes so wrapped up in what Joey has her doing that Sean and I have gotten the brush off. It is wonderful to be able to sleep at night knowing Mom is being tended to in such a competent, compassionate, kind, and gentle manner. These people are angels on earth.

DCF and the Melbourne Police Department have gone silent on our case against the previous facility. I called the investigators several times, but after they got my initial statements, they no longer seemed to care, even telling me since Mom didn't die or wasn't hospitalized, nothing likely would be done.

On the evening after relocating Mom to where she is now, I completely and totally lost my shit. All that pent up emotion came pouring out and I was a mess for a few days. But thanks to my family and some really baller friends, my chosen family, I survived to share my story. I guess I even need to give a shout out to my brother, who I've had to lean on throughout this process, as the pitfalls seem never-ending. Who knew I'd ever say that about Baby Brat, right? Anyhow, thanks, Bro.

That brings us back to the green blouse sitting before me on the table in need of a tag for Mom's birthday. There are so many funny things I would love to write, but Mom would no longer understand them. I am so thankful to have gotten the chance to have had her enjoy my funny tags in years gone by.

These days I give blessings for the little things, like that she even still knows who I am, because the day is coming when she won't. That will be a hard one. But until then, like a wonderful silver lining to this dementia storm cloud, I still have one *To-From* to use whose story has not yet faded into dust:

To: MOM

From: CQ

****

CQ is my oldest nickname, and one with which Mom still greets me. Some days I wonder if she's forgotten my real name, but I like CQ better anyhow.

CQ is short for CQ *Shuson* (pronounced Shoos-on), derived from my love affair with my very first pair of shoes. As the story goes, during my golden-ringleted, toddler years, I would race to the front door every evening to greet my work-weary father, home from a long day at the office. One day he found me already waiting for him in the threshold, full of the devil, dancing in circles, chirping and squealing like a baby squirrel with its tail on fire.

Dad scooped me up and held me at arms-length, while my feet performed a furious mid-air cha-cha. I was chattering a string of mystifying syllables, which he could only make out to be, "CQ shuson! Daddy, CQ shuson!"

Amused and bewildered, he turned me to face my mother and begged a translation. "What on earth is this child trying to tell me, dear?"

My mother broke into a smile at my antics and informed my father that earlier that day we girls had made our maiden pilgrimage to Jakubick's, a veritable promised land of fashion footwear. There, much to my delight, Mom had purchased me my very first pair of black, patent leather Mary Janes, which I now sported with furrowed brow and crossed arms at my father's lack of enthusiasm.

"So," my mother concluded, "your little darling is asking you to please admire her exquisite, good taste, and 'see the cute shoes she has on'. CQ shuson, dear."

Dad roared and set me down, so I could pirouette around the room and delight in my fabulous new shoes. And my nickname was born. Since that very day, they've both called me CQ Shuson, or "CQ" for short.

Mom smiled at the tag when she read it atop the box with the lovely green blouse. She recognized both Sean and me this 81st day of her birth and we had a wonderful visit. Her birthday was a good day and my only hope is there will be more. Many, many more.

She probably will have forgotten Sean and I were even there to share her special day by the time we hit the parking lot, but staff has told us that she carries a smile with her all day long after we've visited. Though she may not remember why she's happy, her heart tells her something good has happened. So, Sean and I try to go as often as we can, though these visits are so incredibly, unbelievably hard.

I drove home after my visit lost in thought with a bittersweet heart. I had left the tag on her dresser next to the flowers

Sean had brought, carnations, her favorite. My hope is that she will pick up the tag and know the tiny dancing girl in the Mary Janes had come by to wish her German mother with the fright of a pantry a happy St. Patty's Day birthday. I sure do hope so.

I love you, Mommy. Happy birthday! XOXOXO, CQ.

Chapter 4: APRIL

On the dewy first morning of April, I was alone at work and grateful to be so. Doug and his ridiculous yak hat were out of town on a business trip, and I was under a deadline to finish a complex engineering project and had no time for April Fool's shenanigans. Had Doug been in the office, he would have been merciless. As my cubemate in years past, Doug had pranked me with fake bugs, transposed the buttons on my mouse, smeared my desk phone receiver with charcoal, and jumbled the letters on my keyboard. My only place of April Fool's refuge had been the ladies' room, and even there I'd found myself checking to see if plastic wrap was covering the bowl before I sat down. Doug was not to be trusted.

Truthfully, none of the significant men in my life were to be trusted when the calendar flipped to April 1st. I had been pranked, deceived, duped, and hoodwinked by every single one of them, be it friend, family, or foe. Even when I was a youngster and my dad's custody weekend fell on April Fool's Day, there had been mischief afoot. Dad and Sean would join forces to short sheet my bed, freeze my underwear, substitute cream cheese for toothpaste or replace the salt with sugar. Things didn't get any better on April 1st after I married, either. Rick enlisted Dani to help him rig the sprayer on the kitchen sink to soak me, sneak slimy gel animals between the bed sheets, or remove all the towels from the bathroom while I was in the shower. The list of tomfoolery with me on the receiving end was infinite, causing me to wonder whether I am an easy target or a very good sport. Though I would like to think the latter is the case, I know in my heart the former is probably closer to the truth.

This year, resting easy with Doug out of town and no current man in my life, I hadn't even given April 1st a second thought. It was only because I was engrossed in the details of my work project that I jumped when my desk phone rang, the unwelcome interruption breaking my concentration. Groping blindly for the receiver, patting a hand around the general vicinity of the phone without taking my eyes from my computer, I knocked it off the cradle, grabbed it up, and shoved it between my chin and shoulder to bark out an irritated, "Hello?" My dad's voice sounded from the other end of the line. He was old school and liked phoning from landline to landline, fed up with dropped calls from his flip phone, which we all suspected he caused himself.

"Hey, CQ, I've got some exciting news! I was talking to your step-monster (a nickname for my stepmother that we used endearingly) about her upcoming birthday, and she said she wants to treat you and your brother to a cruise. So, I found a great deal and booked the four of us on a week-long excursion from April 16-23. I know you said you had vacation time banked, so do you think you can get off?"

Crickets.

"CQ, are you there?"

I had nearly fainted. Dad wanted to take me on a cruise? Though normally a pretty frugal guy, Dad did make exceptions when it came to travel. Wow, he had booked a cruise! I had never been on a cruise!

"Yeah, Dad I'm here! I'll check my calendar right now," I exclaimed, sitting up in my chair and opening my Outlook calendar to see if I had any date conflicts. Suddenly, the April 1st date caught my eye, and I realized I was being suckered. Oh, that sneaky devil; he almost got me! Oh, hell no!

"Yeah, nice try, Dad, but you're not fooling me this year! I know what you're up to, although I admit you had me going for a minute there. Free cruise? Don'cha think that was a little mean?"

"Mean? What are you talking about? I'm serious! We're leaving on Holland America out of Port Canaveral on the 16th. It's what Sweet Pea wants (Sweet Pea was my Father's pet name for my stepmother). We're going to have a ball. Really!"

"Mmm hmmm. Whatever, Dad. Well, listen, I'm really busy and don't have time for fun and games right now, but I'll give you a call this weekend and we can catch up. I gotta run. Happy April Fools' Day! Love you, Dad. Bye!"

As I hung up I could hear him sputtering at the other end, "April Fools' Day? Oh, no! Wait! CQ!" Man, he was really getting into it this year. The old guy seriously needed to consider a new hobby; he was incorrigible since he retired.

I went back to work and safely passed the rest of the day without further incident. That night I congratulated myself and went to bed with dry hair in a fully sheeted bed with no slimy things. Best April Fool's Day ever!

The following morning at work, my desk phone rang again. And again, Dad was on the line. He began speaking before I could even get the receiver to my ear.

"Okay, it's April 2nd, so let's try this again. Please get vacation for April 16-23, because we're going on a cruise for Sweet Pea's birthday.

Crickets.

"Hello? CQ?"

This time my end was silent because I had dropped the phone in a mad dash to my boss's office to submit a vacation request. Holy cow, I was going on a cruise!

Two days later I got a FedEx package from Dad. Inside was a glossy, blue Holland America folder containing room location (Sean and I would be sharing a balcony cabin right next to Dad & Sweet Pea's), a layout of the ship, meal information, destination itinerary, entertainment schedule, packing suggestions, and add-ons list. The folder had a *To-From* penned on the front in my dad's recognizable hand:

>*To: Who's the fool now?*
>
>*From: D.O.D. (Dear Old Dad)*

Who's the fool now? Me! Slap me in cap n' bells and call me the Joker, this fool was going on a paid vacation!

>******************************

While putting the cruise dates in my phone calendar, I was reminded I needed to schedule an appointment with my friend Robert to get my taxes done before I left. Thank God for Turbo Tax and a buddy who's willing to work for beer. Robert liked Sam Adams Boston Lager so I purchased a case in advance and tagged it to read:

>*To: 'Cause you're my taxman, yeah, my taxmahhhhnnnnn!*
>
>*FROM: Thanks for keeping your pants on*

The origin of the tag is something Robert and I chuckle about to this day, a story he insists is too outrageous to believe, though I have pinky sworn the ridiculous scene is the God's honest truth. We refer to the event as *The Incident*, and though many years have passed since it happened, I can vividly recall the details as if they occurred yesterday. Unexpected nakedness tends to hang with a person.

On the day of *The Incident*, two unwitting victims were claimed: me and my accountant Steve, who unfortunately lost my business as a result. I feel kind of bad about that last part, because *The Incident* really wasn't Steve's fault; he had no idea the office space next to his newly leased location was occupied by a nut job. Or at least I hope he didn't. Steve simply needed more space to stack his disheveled, towering mounds of paperwork (I don't know how he ever found anything in that mess), so he had moved across town to roomier digs at a reasonable price. His new rental was half of a one-story house that had been converted into a commercial side-by-side, the poorly marked Suite B, whose overgrown hedge-lined walkway was around the side of a nondescript, peeling, pale yellow rambler.

In retrospect, I feel the least Steve could have done was to install a big sign with an arrow or put in runway lights or something – anything to let his clients know where they were going. But alas, there was nothing to let Steve's clients know that the entrance to his office wasn't through the front door of the house. We could only but assume, and everyone knows nothing good ever comes from that.

So, this scenario of an unmarked Suite B entryway was what I happened upon, running typically late with W-2s in hand, as I pulled up at the address Steve had provided. Walking briskly down the only walkway I saw, my high heeled shoes clipped loudly against the cement path leading to the front door. Six-inch black painted numbers on a placard above my head were the only obvious markings on the facade, so I was oblivious another entrance existed, nor had Steve informed me of such during any of our previous conversations. (I'm beginning to wonder if perhaps this whole thing *was* Steve's fault.)

Other than providing the street address and instructions to "come to Suite B", Steve had said only to give a shout if he wasn't up front to let him know I was there, since his office was around the corner from the door. Given these instructions, I still thought it odd that all appeared dark with no light emanating from the front windows of the little yellow house, I approached the door. Apprehensively, I gave a knock, but got no reply, so I tested the knob. The handle turned, so I went in.

Instead of the typical reception desk in the foyer, the front door opened into a cavernous, darkened room. Standing at the threshold letting my eyes adjust, my internal alarm system was pinging like a high-speed broadband connector, telling me to flee. Ignoring my instincts, like a half-witted teen age girl in a horror flick, I stepped deeper into the inky darkness, letting the door swing closed behind me. Able to barely make out dull images, I saw there wasn't a stick of furniture in the place. In the blackness I could make out only building materials set against the far wall to my left, and then a small sliver of light coming from a partially open door just off the hallway beyond the darkened room. Thinking that must be Steve, but tongue-tied with a mixture of curiosity and fear, I stayed silent rather than calling out. I cautiously crept down the hall to the lit doorway, hearing what sounded to be a man singing. Arriving at the lit doorway, which beckoned for me to look inside, I hesitantly peered in and ogled a sight that made my mouth drop. There, in all his Fruit of the Loom glory, stood a tall, lanky, middle-aged man, a doppelganger for Kramer from *Seinfeld*, sporting a half-lathered face, and wearing nothing but white briefs and black socks. In his hand was a razor, which doubled as a microphone into which he passionately sung *Womanizer* by

Brittany Spears as he shaved. My feet felt nailed to the floor. The image fried my brain, and I was physically unable to move. Looking on compulsively with a mixture of intrigue and revulsion, I watched as the man bopped and crooned to himself in the mirror.

Daddy-O, you got the swagger of a champion!

Too bad for you, you just can't find the right companion!

I guess when you have…

Mid-sentence when he lifted his chin to shave his neck, he spotted me standing there gawking at him. Startled, he let out a scream and crouched to hide his man parts, dropping his razor in the sink as he floundered for a way to get to the door. The door to what apparently was a bathroom.

Pulling myself from the spectacle, I turned to face the wall opposite the door and shielded my eyes as I spoke. "Sorry, my accountant gave me this address, and I must have written it down wrong!" I turned tail to flee, wondering why I had stayed to explain myself. For cripesake, he could have been a serial killer!

"No, wait," the guy shouted, peeking around from behind the door. "Are you looking for Steve? He's in the next office! Just take a left out the front door and there's an entrance around the side. Follow the walkway to Suite B!"

"Oh, geeez, I'm sorry," I shouted in apology, speaking into the air in front of me as I ran for the front door, afraid to look back, adding, "have a good night!"

Have a good night? Really? Lord, those ingrained Wisconsin pleasantries truly worried me sometimes.

I scurried to Steve's office around the side of the house and found him up at his reception desk waiting for me. "Did you have any problem finding the place?" he asked pleasantly.

Talk about a loaded question. It took me a long moment to answer.

Finally I said, "Nah, the half-naked womanizer shaving next door gives good directions."

Steve just laughed. He thought I was kidding. I told him the story and he neither believed me nor apologized. Steve wasn't raised in the Midwest.

That was the last time I saw Steve or his serenading landlord. When Robert offered his assistance with tax preparation the following year, I gladly accepted his help. Though this Wisconsin girl could never acquire a taste for Boston lager, a case of Sam Adams was well worth the trade.

****

With my taxes filed, I went full steam ahead with cruise preparations. Dad had given Sean and me a boatload of instructions, dos and don'ts, must-not-forgets, and better-nots. I had packed and repacked a half-dozen times and was still making last minute adjustments when Sean arrived to pick me up on our day of departure. I came flying out of the house in a flurry of luggage, keys, sunglasses, hat, hair, and handbag.

"Is that all you're taking?" joked my brother as he struggled to grunt my massive suitcase into his car.

"Yeah, why?" I asked, thinking he was serious. "Do you think I'll need a jacket? You're right! Hold on, I'll be right back," I cried, scurrying back into the house.

My brother got in the car and laid his head on the steering wheel wondering what he had been thinking. He should have known better than to mess with me when I was overstimulated.

A minute later I emerged from the house carrying a jacket and an extra pair of flip flops. I threw myself into the passenger seat of Sean's car and had barely closed the door before he started backing down the driveway. Dad was already blowing up Sean's phone wondering where we were. Though Dad had taught us everything we needed to know about being tardy, God help anyone who was late once Dad was ready, his phone somehow never dropping calls when he was in badgering mode.

Forced to answer before we got calls every three minutes of our 30-minute ride, Sean picked up, putting the call on speaker in his truck. He told Dad we were on our way, after which Dad's phone promptly dropped the call. I busted out laughing. With our family dynamic, this was going to be an interesting week. A real test of adult children's intestinal fortitude.

When Sean and I reached the port terminal, we found my dad and stepmother impatiently waiting by the security area, where we joined them. Having dropped our luggage outside with the stewards, we now had only to go through the port terminal's security checkpoint with our carry-on items before going upstairs to check-in and proceed down the gangplank. With everyone together, we queued up in a jovial mood. A week of fun and adventure awaited, and we couldn't wait to get this party started!

Dad and Sweet Pea were the first to plop their brightly colored canvas totes on the x-ray belt and wait for the contents to be scanned. Greenlighted to continue, Dad shouted to us loudly from the other side of the x-ray machine. "We're going to go upstairs to get checked in. Meet us up there. Don't dawdle!" Dad was hard of hearing and refused to wear his hearing aids, so this announcement was made loud enough to be heard in the Ozarks.

Embarrassed, Sean and I looked at the people in line behind us, pretending Dad was talking to one of them. Nobody fell for our sham, but a few chuckled all the same. Dad and Sweet Pea walked through the turnstile, collected their things, and proceeded up to the mezzanine on the escalator. The impatient Port Authority guard motioned for me to advance, so I threw my bag on the conveyor belt, with Sean right behind me.

My floral blue beach bag contained my bathing suit, sunscreen, small toiletries, and last-minute jacket and flip flops. I watched the rope handle disappear through the x-ray tunnel, walked casually through the scanner, and waited for my bag to be ejected. When it was, I thanked the guard, collected my bag, proceeded to the escalator, and had just climbed onto the first step when I heard a commotion coming from the checkpoint behind me. Glancing over, I saw red lights were flashing above the conveyor belt I'd just left, and a bevy of law enforcement were swooping down around Sean. My brother met my startled stare with his own. I threw my hands into the air with a gesture of *WTF, bro*? He returned a shrug of *I have no friggin' clue*. Then, he mouthed, "Just keep Dad up there!" And my stomach sank to my feet. Lord help me, I was ascending to Little Bighorn to battle Custer.

As it turns out Sean, a cop, had forgotten a small caliber handgun was stashed in the hidden pocket of his fanny pack. The week before our trip, he had completed his first shift on a new bike detail for the police department and had used the fanny pack to carry the small firearm. While packing for our cruise, he had been looking for something small enough to hold his personal documents for when he was on or off the ship, and had landed on the fanny pack. With its many zippered pockets, the pack was perfect for carrying important items and safeguarding them against thievery. A good plan. Except, he forgot about the wee gun concealed in the back pocket.

Also unbeknownst to us and adding to the drama of the moment was that our ship, the Zaandam, had just encountered issues with attempted smuggling not a week before our trip. Zaandam staff had fortunately been successful in thwarting the crime, but Holland America wasn't taking any chances in keeping their noses clean. Ship security was to be on high alert, something the captain of the ship had made clear. Crystal. Clear.

As I reached the top of the escalator, Dad and Sweet Pea were already walking over to investigate what was causing all the commotion downstairs. There was nothing I could do to shield them from what was going on, and oh, weren't they surprised when they saw who was in police custody.

Immediately, my father launched into a tizzy fit and said he was going to march down there and "straighten things out". Translated: we were all about to get incarcerated for the rest of our lives. Thankfully, this day I had Sweet Pea in my corner, and together we were able to restrain the beast, which was much like trying to keep a six-year-old on a sugar high confined to a park bench at Disney while the rest of his classmates were riding Space Mountain. If we let Dad out of our sight for one second, he would have made a beeline for the escalator.

Hours passed with Sean behind closed doors, while the authorities checked his credentials, his story, his squeaky-clean background, telephoned his police chief, met with the port's chief, and in the end our destiny rested on a decision from the ship's captain himself, who had to be called down from the bridge. When I was told this, I imagined Captain Kirk pacing back and forth in his pea green uniform shirt at the helm of Starship Enterprise.

The verdict took forever, and neither Dad, Sweet Pea, nor I could board the ship in the interim. Since I was booked as my brother's roomie, I was guilty by association, and since Dad and Sweet Pea had paid for our passage, they were in the same boat. (Get it? Ha!) Containing our father for lo those many hours had me fit to be tied and I remembered afresh why I went poohicidal on Sean's bear when we were young. This time it was him I could have flushed out to sea.

Just a half-hour before the ship was ready to set sail, the edict came down that we would be allowed to go. By the grace of God the gun hadn't been loaded and there was no ammunition in either the fanny pack or any of Sean's luggage (nor ours). Sean, meticulous about his firearms, had unloaded and cleaned the gun after his shift, putting the unloaded gun back in the pack while placing the ammo in a secured hard box in his home safe. I've never been so grateful that my brother was a goody two-shoes.

Besides being allowed to sail, the other bonus was that less than 4 hours into our trip I had my first *To-From*:

> *To: Fanny Packin'*
>
> *From: Daddy Grabbin'*

Unfortunately, when our bags arrived at the room, they'd been searched, and all my crisply ironed evening clothes needed to be re-pressed. For this, I made my brother pay my bar tab and I spared no expense at quenching my thirst.

****

Once out at sea, things on the cruise began to settle down. Joining us at dinner was another couple, Ed and Louise, longtime friends of my dad and Sweet Pea. Ed, one of my dad's dearest friends, had surprised his wife Louise with the cruise for their 35th wedding anniversary. Louise had been overjoyed. Like me, Ed and Louise had never been on a cruise, and Louise had always wanted to go.

When the happy couple joined up with us, they were in gay spirits. Having been among the first to board, Ed and Louise had been too busy exploring and enjoying the perfect weather, a welcome relief from the frigid Wisconsin tundra from which they had come, to notice we had been detained. We four decided we would keep that little tidbit to ourselves unless asked, and they never asked, so we never volunteered. What happened at the port stayed at the port.

At dinner, Dad cornered Ed and launched into his "Timmy's Ticket to the High Seas" lecture series, a prerequisite for anyone sailing with Dad on their maiden voyage. Having traveled all over the world, my dad was a treasure trove of information on how to do a trip cheap, how to do it right, and how to do it without getting the trots. You see, if Dad had learned anything from his many experiences abroad, it was that the integrity of the bowels was the key to success. Ironically, he most enjoyed sharing this information while up on his soap box pontificating, the definition of which he once told me was diarrhea of the mouth. Perhaps that's why Ed didn't listen.

For two days everything went exactly as planned. Everyone was having a lovely time, and after several enjoyable days at sea, our delighted entourage arrived at the first port, Cozumel. We all disembarked and took the bus to town, shopped, toured, and had a great time. We arrived back on the ship in the late afternoon and decided to grab some sun before cleaning up for dinner. Ed spread out a beach towel on the deck chair next to my dad and they engaged in pleasant conversation. Then Ed reached into his pool bag, pulled out a huge fig, and began devouring it.

"Tim," said Ed to my dad, "you've got to try this. I got it at that market in town and it is just delicious!" Juice from the plump fruit was running down his hand and he was like a kid with a melting ice cream cone. He was making a mess but delighted with himself.

My dad eyed his friend warily. "You didn't get that from the ship? I don't think that was such a good idea, Ed. Remember my warning about certain foods? Figs are extremely rich, especially if you're not used to them, and please tell me you washed it first."

"Don't be ridiculous. It's all natural–a fruit for cripesake. It's fine." He smacked his lips and polished off the last bite.

About a half-hour later, Ed's tummy began a riotous symphony. He became atypically quiet, and his color grew strange. He excused himself and told Louise he was just going to bop up to the room and would be right back. He walked away at a rapid clip, stomach growling like it contained two angry mountain lions battling over a piece of meat. Dad just shook his head as he watched his friend sprint across the deck. There just wasn't reasoning with some people.

By the time Ed reached the elevator, he was in a panic. He thought about using the stairs, but he had a bad knee and didn't think he could make it up five flights fast enough. He was on Level 3, his room was on Level 8, and there were no elevators waiting at the ready. He pressed the elevator up-button so hard he nearly drove it through the wall and into the ocean. He watched the numbers above the bank of doors in desperation, praying like a gambler at the craps table (no pun intended) for one to hit number 3. "C'mon, three," he cried.

Finally, the bell for the middle elevator dinged, and the doors parted. Ed bolted inside and crushed the button for the eighth floor. He danced in place as the doors started to close. Then, just as the doors were two inches from locking together, Ed saw the rubber end of a cane and a gnarled arthritic hand jam into the crevice. The doors reopened and in hobbled a hunched, crotchety old woman who threw Ed a nasty glance.

"Sixth floor!" she barked, as the doors began to close once again.

Ed reached over and punched the 6-button, his stomach protesting loudly and garnering the attention of the old woman. Ed clutched his belly, willing everything to stay put with every fiber of his being. Unfortunately, his innards had reached maximum capacity, and the fig had to go. Without further ado, Ed's intestines dumped their load as the elevator announced their arrival on the sixth floor and the doors rolled open. The old woman stared at Ed with unguarded disdain, released a disgusted breath, and shoved her cane in front of her as she shuffled by.

"Mister," she exclaimed, poking a crooked finger at him as she passed, "you've got a problem!"

"Ya think?!" Ed spat, as the elevator doors closed behind her.

Oh, did he ever. Swim trunks were no match for the load in his shorts, which now ran down his long, tanned legs, over his flip-flops, and onto the elevator floor. When the elevator opened at level eight, Ed poopy danced out the door and made a beeline for his cabin.

Meanwhile, back at the pool, Louise was beginning to worry. She decided to check on her beloved, who wasn't looking so good when he left. Arriving at the 3rd floor pool elevators, she noticed that the middle elevator was closed and there was some kind of maintenance going on. She hoped it wasn't anything mechanical, but her woman's intuition told her there was cause for concern. It wasn't wrong.

When the doors of Louise's elevator opened on the eighth floor, she beheld a sight for which nothing could have prepared her: from the middle elevator to the doorway of her and Ed's cabin was a Hansel and Gretel trail of brown, at the end of which was Ed, scrubbing furiously with a soapy washcloth. Louise was horrified. But there was no time to waste. She sprang into action, throwing herself down on the floor beside her hubby, desperate to remove the evidence before any of their neighbors spied it. Kneeling beside Ed on the hallway floor, swabbing the deck like a mad woman, Louise delivered a blistering tongue-lashing about how Ed never listens. She took this opportunity to cover about 35 years' worth.

At dinner that night, Ed found a wrapped package on his assigned seat at the dinner table. The rest of the group was snickering and watching as he picked up the package and read the tag, which said:

To: Mister, you've got a problem!

From: I bet you'll listen now

Ed tore the wrapping off a package of Fig Newtons and, the good sport he always was, shook his head and laughed with the rest of us.

Thankfully that was the end of misfortune for our at-sea adventure. The remainder of our journey was filled with good times, big wins in the casino, forging new friendships with fellow cruisers, and a boatload of great memories.

As a footnote, according to Louise, Ed never ate one of the cookies and hasn't touched a fig since.

****

Before I knew it, I was back in my cubicle and buried in work from being away for a week. Yawning, I'd just gotten back to my desk with a fresh cup of coffee when one of my engineer co-workers came over with a question. I noticed she looked frazzled and more than a little tired. I assured her I would take care of the error she had brought me earlier and there was no need to worry.

"No, it's not that," she said in reply. "I think I have a squirrel in the attic, and it's had me up for two nights now scratching and gnawing. I can't get a pest control company out until Monday and it's grossing me out. I don't know what to do!" She cried, nearly bursting into tears.

Poor thing! Been there, done that. I had once been the woman coming into work baggy eyed and frazzled, after hearing scratching in the attic.

"I've got you," I exclaimed. "Will you be at your desk after lunch?"

"Yeah, why? Do you know someone that can help?" she asked excitedly.

"Not someone, but something. I just need to run to the store first. I'll explain later, but you need to promise to follow my instructions exactly. No deviating!" I used words her engineer's mind would follow, ensuring she'd listen. I hadn't and the result had been disastrous.

Years prior, my critter nightmare had started during a 3 AM potty run while I was still married. I'd heard something scratching at the ceiling above the bathroom, and I'd woken Rick to listen. He'd groggily dismissed the noise as a squirrel and told me he'd address it in the morning. As he turned over and went back to sleep, the idea of having a disease-ridden rodent wandering carefree under my roof just wigged me out. I didn't sleep all night.

To appease me, the next day Rick pulled down a couple soffit covers to free the interloper, replacing the covers that evening, assuring me the filthy creature had gone about its way. Didn't work. The clawing continued, got louder as the week progressed, and soon the din began waking us both out of a dead sleep. The little beast was now burrowing in the corner of our bedroom directly above our headboard. I was beside myself.

Without the funds to call a pest control company, I decided to consult the maintenance guy at work. James had lived in the south his whole life and was a veritable plethora of information, mostly useless, but some good. True to form, James said he had a surefire solution – mothballs - guaranteed to rid any attic of squirrels. Delighted, off to the store I went on my lunch hour, realizing only after I arrived that James had not provided me with any instructions for use or quantity to buy. Since mothballs were so cheap, I decided to buy all they had – three, large 24-ounce boxes.

Arriving back at home before Rick and not wanting to waste any time, I scrambled up the ladder I'd set below the attic entry and warily peeked through the attic access cover, scared senseless that the horrid little creature was going to fly out of nowhere and attack. Thankfully, all was quiet. I contemplated how to proceed with my stash of mothballs, and never having had cause to use them prior to this time, my rationale went like this:

1. *Okay, there's all this fluffy insulation stuff up here, and it's supposed to protect the inside of the house from the elements, so it should certainly contain the vile odor of these mothballs, right?*
2. *Now, I think I remember hearing that mothballs dissolve over time, so I should be able to just chuck them around and they'll do their thing and then evaporate, right?*
3. *I wonder if it's the smell that drives the little beasts out, or do they eat them? Ewww, gross!*
4. *Whatever, I'm using them all. If a little goes a long way, a crapload is the way to go. I wonder if I bought enough?*
5. *Rick is going to be so proud of me for handling this myself! God, I'm good!*

And with that, I ripped open all three boxes and threw handfuls into every nook and cranny of the tiny attic of our 900-sq-ft house. Satisfied and extraordinarily pleased with myself, I put the ladder back in the garage, cleaned up, and went into the kitchen to make dinner.

Halfway through frying pork chops, I began to get whiffs of a mothball smell. I kept washing my hands, thinking that's where the odor must be coming from. Only, it kept getting stronger, and before long it was downright overwhelming. Soon mothballs were all I could smell. Peeew!

Rick arrived home after picking up our daughter Dani from soccer practice.

"Mom, what is that smell?" Dani shrieked, holding her nose.

"Yeah, hon, it smells like my grandmother's attic in here!" Rick agreed.

I proudly explained what I'd done, and Rick was momentarily speechless. That wouldn't last. Trying very hard to remain calm, he finally managed, "So, you used all three boxes of them?" His voice raised a couple octaves on the 'three', and I knew instantly my blonde gene had screwed me again.

Yep, apparently, my calculations were a little off. As I would discover during James's *Mothballs for Dummies* lecture the following day, a couple pieces in a square of cheesecloth tossed into the center of the crawl space with a retrieval string would have done the job. Three boxes were enough for an entire barrier island, and now, since I'd spewed them willy nilly in every nook and cranny of the cramped attic, there was no hope of remedy. We would have to ride out the stench and wait for the balls to disintegrate. Yikes. But, that shouldn't be too bad, right?

Wrong. Very, very wrong. By nightfall that first evening, there was a stifling cloud of Naphthalene coming from our attic that was so thick I'm certain we asphyxiated every stray critter in a fourteen-mile radius. The stench was virtually pulsating from our house and embedding itself in every crevice of our beings. The gagging smell of mothball would come wafting out of my purse at the grocery store, out of Dani's cleats on the soccer field, and even overpower the stench of brush fire in Rick's bunker gear. There was no escaping it, it would last for weeks and weeks, and it was everywhere! But at least I could rest knowing I had a pest-free attic, right?

Fast forward a month. I'm outside on a pleasant Saturday afternoon doing some yard work (anything to get out of the house), when I hear a painfully familiar scratching coming from the porch roof. I look up, and what do I see? A humongous, disgusting, ghastly, horrible, repulsive, furry, gray rat! I nearly vomited, as I watched the vermin launch itself like the Caped Crusader into the adjacent yucca tree at the corner of my flower bed, skitter over to our palm, brazenly scamper through the branches, peer down at me, stick out its tongue (I swear), retrace its path, and then run back across the porch roof and into our attic through an uncovered soffit hole. Oh. My. God! I nearly died.

First thing Monday morning, I made a beeline for James's office. I read him the riot act and then stood there, arms crossed, waiting for his explanation. Amused, he drawled, "Well now, darlin', mothballs don't work on rats!"

"Are you freaking kidding me?!" I shouted. I thought my head would explode.

After I calmed down, I decided to break down and call in the professionals. I phoned an exterminator, who said he would come by the next day. Relieved that this dreadful nightmare would finally be over, I slept peacefully through the scratching, gnawing, thumping, and mothball stench for the first time in weeks. Finally, we would get some peace!

Rick called me at work the next morning to excitedly tell me the exterminator had put down poison. This time it was my response that wasn't quite what was expected, but there was no speech delay involved. "Poison? No! I wanted traps. Traps!" I shrieked in the middle of the cube farm. I had been watching too many of those hoarder TV shows, and they had left me with visions of the horrid, yellow-toothed rodents dying up there by the dozen, leaving us with decomposing rat oozing from the ceiling and splattering into the gravy boat on Thanksgiving.

As I hyperventilated, Rick frantically tried to explain that there was no need for alarm – the toxins would cause the varmints to come out looking for water, they would die outside, and all would be good. See? I was momentarily quieted…until I spotted the storm clouds looming on the horizon. Now came visions of the repulsive creatures hanging by their craggy nails out the soffit holes, their long, emaciated tongues lapping rainwater off the roof, until their bloated rodent bodies exploded a mushroom cloud of parts and goo across every square inch of my attic.

A week later, sleep deprived and grumpy as hell, I'd given up. The little bastards could gnaw the house to shreds, I didn't care anymore. I would be shunned by society, living in rat squalor, captured on some pathetic reality TV show labeled the Rat Woman, ruined for life. Whatever. I was over it. Wheeling my trash bin out to the curb before jumping in the car to go to work, I saw our neighbor sweeping something peculiar out of his garage. I hollered a friendly greeting out the passenger window as I drove by and got a closer look at what he had there. My heart leapt – it was a dead rat! A dead rat! Yes!

I did the dance of the happy fairies behind the wheel as I drove by, leaving my neighbor standing there looking bewildered. Ah, life was grand! I could look forward to once again catching those elusive Zzzs.

Until the day we sold the house, we never had another creature of any kind in the attic. Whether this was thanks to the mothballs or the poison, I am not sure, but I figured perhaps the mothball remedy might help my friend make it through until Monday when her exterminator came. So, I bought a small box of mothballs, a package of cheese cloth and some string, wrote out explicit instructions in bold sharpie pen, underlined all the important parts, and left it on her desk with this *To-From*:

To: There's something in my attic!

From: Here, try this; it'll kill somethin'!

My coworker reported on Monday that by Sunday the noise had stopped. She'd been able to sleep through the night and, sure the mothballs had done the trick, she had canceled the pest control appointment pending any more noise. She thanked me profusely and said the only thing bothering her now was that her attic reeked of mothball. She asked me if I had any remedies for that.

Nope. Not a one.

Chapter 5: May

To: Gigi

From: Spawn & Grandspawn

You are invited to Mother's Day High Noon Tea at the spawning grounds. See you there!

This invitation arrived on May 1st from my daughter and 4-yr-old granddaughter, my two favorite pieces of work. Both are spicier than the devil's pepper patch, and I wouldn't have them any other way. I replied that Gigi would be delighted to attend. And I did. It was lovely.

My daughter, Dani, was born when I was twenty-seven. From the time I first found out I was pregnant I was over the moon. Even as a very young girl my greatest desire was to be a mother, never imagining my life being complete without having a beautiful, perfect little human who called me Mom. And I wanted to be good at it.

Having helped raise my little brother and babysat every kid in the neighborhood from the time I was eleven, I had always assumed I was thoroughly prepared for becoming a parent. Time would reveal that I was clueless. Oh, so clueless. Mothering lows would bring me to the depths of despair and the highs would fill me with unimaginable joy. Parenthood would prove to be the ultimate roller coaster for which nothing could have prepared me.

My pregnancy was perfect until it wasn't. A more elated mother-to-be doubtfully walked the planet. I ate healthy, exercised mindfully, followed all the rules, and by the end of my first trimester had become my doctor's prize patient. Nothing phased me and my short-fused Irish temper became non-existent. I felt better than I'd ever felt in my life and saw nothing but love and joy in the world. I became so sappy it was honestly disgusting.

Then a week before my due date I was hospitalized with eclampsia, a condition that occurs in pregnant women causing an increase in blood pressure which can be detrimental to the health of the mother and the unborn child. My blood pressure skyrocketed, and my body ballooned with fluid. My usually thin ankles and wrists disappeared, my face grew as big as a watermelon, and when my brother stopped by to see me in the hospital, he couldn't hide his shock.

"My God, you're an Oompa Loompa!" Sean exclaimed, and I again thanked my younger self for flushing his Pooh bear.

The toughest thing about having eclampsia was that I didn't feel sick. With my body retaining a layer of water, it was like being encased in bubble wrap. I couldn't feel a thing. And with all the nesting hormones pumping, the sickness came at a time that I was filled with energy. The dichotomy really screwed with my mind. How could I be sick when I felt so great?

But I was sick. Really sick. And my husband Rick wouldn't tell me until three years later the doctors told him they were worried they'd lose both me and the baby. In the final moments of my 29-hour labor, my normally low 90/60 blood pressure spiked to 191/109. The baby was in distress, and my doctors feared I was going to have a stroke. These facts were kept from me, as no one wanted to add even a sliver of additional stress, fearing it would send my body over the edge.

When it was time for me to push, the midwife told me, "The baby may not cry at first," and Rick, robed and masked at my bedside, was uncharacteristically pale and silent, a neonatal team just feet away on standby. In the chaos of the moment, I was oblivious to all of it, including the moment Rick had been quietly taken aside to be told he might have to choose which one of us to save. Rick never shared what his decision might have been, had I been asked, I would have chosen Dani.

Blessedly, nobody had to worry. Dani let out a garbled cry before she was even out of the hopper. It was the sweetest, most demonic sound I'd ever heard. She was none too happy to have been thrust into the world and wanted everybody around her to know it. Unfiltered and spunky from the get-go.

In those first few hours after childbirth, my blood pressure continued to spike, so the nurses whisked Dani off to clean her up while they got me stabilized. As soon as I was in the clear, they allowed Rick to wheel me to the nursery window to have a look at our little miracle. I will never forget the sight. On the other side of the glass were over a dozen newborns lined up for ecstatic spectators. All little cherubs were sleeping peacefully except for one, who was so flushed with tantrum she looked purple, having worked her wrinkly bottom so far down the Lexan bassinet that her red, pruney feet were sticking up in the air.

"Wow, look at that one!" I whispered to Rick between guffaws of laughter, unable to read the babies' name cards from my angle. "What a set of lungs; I can hear her all the way through the glass!"

"Yep, just like her mother," Rick replied with a chuckle, enamored as I was with the gaggle of babies. He'd wanted to be a dad every bit as much as I had wanted to be a mom and couldn't have been more excited in the moment.

"Shhhh," I admonished him, putting an index finger to my lips. "Her parents might be here and hear you!"

"Tool," he cried. "That one is ours!"

****

To: My child will never act like that; what's wrong with those parents?!

From: My child will never act like that; what's wrong with those parents?!

Dani spent the first six weeks of her life like the way she spent her first hours. She cried all night and all day and nothing we did helped. Rick and I never knew humans could function on so little sleep or with so little food. I swear the nourishment from licking the envelopes on bills for those first few months was all that kept me going. It was brutal.

Though I loved that little face more than I could put into words, motherhood was not turning out to be at all like I had imagined. Nursing was a nightmare. I struggled to get Dani to latch (attach to the breast so she could feed), and in those days they didn't tell new moms this was even a thing. Nothing in the dozens of books I had read mentioned anything about latching or failure to latch. As far as I knew, the baby just came out, you dangled dinner and that was that. I was left to assume it was a natural occurrence. Yeah, no.

And the pain! When Dani did latch, she did so with such vigor I had to bite a washcloth to keep from shrieking in anguish. I couldn't imagine how women through the ages had done this so nonchalantly. After just two weeks my "girls" were bleeding and looked like I had sent them through a meat grinder. The baby books had told me about "toughening up" for breast feeding by rubbing with a towel, which I had done, but no amount of towel rubbing could have prepared me for this abuse. It was agony!

The morning of my first postpartum check-up I awoke with a fever and felt awful. I called the doctor's office in tears to cancel, but they told me to come in anyway. And I'm so glad they did.

Rick, Dani, and I all went to my appointment. I had grown close to the staff over the course of my pregnancy and wanted to show off my new bundle, the fruits of our combined efforts. We hardly got through the office door before we were encircled, everyone delighted to welcome Dani into the fold, taking turns shuttling her from one set of waiting arms to another. This continued until the three of us were ushered down the hallway to an examining room, where Debbie, the nurse midwife who had delivered Dani, was already waiting.

"So, how's our favorite new mommy?" Debbie asked cheerfully as I climbed on the tissue-covered table in the examining room.

I immediately broke into woeful sobs.

"Awful. I'ma horrible mom!" I blubbered uncontrollably. "Nursing is excruciating, and my baby hates me. She hates me!" I wailed, a river of tears rolling down my cheeks, soaking the front of my favorite maternity shirt. Unlike every other mother I knew, I still couldn't fit into my pre-pregnancy clothes, only adding to my misery.

Obviously used to new mommy hysterics, Debbie didn't even bat an eye. She asked Rick to take Dani to the waiting room so we could talk alone, and after they left, she patiently waited for me to calm down. When my wails subsided to hiccuppy sniffles, she asked me to explain my troubles. I told her about my breastfeeding woes, which she all but disregarded, repeating the advice I'd read in the prenatal books about toughening up the nipples before birth.

"But I did all that!" I cried as I undressed for the exam, starting to bawl anew. "Was I supposed to use sandpaper?" I shouted between sobs as I reached for another tissue.

Then Debbie caught sight of my exposed chest and gasped aloud at what she saw.

"What did you do to yourself?" she exclaimed in shock, recoiling. I looked at her questioningly.

"I told you!" I cried, exasperated.

"Dani did all that?"

"Yes! She bites!" I sobbed.

Debbie eyed me suspiciously, seeming to weigh whether I was telling the truth. She inspected the damage closely, commenting aloud, "Goodness, there's a good infection started here. We need to get some antibiotics started immediately."

She began writing out a prescription, talking to me as she scribbled on the pad. "Now, as far as the issue causing this, some infants are biters, but it's really very rare. I think you may just be overly tender because of the infection, and there's probably also a palate or tongue issue interfering with her ability to get a comfortable fit. Let me get Rick to bring Dani back in and I'll see if I can determine what the problem is." And with that, Debbie went out to the waiting room to fetch them.

Returning to the examining room, Dani gurgled happily, feet kicking about in her baby carrier. She loved that thing. Debbie cooed at the adorable infant and then slid her index finger over Dani's drooly gums. Dani chomped down so hard Debbie let out a holler, startling everyone in the room and causing Dani to jump and burst into tears.

Grasping her red-tipped, throbbing finger, Debbie looked at Dani apologetically and talked soothingly to her while offering a pacifier. "Oh, I didn't mean to scare you, sweet girl. That's a ferocious bite you have there!" Dani took the binky between protests, working it with a vengeance while she eyed Debbie with knitted brows.

When Debbie turned to chat with Rick and me, her expression and tone were far more sympathetic than they had been earlier. "Well, she's a biter, alright. My first one!" Debbie said with a laugh. "But that's good news. Now that I know what the problem is, we can work with this," she added, smiling sweetly at Dani, but keeping her fingers well out of reach.

Work with it we did, beginning with bottle feeding only from that day forward, and within days we were all happier campers. Once getting the nutrition she needed minus the stress and extra effort, Dani's disposition turned sunny, and the whole family got some well-deserved rest. For eleven months I pumped milk like a guernsey cow, and we went through a score of rubber nipples as Dani gnawed through them like a teething gator.

Crisis averted, life in the Pierce household was smooth sailing and time passed quickly for our happy little family. In the blink of an eye sippy cups replaced bottles and our adorable little girl entered toddlerhood. The terrible twos proved not to be terrible at all, so Rick and I grew cocky. Dani didn't do any of the naughty things we saw other misbehaved youngsters do. We attributed our child's exceptional behavior to our exceptional parenting and assumed we were home free. Toddlers were a breeze, and this parenting stuff was a cinch!

God must still be laughing.

My motherhood lucky streak came to its end on a Monday morning in the grocery store when Dani had just turned three. I was doing our weekly grocery shopping and was almost finished when I circled back around to the cereal aisle to get oatmeal. Dani had been on a streak where oatmeal and peaches were the only two things she would eat. Her pediatrician told us to go along with the phase until it passed, ecstatic that these were the foods she was stuck on. Most kids, he said, had far worse choices than this. So, oatmeal and peaches it was, resulting in permanent orange stains down the front of every piece of clothing she had, including the red, yellow, and navy polka-dotted top she had chosen that morning to go with her peach and chartreuse shorts. Wanting to encourage her independence, I had begun encouraging her to pick out her own outfits, mismatched though they might be, so long as they were weather and event appropriate.

Rolling down the cereal aisle with my mounded trolley and Dani in the seat, I pulled to the side to let an elderly woman pass by with her motorized cart. While we waited, I reached into my purse for a spare hair elastic to remake one of Dani's pigtails, which she had ripped out somewhere along the way, leaving one side of her baby fine hair dangle and become knotty. As I rummaged through the dregs at the bottom of my bag, Dani strained to reach over me, laser-focused on something behind me on the shelf.

"Mommy," Dani shrieked as she willed her arm to lengthen. "Ceeweeals! Ceeweeals!"

Giving up on the elastic, I extracted myself from the purse to see what had my toddler so excited and realized with dismay we were parked directly in front of the sugary cereal whose commercial always caught Dani's attention when she watched *Eureeka's Castle*, an animated version of Mr. Roger's Land of Make Believe. She had recognized the box and was trying desperately to get to it, looking adorable with only one lopsided auburn pigtail jutting off her head like a lone palm on the edge of a deserted island.

Having just been through the wringer with a girlfriend whose daughter was suffering from a whole host of digestive, behavioral and health issues the doctors had determined was tied to a red dye allergy, an additive most commonly found in processed foods like hot dogs and highly processed cereals, there was no way I was giving in and buying this stuff.

"No, baby," I said calmly, kissing her sweet head and wheeling swiftly away from the cereal. "We're getting oatmeal. Look! Your favorite!" I exclaimed, arriving at the oatmeal section, and holding up the familiar package. She was not impressed.

"Ceeweeals! Ceeweeals!" Dani cried, reaching back to the boxes at the other end of the aisle and struggling to stand in the cart's seat. Her shouts grew louder and more impassioned, attracting looks of disapproval from all the nearby shoppers. I recognized that look; it was the same one I used to give to moms in similar situations in the days before I became one. Karma was a bitch.

Finally wriggling her chubby legs free, Dani was able to stand up on the seat of the shopping cart and, without warning, launched herself at me. I grabbed her midair, limbs flailing in every direction. I set her down on the ground to get a better grip and as soon as her feet hit the floor she bolted for the cereal, her battered pink high-top baby sneakers moving so fast I couldn't catch her.

When she got to the spot below the cereal she wanted, Dani reached up to the shelf and screamed to have the box. On tiptoes, shirt hiked up to her neck exposing her little Buddha belly, she strained with all her might to reach the shelf. Flinging aside boxes on the lowest shelf, she stepped up and raised one knee attempting to climb on the next level, which hovered high above her little head.

"No, baby," I said again while I reached out to grab her.

This triggered a full nuclear meltdown. Dani burst into tears, yanked her arm away from me, flung herself down in the middle of the aisle, threw her head back onto the terrazzo and screamed loud enough to wake the dead. When I bent down to pick her up, she rolled out of my grasp, making me chase her down hunched over like a mother guerilla, exposing the torn band of my worst pair of underwear over the top of my stretched-out, bleach-speckled pink maternity leggings, which I normally never wore out in public. And if that wasn't mortifying enough, when I finally did seize hold of my errant child, she arched her back, causing me to nearly drop her, eliciting a terrified scream in a vibrato that reached into every corner of the earth.

Having devolved to a battle of wills, the situation was beyond repair, and I would be damned if I was going to give in and reward this ghastly behavior. Abandoning my full cart of groceries right there in the aisle, I hoisted my purple-faced toddler under my arm and carted her out of the grocery store like a bag of dog food while she screamed and thrashed. I gave looks of apology to passersby as I struggled to get my shrieking youngster to the car, which felt like it was parked in Africa.

The fight that ensued to buckle Dani into her car seat was epic. Somewhere in our struggle she became more horse than human – all muscle and no fat. By the time I was finished I was panting, bleeding, and dripping with sweat. And still the tantrum showed no signs of weakening. I had to give her props – she was one tough cookie!

The whole ride home Dani screamed and fought in her car seat. At stoplights the motorists in the lanes next to us would stare and shake their heads, able to hear her yowling protests through both sets of closed windows. If I suffer hearing loss in my elderly years, it no doubt began here.

Once at home, the battle waged on to get her out of the car and into the house. By the time I was through, I had a lump on my head, and we had both lost a shoe. I took her straight to her room and placed her in her crib. She seemed to be tiring, so I calmly asked her if she was done. The answer came in a fresh round of wails and screams, so I left the room, quietly closing her bedroom door behind me. I needed a "mommy minute".

In the hallway, I slid down the closed door to the carpet, and leaned my head back against the doorframe. I listened as my child's sobs subsided into silence and when I peeked in, I saw she had fallen asleep. I watched her for a moment as she slept looking angelic before I dragged my weary body out to the living room. I was spent.

Disheartened, I knew my parental bubble had burst. I flung myself on the couch to contemplate where I'd gone so tragically wrong. My dreams of becoming a supermom were shattered, and I had no idea where to go from here. At least every direction was up. At that moment I wondered if I'd done anything right and was certain that I hadn't. It was the same feeling I had experienced that day in Debbie's office when I'd bawled my eyes out at my failure to breastfeed.

Like I was the worst mom ever. And sitting in the living room that day with no groceries in the house and a worn-out toddler having cried herself to sleep over an unpurchased box of sugary cereal, nobody was going to convince me otherwise.

In time I would learn that having your idyllic parental vision board go down in flames, leaving you feeling bereft and defeated, simply comes with the territory. When I became a grandparent, I witnessed Dani go through the whole cycle, and there wasn't a bloody thing I could do but watch as history repeated itself. During her pregnancy, Dani informed me of all the things her child would never do, just as I had done during my nine months of gestation with her. Then I helplessly watched as my daughter's precious list of *My Child Will Never Dos* imploded when my granddaughter was denied a meal of rainbow sprinkles for breakfast. Or told to put on underwear. Or shoes. Or that it was Thursday. Dani fretted weekly, sometimes daily, that these toddler tantrums meant she was the worst mother ever, while her husband Shawn agonized that everything he did was ruining his child for life. Nothing I say or do during those difficult moments can convince them they are doing fine and that they are exceptional parents; they will have to come to that realization in their own time.

Until then, I have found the best solution for all of us is to schedule lots of granddaughter sleepovers so her battle-weary parents can wallow together in peace. I know there will come a random day in the future, when something will flip the switch and cause them to realize the annihilation of the *My Child Will Never Do That* list is not an indicator of bad parenting. It is simply a rite of passage through which all parents, no matter how good or bad, must cross. With that stunning revelation will also come the realization that the only thing that defines a great parent is when one gives a child their very best with a loving heart, no matter what that looks like on any given day. There's going to be mistakes. And sometimes they seem monumental. For those we can only apologize, learn, move on, and try to do better tomorrow. That's called love. And love is what makes a super parent super.

****

To: Vinegar Toes

From: You inherited your mama's stinky cleats!

With this tag my granddaughter received a bar of her favorite raspberry soap. Already at four, my granddaughter is known for her stinky feet. It doesn't matter whether she wears socks, or what material her shoes are made of, or if she's even wearing shoes at all. By the end of the day those adorable little piggies are going to stink. And it's going to smell like vinegar.

The poor little darling has her mama's feet. When Dani was young and played soccer, I once mistook the odor that came off her cleats for a dead animal. The stench was seriously that bad, though not solely her fault. Florida was experiencing a particularly rainy fall that year, which kept the soccer fields flooded and had the kids playing in the rain all season long. Dani got drenched on the field time and time again, playing in mud up to her ankles, her poor little toes pruned and wrinkled like raisins by the time she stripped off her socks.

Not wanting to get the muddy mess in the house, I took to having her strip in the garage the minute we got home and toss her soccer clothes straight into the washing machine. I would then immediately start the load; anything to keep the funk down to a minimum. My methodology worked;

however, I never noticed the lack of soccer socks coming out of the laundry.

Had I been more aware, I would have recognized that my little darling girl was squirreling away her dirty, nasty, funk encrusted game socks in her bag for weeks. Weeks! As were all her teammates. Unbeknownst to us parents, the girls had made a pact in the beginning of the season that they wouldn't change their socks until their team lost a game. After they went undefeated for the first two games, no girl on the team wanted to risk ruining the mojo. The two-game streak stretched to two months with no sign of letting up. That's a lot of sock stench. Do the math.

The Saturday after the tenth straight win, I was out in the garage doing laundry, when I was hit by a smell so foul it made me gag. I began sniffing around the periphery of the garage, taking a whiff here and there, but couldn't locate the source. I sprayed some air freshener, opened the garage door, and ran a fan. Nothing helped.

The following day, the odor in the garage was worse. I went in the house and found Rick.

"I think an animal got in the garage and died somewhere. It reeks out there. Bad! Maybe we have another rat!" I cried.

"Don't be ridiculous," he replied, shooing me away with his hand. "It's probably just musty from all the rain."

"I'm serious," I kept on. "Go out there and smell for yourself!"

Knowing I wouldn't relent, Rick sloughed out to the garage with me hot on his heels. Not expecting to change his tune, he inhaled deeply with mock exaggeration and then confirmed my disgust with a surprised hearty "Pewwwwwww!".

Unable to stand the awful smell, we spent the entirety of the next several hours of our Sunday emptying the contents of the garage onto the driveway trying to locate the dead vermin causing it. We settled into a routine of picking up a box or container, giving it a good sniff, and then setting it outside in the elimination pile, deeming it devoid of emaciated carcasses. This continued for the better part of two hours, ending when I picked up Dani's soccer bag. I only got the bag hoisted a couple inches off the ground before the stink assaulted my nostrils. Mother of God, did it reek!

"Found it!" I hollered to Rick, who stalked over, delighted to investigate the kill.

"What is it?" he asked, looking around excitedly. Boys love all that icky stuff.

I held the soccer bag out to him at arm's length, terrified to look. "It's in there," I shouted, thrusting the soccer bag at him.

Not knowing what horror awaited inside, I took cover behind Rick, peeking over his shoulder as he slowly unzipped the nylon sack. It was like Satan himself belched the funk of rotting meat and hellfire from the opening. We both cringed and covered our mouths. With two fingers, he extracted a crusty, stiff sock. It could have stood up in the corner by itself.

"She's your child when she does this stuff," I said to him, shaking my head.

"Yep, that's my baby!" he exclaimed proudly, throwing the nasty sock in my direction. I jumped aside and let it fall to the ground, then lifted it into the washing machine with my foot.

"Well, you and your baby have a mess to clean up on the driveway. Daniellllle!" I hollered into the house.

Dani was angry at me for a week for washing those nasty, stinky socks. But lucky for me, her team won again the following Saturday, freeing me from the doghouse. As a matter of fact, her team's winning streak would continue for the entire season, so it was a darn good thing we found out about the sock pact when we did. I fear her feet may have rotted off if we hadn't.

Ironically, that's not the only happy ending to this story. Somewhere on the way to adulthood, Dani became obsessed with keeping her feet clean, no longer able to stand when they are dirty. I don't know when on her journey this happened, or how, or if it had anything to do with the sock episode in the garage that Sunday. Regardless, if there is a foot stink in her house, Dani can no longer be held to blame, something we all hope will someday rub off on Little Miss Pickle Foot.

****

To: I can't do this without you

From: I love you, too!

The precise moment I knew I'd done okay as a mom came unexpectedly in a text after a failed search for a prom dress. Parenthood never ceases to amaze.

The extenuating circumstances surrounding my epiphany began when my daughter Dani was little and I made her a promise that should she want them, I would buy her two dresses where price was no object: one for her senior prom and one for her wedding. Two dresses I always longed for but never had. Since I was never asked to prom and eloped in lieu of having a formal wedding, all my fantasy formal dress dreams had to be lived out vicariously through her.

Before Dani's senior prom came along, we were able to practice preparations with events such as homecomings and junior prom. I would schedule her appointments for hair, makeup, nails and toes, and the two of us would dress shop for weeks. Our tradition would be to go to every store, have her try on everything she fancied, set the favorite picks aside, and then eliminate them one by one until we settled on that single dress that was just exactly right. The One. And it was always perfect.

As the years went by and word of our dress outings spread, some of Dani's friends would join us on our excursions. We would make a day of it, have all the girls try on whatever they pleased, and then everyone would compare notes and provide input. I never got offended or upset if the other girls' opinions differed from mine, I expected it. All I cared about was that at the end of the day Dani was happy with whatever gown she chose and felt beautiful wearing it. And every year I was honored beyond words that regardless of who was with us, my opinion was the one that mattered most to my daughter. It touched my heart and still gets me teary eyed.

Perhaps because she is my most precious gift, I have an uncanny knack for picking out what looks perfect on her. This skill must be a mom thing. In the days before my mother got sick, she did the same for me. I could spend hours shopping for something to wear to an event, find nothing, go pick Mom up, bring her to one of the same stores I'd combed through, and she would have me beautifully outfitted, accessorized and shod in 10 minutes. From the sale rack. It was like voodoo.

So, with Mom skills and an unscathed track record in my corner, I was stoked when the time finally came to shop for Dani's senior prom dress. We excitedly tore up the town two months in advance. We started at the mall, went to every dress shop they had, scoured the dress racks in all the bigger department stores, and she tried on everything. But at first blush there wasn't a single dress that fit the bill. Undaunted, we branched out.

Weekend after weekend that spring, we went looking. We tried the finer ladies' shops downtown, the exclusive little boutiques in the village, the giant retailers, and the outlet stores, but still nothing. We started to get nervous. I felt like the Fairy Godmother that had lost her magic. With less than three weeks left till the big night, Dani was empty-handed. It was crunch time.

Rick and I were separated by then and he was in a relationship with a younger woman named Lesley, to whom he is now engaged. I've liked Lesley from the get-go, appreciating that she is a much better match for Rick than I ever was. Knowing we were struggling to find a prom dress and thinking perhaps the larger malls out of town might have a better selection, Lesley offered to take Dani on a shopping trip to Orlando the following weekend. I had to work my second job at the country club, and there was no way I could get off, so unfortunately, I couldn't go with them. My mother's heart wanted only for Dani to be happy and find something fabulous, but inside I was absolutely devastated I wouldn't be there.

When Saturday came and Dani and Lesley headed over to the city, I tried my best to suck it up and not let it bother me. It didn't work. I dragged myself through my shift at the country club with a heavy, heavy heart. Towards the end of the evening my phone vibrated with a text from Dani. I took a deep breath and prepared myself for what would surely be elated news about a dress. I opened the message and read…

"Do you think we can go out looking one more time next weekend? I can't do this without you."

I can't do this without you. I read the words again through tears. And again. And again.

"You bet we can! I love you!" was all I could text before the water in my eyes made it impossible to see.

The following Saturday Dani and I went to a local bridal shop on a suggestion from one of my coworkers. Dani tried on dozens of bridesmaid dresses, and finally put on a sequined pink gown that we both thought was pretty. She really wasn't much of a pink girl, but the gown looked beautiful and had her smiling. At last.

Deciding we had found The One, Dani headed back to the dressing room to take it off. That should have been the end of it, but something in my mother's intuition led me back to a rack we'd already rifled through multiple times. This time, a bright lime green, lace and sequin sheath seemed to appear out of nowhere. My mommy voodoo told me it was perfect.

"Hey, Dan, don't get dressed yet. I found one more you need to try on. Here," I said, as I handed her the gown through the dressing room door.

"Seriously, Mom, lime green?" she exclaimed when she saw it, looking at me like I had to be kidding.

"Just try it on; I have a good feeling about this one!" I insisted. I just knew I'd found it. The One.

While I waited for her to come out of the dressing room, I watched a happy mother-daughter pair shopping for wedding gowns. They looked like they were having the time of their lives. I couldn't help but smile, imagining the day Dani and I would be on the same journey. Just then, Dani emerged from the dressing room in the spectacular lime green sheath, rousting me from my daydream and causing the mother-daughter pair to let out an audible gasp when they saw her. She looked stunning.

There were tears in her eyes, and I couldn't speak for the lump in my throat. She turned to me looking so beautiful I thought my heart would burst. "It's The One, Mom!" she exclaimed.

On the day of prom, she was a vision. I don't believe I had seen her smile that much in all her eighteen years. Nor had I. She said that dress made her feel like the most beautiful girl in the room that night, and that's probably because she was.

She loved that green dress so much that she many times said she wanted to have one just like it made in white for her wedding. I told her that would be fine but knew another dress would be waiting to dethrone its predecessor. Either way I didn't care, so long as I could be there to help her pick out whatever made her feel like the most beautiful woman on earth. Which, of course, she is.

I can't do this without you. A daughter's love in six words. I kept that text message and read it every day until my phone broke, a physical detail that makes no significant difference. I have no need to read those words in a text; I can pull them up whenever I desire. Those words are, and forever will be, imprinted on my heart.

Chapter 6: June

The small group of friends that comprised my "Breakfast Club" met at the usual spot Sunday morning and by the time the dirty dishes were cleared, I was booked on a cross-country road trip, leaving within the month. In less than two weeks' time, Spider Slayer Clark and I would be driving a used Hyundai Sonata from Florida to Arizona as a favor for our friends Glenn and Paul. The Sonata had been purchased by Glenn as a gift for his mother, who had recently totaled her car and couldn't afford to replace it. The good son that he was, Glenn had shopped around and found the Sonata, but needed a way to get it to Tucson.

"I know this may sound crazy," Glenn had said to the table when we'd first sat down for breakfast. "But would any of you be up for driving a car to my mother in Tucson? I would pay for everything. Paul drove out the last one and said never again." Paul confirmed Glenn's words by nodding like a bobble head.

Without so much as a pause, Clark and I shouted in unison, "I'll do it!"

Laughing, Clark and I pointed a finger at each other and screamed, "Jinx!"

"No, I'm serious," said Glenn. "I need Mom to get the car as soon as possible, and I don't want to have to hire a truck to haul it out there. Trucking is too expensive and would defeat the purpose of the money I saved on taxes and registration buying it in Florida."

"I am serious! I'd love to do it," said Clark, who had never been west of Atlanta and loved to drive. "And I could probably leave next weekend. I'll check with the boss tomorrow and let you know in the morning. I really don't think it'll be a problem." Clark worked for a homebuilder, and summer was his slow season.

"I'm serious, too!" I exclaimed. "I have the vacation time, and you know I love road trips. Hey, how about if Clark and I go together?" I looked excitedly from Clark to Glenn.

"You two would have to room together," Glenn clarified, giving us a critical look. Clark was a notoriously loud snorer and Glenn knew that didn't sit well with me. I needed my bedroom dark and silent for sleep.

"Clark, I'm good with it if you are. It's only for a couple days. You in?" I asked.

Clark gave a thumbs up and that was good enough for Paul whose thumbs began flying across the keypad on his phone making preparations. By the time our server delivered the check, he had everything reserved and ready. The youngest in our crowd barely into his forties, Paul loved technology and having a mission that involved anything online. He would have made a fantastic travel agent. Working as a marketing representative for an insurance conglomerate, he was missing his calling.

"Okay, you're all set!" Paul beamed, hitting the last button to reserve our hotel in Tucson. "You're going to end on a high note. I got a fantastic deal at the Marriott using some travel advantage points before they went to waste. A suite with two bedrooms!" He was in his glory.

"Good job, Paul. Hey, we can call this 'Blondie and Clyde on the lam'," joked Glenn. He loved old classic movies and *Bonnie and Clyde* was one of his favorites. Chuckling, he was proud of himself and the witty quip.

"I like it!" I exclaimed, knowing the moniker would undoubtedly be making its way onto a *To-From*, though a little afraid of the pending story that might accompany it. My Spidey Sense told me a noteworthy adventure was on the horizon, which was both exciting and terrifying.

I wedged myself between Glenn and Paul as we walked out of the restaurant into the blinding Florida sun, one arm around Glenn's shoulders, the other around Paul's waist. They were quite a pair. When I first met them, I couldn't figure out the dynamic, as they were opposite as opposite could be.

Paul, several years Glenn's junior, was tall, brunette, and dramatic. Unfiltered like me, you always knew where you stood with Paul. I loved that about him. Paul's passion was his yard, which housed a lavish garden full of fresh seasonal veggies, herbs, and flowers. Whenever I visited them at home, the IHOP, Paul would greet me at the front door and whisk me immediately out to the patio for a proud nickel tour of his latest blooms, setting aside a bag full of pickings and cuttings that I never failed to kill. Then he would take me inside to show me his latest designer messenger bag acquisition, his other passion. Paul's collection of bags rivaled that of Bloomingdale's, and I was forever envious of them all, though I never would have used them. My go-to purse was a lined, zippered coconut I'd purchased from the Milwaukee Zoo.

More like me in the realm of bags, Glenn used a dark canvas, nondescript backpack for his work bag, and it looked a little worse for the wear. Paul's polar opposite, Glenn was shorter, blonde, reserved, and could have passed for my sibling. Only eight days younger than I and working as a software engineer in the manufacturing industry, we had bonded from hello. He'd been friends with Phyllis for years before I had been invited to join the Sunday Morning Breakfast Club, which was how I came to know him and Paul. Glenn started calling me Blondie after our very first breakfast together, interspersing it with Blonde One, names of endearment I adored. He teased me unrelentingly about being The Much Older Sibling, causing people who didn't know us well to pause wondering just how old I was, much to his delight. Glenn had a heart of gold and was a loyal friend. He hated strife and delighted in playing the role of psychologist and peacekeeper. He would sit with knitted hands, steepling his index fingers against his mouth, while I ranted about a personal or work predicament, then offer his opinion in incremental bites like lines of code for software. As a fellow Virgo, I appreciated Glenn's organized delivery and sound advice.

Another commonality between Glenn and I was that we were gift givers and spoiled the ones we loved. For my sixtieth birthday he and Paul found me a stunning blue sapphire and diamond ring, necklace and earring set that they presented to me in a giant blue box with a silver bow. The tag read:

To: Elderly Blonde One

From: MUCH Younger Brother and the Youngster

The gift took my breath away. It was extraordinarily thoughtful, though not surprising given Glenn's generous ways. Nobody can ever say I didn't surround myself with good people.

Driving home from the diner after Breakfast Club, I was filled with anticipation for what felt like the gift of a mini vacation. Our travel schedule would be a whirlwind, but that was all the fun. Clark and I would have three days to get from Melbourne to Tucson, where on the third evening we would hop a non-refundable flight home. Our plan was to set out first thing Friday morning, drive a total of 14 hours with a 2-hr break mid-day to grab lunch and take in some local culture wherever we were at, get a 6-hr snooze at night, breakfast on the fly and repeat. Everyone I spoke to about the trip asked me if I knew exactly how ambitious this whole timeline was. Of course, I did. It looked reasonable on paper.

On Monday morning both Clark and I got work approval for the time off and we were good to go. Paul confirmed our hotel reservations and flights, ecstatic to have another rewarding task. We were set!

Bright and early the following Friday morning, Clark and I met at Glenn and Paul's to begin our adventure. Just after dawn we waved goodbye to our friends from the windows of the Sonata, a cooler packed with snacks, the world our oyster. Clark was at the wheel, and I was nestled in the passenger seat with my blanket and game of laptop Candy Crush. We were ecstatic. This was going to be great!

And it was. For almost ten whole hours.

Just over the Louisiana border, Clark, in a voice laced with concern uttered, "Uh oh. That's not good," and our happy road trip bubble burst into smithereens.

"What's not good?" I cried, sitting bolt upright in my seat.

Clark replied not in words, but by pointing to the dashboard, where a yellow light was shining. The amber glow was in the shape of a tiny battery, looking ever so happy and proud of itself. As if reveling in the newfound attention, the wee light seemed to grow brighter and brighter with each passing mile, in eerie contrast to the ominous black clouds that roiled overhead. Until the moment Clark had interrupted my Candy Crush game, I had been too absorbed to notice the darkening sky.

Foreshadowing the events to come, a tremendous boom of thunder rang out just as every icon on the dashboard lit up and then went completely dead along with the engine. It was as though the car had exhaled for the last time, giving one last mighty breath before it expired. Lightning snaked across the angry sky, illuminating our faces and the Sonata's interior in brief flashes. It reminded me of the strobing lights of a Class B horror flick, and I half expected a sketchy dude with a chainsaw to come knocking at my window. Another crack of thunder exploded in our ears, causing us both to jump, after which rain poured down in sheets from the heavens.

"Where are we?" I asked Clark, trying to see a sign in the inky darkness. I could tell only that we were on the downward slope of a hill.

"About half-way across the LPC," grumbled Clark, leaning forward in his seat, craning to see out the windshield as he fought to steer the dead car.

"Oh, crap," I cried. I'd been warned about this.

The LPC, Louisiana's 24-mile Lake Pontchartrain Causeway, was the world's longest bridge over water and the worst place on earth to break down. The bridge was divided into two parallel one-way bridges, one going east and a separate lane across the waterway going west, each with a single exit halfway between the two ends. Because of the layout, it wasn't uncommon to take a whole day to get rescued if you needed a tow. This was not what Clark and I needed on our tight travel schedule. There was no wiggle room for such nonsense.

Fortunately, during the next flash of lightning, we saw that the one and only westbound exit lay dead ahead of us, and since we'd just crested the top of the causeway, it was straight downhill. Also in our favor was that we'd been traveling at a decent clip before the engine stalled, so we stood a good chance of being able to coast all the way off the exit without having to push. Not that pushing was an option in the atrocious weather conditions.

Praying to Isaac Newton for momentum, we urged on the little engine that couldn't. And it worked. We taxied with just enough force to get into the wayside, coming to a rolling stop in a parking spot next to some 18-wheelers.

"Well, that was fun," I said to Clark, who shot back a scowl in answer. "How good are your automotive skills?" I knew he tinkered a lot with lawn equipment and his motorcycle, so I prayed it was decent.

"I think we've only got a battery issue, so I'll pop the hood and see if one of these truckers has some tools I can borrow. I want to wait a minute to see if this rain will let up."

Thankfully it did. When the downpour subsided to a drizzle, Clark hopped out and spoke with one of our friendly trucker neighbors and borrowed a screwdriver. I left him fiddling with the battery while I wandered around the wet parking lot waving my phone in the air trying to locate a cell tower signal. Finding a good spot while standing atop a giant rock, I phoned Glenn, who patched in Paul, and together in minutes they Wikipedia'd a diagnosis, found a nearby dealership, scheduled a service appointment, located the nearest lodging, made a reservation for us and had a tow truck en route. Talk about efficient! Unfortunately, their efforts were in vain. On my way back to Clark to give him the news, I heard the Sonata start and got admonished upon arrival for overreacting. Sheepishly, I called Glenn to cancel the tow, the appointment, and the reservation, and we got back on the road.

Having now wasted our 2-hr lunch window, we canceled plans to stop, deciding we could still make Houston by midnight if we drove straight through. Cautiously, Clark turned on the radio, I resumed my game, we lunched on cooler snacks while we got resettled. Two hours passed and all was well. Our spirits lifted, and we had just begun to think the worst was behind us, when the skies opened, the water poured down, the dashboard lit up and the power went out. It was the world's worst déjà vu.

We limped off the exit this time just east of Lafayette, Louisiana. I called Glenn, who called Paul, who found a mechanic, scheduled an appointment, made reservations for a tow and contacted a hotel. I was half tempted to have them schedule me a dental cleaning and a mammogram while I was there. These guys could rule the world!

While waiting for the tow, Clark borrowed a screwdriver from the kid working behind the counter at McDonald's and got the car started. I couldn't decide if I was elated or pissed. I called Glenn to cancel the tow, but I insisted on keeping the service appointment and hotel reservation. We drove the Sonata across town to the garage, much to the annoyance of Clark, because the car seemed just fine again. I didn't care; I wasn't taking any chances.

At the garage, Clark spoke with the mechanic while I dragged our cooler into the waiting room and got comfortable. Clark joined me and we snacked. We drank the previous night's coffee from the grimy pot. Clark fell asleep and snored in the chair as a toddler investigated his gums. I read an old motorcycle magazine and sat. And sat. And sat. And sat. Finally, three hours later they gave us the news. They found … nothing. Not a bloody thing. Free of charge they sent us on our way. Clark fumed and refused to talk to me. Certain I'd made the right decision, I restarted my game and ignored him.

As we got settled in, we got a call from Glenn and Paul and ironed out a revised travel plan, since we were now way behind schedule. Clark and I told Glenn and Paul we wanted to drive as long as we could, as far as we could, stopping only to gas up and pee, estimating we could still make our plane out of Tucson. We told Paul not to bother with hotel reservations, we'd find one ourselves wherever we decided to rest, and by taking turns driving, we were confident we could make the schedule happen. Glenn and Paul applauded our efforts and vowed to call us every couple of hours for updates.

An hour passed, day became night, and the rain subsided. We played silly games to pass the time, like I Spy and License Plate Bingo. We ate from the cooler, so we didn't have to stop. Then, just as we came upon Lafayette, Louisiana, the dashboard lit up and the power went out. People could have heard my screams in Guam.

Limping off the exit to Target, we didn't have the heart to call Glenn and Paul. Instead, Clark went in and purchased a pair of pliers and together we performed Sonata CPR. Partially successful, we got the jalopy to sputter to the next major exit, where we coasted to our fourth (and final) destination of the day. The Red Roof Inn.

Now, I've been in some shady places during my travels, but this place took the cake. All the lights in the parking lot had been shot out and broken glass was everywhere. Fast food wrappers littered the ground, there was discarded bedding and trash in the bushes, and the paint on the building was so old I couldn't tell what color it once might have been. Doors stood open or hung cattywampus in the jams of rooms that I hoped were uninhabited, and an inch of grime mixed with mold covered every handrail and window sill. Even the air smelled rank. It was nasty.

Normally I would have turned tail and run, but Clark and I were exhausted, dirty, frustrated, and done. Willing at this point to settle for anywhere with a bed and a shower, we located the front door, which was so grimy and disgusting neither one of us wanted to touch it. Grabbing hold of the broken metal handle using the bottom of my shirt for a glove, I went inside while Clark stood watch. The lobby had a bulletproof glass cage with a slide-out drawer and a clerk that eyed me warily. Her look and expression told me in every way I did not belong there. She seemed aghast and annoyed when I accepted the only room she had available, begrudgingly swiping my credit card. My thought went to the porn that would surely be purchased with it by daybreak, but I was just too damn tired to care. I took the metal key when it was offered and headed out the lobby door, this time using my butt to push it open.

"Room 106," I said to Clark, using the little strength I had remaining to point in the direction of the corridor to our left. "It's down this way."

Wheeling our suitcases behind us, we passed under a stairwell with a stench so foul it made me gag. Like spoiled milk mixed with rotten meat, the rancid odor emanated from a sticky reddish-brown substance a maintenance man was trying to power-wash off the sidewalk. A bit disconcerting at 10:30 at night. Who power washes at 10:30 PM? And why? I tried not to think about what mass murder was on the bottom of my Vans and wheelie bag.

Clark and I exchanged a look and picked up our pace. Twice we passed Room 106; once because the 6 had peeled off, and the second time because it looked occupied. Standing before it for the third time, we peered inside through the window, which had only one dingy gray-backed once orange curtain hanging from a bent rod. The room's television was on, one bed looked slept in, and a fresh cloud of cigarette smoke hung in the air.

"Clark, this can't be our room!" I whispered in a panic as Clark opened the door.

"It must be. See, the key fits," he replied as he popped open the door and unceremoniously pushed me into the room like a miner's canary. He never moved a millimeter from the threshold.

"Nice," I barked.

Warily, I looked around. The floor had no covering except for bits of old linoleum glue, dirt and fur balls. The rumpled bed had a butt mark on the side where the worn comforter had been thrown back, and the door to the bathroom was half closed. Or half open, depending upon how you chose to look at it.

"Clark, I think somebody is in the bathroom! I'm scared!" I rasped.

Clark said nothing, just gave me a "be brave" look and waved me on with his hand. He hadn't budged from his spot in the doorway and was braced to flee, looking like a frightened cat in his Captain America shirt. Some superhero.

Cautiously, and with great hesitation, I inched forward to the bathroom. When I got within a few inches of the door, I listened for movement and hearing none, I carefully nudged the door open with my outstretched foot before leaping back. I half expected a bloody murder scene with a body in the tub. Instead, there was a cigarette butt floating in the toilet and a half-dead roach trying to right itself on the disgusting tile floor. That was enough. I lit out of there like my hair was on fire.

We called a taxi from the Waffle House next to the mangy hotel and had him take us to the Fairfield Inn across town. We scored a free upgrade to a giant suite with a kitchenette from the front desk clerk who said I "looked like I could use a break". I bet I did. While Clark called Glenn to update him on what had happened, I passed out on one of the suite's two king beds and slept like the dead.

At 5 AM, Clark and I woke, showered and were down in the lobby ready to stuff ourselves on complimentary breakfast when they opened at 6 AM. Bursting with waffles and eggs a half-hour later, we took a taxi back to the car. Overnight, Glenn and Paul had determined our auto issue stemmed from the alternator, so they had scheduled an appointment in Lake Charles at a dealership, arranging for a tow truck to meet us at the car at 7 AM to transport us there. Lake Charles was about an hour's drive east of where we had landed. When the taxi pulled up at the Red Roof Inn, sure enough, an enormous, ancient flatbed tow truck sat waiting, the driver a dead ringer for ZZ Top.

ZZ was quite the character. A mountain of dude well into his sixties, he was wearing faded denim overalls with only one functional buckle. The broken side of his bib hung down to his waist, revealing a worn, stained t-shirt in an indeterminable color. He and his clothes were covered in a layer of grease that looked like it would have to be chiseled off, in contrast to his shaggy, layered, snow white beard, which was pristine.

ZZ set about loading the car in a no-nonsense way as soon as we got there. He was done in minutes, signaling to us that we were ready to go and motioning politely for us to clamber aboard. I opened the ancient cab door, which protested with a rusty squeal, and pushed Clark ahead of me to sit in the middle. It was payback for the Room 106 incident.

The interior of the cab looked just as I had imagined it would. Decades of grimy receipts were piled and falling from every surface and stuffed into every crevice. Aged, yellow foam stuck out of holes in the cracked vinyl of the single bench seat, which was the same indistinguishable color as the owner's t-shirt. Everything about the truck exuded years upon years of hard work, loyalty, and dedication. I wondered how many rescues this old girl and her owner had performed. Likely thousands.

ZZ hopped in without further ado, started up the engine, looked us over and apologized for the condition of the cab in a thick southern drawl. "She isn't fancy, but she's dependable," he said. "So, if ya'll want air conditioning you're gonna have to open a window. But it's still early, so we should be in Lake Charles before it gets too hot," he added, giving Clark and me another once-over followed by a puzzled look.

"So, what brings ya'll here? Vacation?" ZZ asked. I nearly choked on my coffee. Did people really come here for vacation? Wow.

I dislodged a dirty wrench from the seat cushion below my bottom, while Clark provided ZZ an abbreviated version of our tale of woe. ZZ chortled with good-hearted laughter and applauded our determination. "Yeah, I could tell yous weren't from 'round here. 'Cuz you sure don't look like no pimp (speaking to Clark), and you (thumbing in my direction), you ain't no crack 'ho!"

I did choke on my coffee that time and Clark convulsed with laughter. When I was able to compose myself, I whipped out my pocket journal to quickly memorialize the tag for one of Clark's future gifts (like I could ever forget it):

> *To: You don't look like no pimp*
>
> *From: Ain't no crack 'ho*

In the end we had to stay two nights in Lake Charles waiting for parts to repair the Sonata. Though I had to burn down two extra vacation days, the lavish free dinners and drinks we scored from Clark's mad poker skill winnings at our hotel's adjoining casino made up for it.

The Sonata was delivered to Glenn's mom in Tucson at the cost of a new Escalade, but she was delighted and therefore so was he. Plus, I had learned that even in the worst of times I don't look like no crack 'ho. Mama always told me good accessorizing would pay off. By gum, I guess she was right!

****

> *To: S'ALGOUD* the sock man (*Douglas spelled backwards, pronounced "S'all good!")*
>
> *From: The Very Important Business Woman*

I put this tag on a pair of naughty socks I bought for Doug while on my first (and only) business trip. I knew he'd love them, and he did. Doug was sock obsessed.

I had found out I was going on the aforementioned business trip only two days after returning from Tucson. My company had decided to send a group of us from the Engineering Department to Dallas for training. When the boss told me about the trip, you would have thought Publisher's Clearinghouse had shown up at my desk and awarded me the grand prize. I'd wanted to go on a big, important business trip since I first started working at Foodlane Bakery when I was 15. Having had to wait over 40 years for this, I couldn't have been more thrilled it was finally going to happen.

Doug was out of the office at lunch when I received this earth-shattering news. Busting with excitement, I tackled him like an overjoyed chihuahua the moment he returned. "Douglas, they're sending me to Dallas! Dallas! Can you believe it?"

Doug, acting surprised, froze a big fake smile on his face and talked through his teeth, "Do they know who they're dealing with?" In reply I shot him a wordless glare.

Already tired of the subject and disinterested, Doug changed the subject to something he found more exciting: socks. Doug loved socks. "Dude, have you seen Peter's socks today? They're awful. Baby-rat pink!"

This time I was the one unenthused. "I'll be sure to run right over and check them out," I said snidely, both of us knowing I absolutely would not.

I wish I had a dime for every time I got roped into a conversation about socks with Doug. He never tired of the subject, and I never understood the fascination. Time and time again he'd try to explain to me that guy accessorizing was all about the socks. Doug contended that combining comfort with functionality was key to a good sock and a happy man. Nearly every day he would plop himself down in the chair next to my desk, hoist a pant leg to display his footwear, and pause for me to congratulate him on his selection. He never received it. I just couldn't get into socks.

No matter how many ways he tried to sway me, I never understood his footwear obsession. I got the whole comfort thing; I wasn't a Neanderthal, after all, and loved sliding my sore piggies into some comfy slippers after a long day. And I appreciated that men were simple creatures whose existence revolved around comfort – comfort of their feet, their bellies, their egos and their "man unit" – but the design on my man's socks was just not a high priority. One stripe combination looked like all the rest, most reminding me of illustrations from a Dr. Suess book. Plus, how was I supposed to get excited about something that was hidden from sight and adorned the foot? I mean, seriously, should I be in the position of viewing a man stripped down to his socks, his choice and style of foot covering is not going to be on the agenda. Guaranteed!

I was in the middle of making this point once again when Peter in his baby rat-pink socks stopped at our cube to ask me a question. As he leaned over my desk with an engineering drawing to point out an issue, I saw Doug over his shoulder going ballistic pointing to his exposed sock. Doug began pantomiming whiskers and eating with tiny paws. I struggled to maintain composure as I listened to Peter explain his conundrum, simultaneously gesturing wildly to Doug behind Peter's back to quit the asinine behavior.

The minute Peter left, Doug shouted, "Did you see them? Did you see them? Baby-rat pink, right? Tell me I'm right! I'm right, aren't I? C'mon, you know I'm right!"

"Okay, yes, Douglas. Baby-rat pink if I'd ever seen it. You're a 'shoe-in' for a job creating crayon colors. Congratulations," I said mockingly. He puffed out his chest and was happy all day. Men are the oddest creatures.

The rest of that week passed quickly, and the day of my important business trip was soon upon me. I'd been in a frenzy for days getting ready. I'd bought new shoes, got my hair done, had a manicure, tastefully accessorized my outfits and stocked up on my favorite vanilla lotion. Co-workers were convinced I was secretly going on another cruise.

There were five of us from the engineering team flying together. The morning we left I had been up primping for hours to make sure my look was perfect, practical, and polished. I was a professional working woman of the world on a big, important business trip and I wanted everyone within eyeshot to recognize it. Before leaving for the airport, I checked that my documents were in order, and I was wearing clean underwear. I'd waited for this moment my whole life!

Once at the airport, the six of us checked our bags and proceeded to the security area, where we were de-shod and stripped of shiny things. Normally a fan of big earrings and lots of bling, I'd made sure my accessories today were understated, easily removable, and that I had no weapons on or about my personhood. I was not going to screw this up for anything!

Proud of myself for covering all the bases, I put my company issued laptop and carry-on bag in the gray plastic tub with my shoes and strode cheerfully and confidently through the metal detector. I had not a worry in the world. Suddenly, an alarm blared, red lights at my x-ray station strobed, and everyone in the area rubbernecked to get a glimpse of me. I was horrified.

A huge, uniformed security guard stepped in front of me and briskly ordered me into a clear, bulletproof cage. He keyed his radio and said he had a "10-37" in custody. A 10-37? Must be code for "beautiful, professional woman of the world on a big, important business trip". I tried to look calm and dignified. Not easy when barefoot, devoid of accessories, and displayed behind glass like a zoo animal. My travel partners, of no help whatsoever, laughed, pointed, and proceeded to our gate unfettered. I began to understand why gorillas flung their pooh.

I was contemplating jumping up and down like a puppy in the pet store window (pick me! pick me!) when an older gentleman was ushered through the clear door at the opposite end of my cage. We looked at each other silently for a moment and considering we might be stuck there for a while, I decided to break the ice.

"So, what are 'ya in for?" I asked brightly. I felt like I should have a toothpick hanging out of the side of my mouth and be leaning against the wall clad in a striped jumpsuit.

"Metal hip," the gentleman replied. "You?"

"I'm a 10-37," I said with a proud smile. It was not returned.

The guard reappeared on my end of the cube, unlocked the door, stood blocking the entrance, and barked, "Palms, please!"

"Pardon?" I replied.

"Palms please!" he repeated in a louder voice, like increasing the volume would clarify things.

Hesitantly, I presented my palms in front of me. Like a striking rattler, he swabbed them with a cloth square and strode off, locking the door behind him. I stood there baffled. Still holding out my palms, I looked at my cellmate and said, "Do you suppose he rubbed something on, or washed something off?"

Not uttering a word, Metal Hip Guy backed up several paces and eyed me suspiciously. I felt like I was carrying anthrax. Then, a guard unlocked Metal Hip Guy's door and set him free. I watched him go with envy, and in return he shot me one last accusatory glance. I had the overwhelming urge to moon him.

I watched the lines file through the detectors, wondering if I was ever getting out of there. Finally, my guard returned, unlocked my door, and announced that I was free to go. Still confused, I asked him what I'd done.

"Nothing, ma'am. The scanner detected a suspicious odor, but the swab came up negative."

Suspicious odor? Vanilla lotion? Next thing you know, they'll be recording my purchases from Victoria's Secret, as they do with Sudafed and Nyquil. Like I have enough culinary skills to cook up crystal meth. I can't even make a decent cup of coffee with a Keurig, for heaven's sake.

The little airport mishap behind me, I was ready to start again and prove to the world I was a capable, poised, professional businesswoman. I caught up with my team at the gate and endured their ribbing and chiding until we boarded. Once in the air, all was forgotten, and the remainder of my flight was quiet. We debarked, retrieved our bags, picked up our rental van and headed to the Embassy Suites in Dallas. I was delighted. This was great!

At the Embassy Suites, I checked in and headed straight to my room, which was fabulous. I unpacked immediately, before they could change their minds and banish me to the Red Roof Inn with the pimps and crack 'hos. I unwound, unpacked, laid out my outfit for the next day, lined up my toiletries, checked that the hair dryer was operational, placed a wake-up call for the morning, and set the alarm on my phone, the clock radio, the television, and my computer. We were supposed to meet downstairs for breakfast at 6 AM sharp, and I was not going to be late. I washed up and went to bed. It was 7:30 PM.

Bright and early the next morning, 4:45 AM on the dot, a crescendo of bells and whistles blasted me out of the sheets. The first morning of my big, important business trip had arrived, and I arose to prepare. A nice, long, hot shower at somebody else's expense awaited, and not having to worry about the dishwasher or washing machine sucking up the hot water while I had a head full of conditioner was something I wanted to relish!

I flipped on the bathroom light switch and the mirror light bulb blew. "Crap!" I cried, flicking the light switch up and down. It was so dark in the tiny bathroom without a light I couldn't distinguish anything. Though this wasn't as big of a deal regarding a shower, which I could manage in the dark, it was a huge problem for styling my hair. The blow dryer was bolted to the bathroom's far wall with no way to take it into the other room where there was a mirror and adequate light. My brain raced for a plan.

I thought about calling the front desk, but at 5:00 in the morning? That would surely piss somebody off. I'd worked the front desk at enough hotels to know you don't mess with the front lines. One disgruntled staffer in housekeeping could just about guarantee lice in my pillows and chiggers in my sheets. Nope. Not worth the risk.

Spying the desk lamp in the bedroom gave me an idea. I would MacGyver the bathroom light by swapping the burnt-out bulb with the one in the desk lamp until I could get maintenance there to fix it. I congratulated myself on my ingenuity and wasted no time on implementation. I unscrewed the bulb from the desk lamp and placed it on a washcloth on the bathroom sink to keep it from rolling. Then I climbed up on the high bathroom countertop and carefully stood to get to the vanity light. No easy task. Steadying myself, I reached over the top of the glass shade and started unscrewing the blown bulb. Things were going swimmingly, when suddenly…crack…the blown bulb shattered, sending shards of razor-sharp incandescent glass all over the bathroom and slicing a deep 1/2-inch gash in my right hand at the base of my thumb.

"Ooowwwww!" I hollered. And blood gushed everywhere. Shit! I didn't even have a band aid!

Vowing I would bleed to death before calling for medical attention, I jumped down from the counter and got in the pitch-black shower, hoping the water would help clean out my wound. The warm stream only served to make matters worse, causing the gash to gush a river of blood, so I got out, dried off haphazardly with one hand, and foraged for a dressing.

First, I tried wrapping the wound in a washcloth, but had to abandon the idea with no way to secure the end. Out of other options, I settled on using toilet paper, blowing through about a half a roll before the blood stopped soaking the layers faster than I could lay it. I tucked in the end and surveyed my work. I looked like I'd been patched up by a three-year-old. Lord. But it had to do. I was late now and in a rush.

My hair was sopping from the hasty shower, so I grabbed the hair dryer, pulling the cord as far as it would go into the hallway. Though I could see half my head in the bedroom mirror, I couldn't work a brush with my wounded appendage. I broke out in a sweat. I switched hands. I whimpered. I ranted. And then just when I started making some headway, the end of the toilet paper bandage came loose, got sucked into the nozzle of the hairdryer and started on fire.

"Really?" I shouted, lunging to unplug the dryer as sparks and smoke poured out of the vented openings, forming a smelly gray cloud. FML!

Not wanting the fire alarm to go off and empty the hotel, I threw the hairdryer on the vanity and slammed the door shut to the little bathroom of horrors. I ran to the bedroom mirror with a bottle of hairspray and crimped my half-damp head in an attempt at a beachy look, slapped on my make-up and threw on my clothes. Not the least bit successful, I looked more like an 80s drag queen than a sophisticated business woman. To top it off, the nasty cut bled through the last of the toilet paper layers as I rushed downstairs to breakfast. I looked a mess.

It was 6:15 AM when I arrived at breakfast disheveled and breathless, the last member of our team to join the group. Without even looking up, my coworker Ben handed my coworker Ryan $5 and an "I told ya so" was exchanged. Then, as if things couldn't get any worse, Ryan spied my dirty bandage, now covered in blood and makeup.

"Mrs. Pierce, are you bleeding?" (Ryan had been calling me Mrs. Pierce since he learned I was once a 7th grade teacher, and I reminded him of his.) He looked alarmed.

"Am I?" I tried to look surprised. "Oh, this?" I held up my war wound, and Ryan blanched down to his socks. He couldn't stomach the sight of blood. He ran for the garbage can and heaved, much to the delight of Ben from whom he'd just fleeced $5.

When Ryan regained his composure and returned to the table, I regaled them all with events of the morning. They laughed and took pity, packing me a muffin to-go while I begged for some antibiotic cream and bandages from the front desk. Gratefully, the clerk found me amusing and was happy to schedule a maintenance call to fix the light in my bloodied bathroom. I don't even want to know what they imagined I'd been doing in there.

For the rest of the trip the team was unrelenting in their teasing and couldn't wait to share the whole debacle with Doug as soon as we got back. Doug joined in the fun, and a few mornings after my return, I found a small box on my desk with the following *To-From*:

To: The Vanilla Terror

From: Toilet Paper Conservation Society

With some apprehension, I carefully opened one flap of the box to peer inside as chuckles erupted from the cubicles around me. Inside the box I found a package of Band-Aids, antibiotic cream, and a battery-operated push light. No respect for a bloody 10-37.

****

As if this Chariot Year hadn't lived up to its reputation with abundant travel, turbulence, and challenges, it was about to deliver another blow. By month's end, both Doug and I would give our notice to explore new job opportunities. Doug was headed to Colorado, and I had accepted an offer at the same manufacturing company as Glenn. The opening with Glenn's company had come up just 24-hours after I'd been whining to all my friends about losing Doug. Glenn had put his neck on the line to recommend me and I'd virtually been hired on the spot. The Chariot Year didn't mess around. I only prayed I could live up to everyone's expectations and weather whatever storm was being cooked up next.

Fingers crossed.

Chapter 7: July

My two-weeks' notice passed in a flash, and before I felt ready, I was packing up my office and tripping down memory lane. Each memento, award, gift, or gag I removed from my cubicle and placed into a cardboard banker box brought with it a flood of memories. There was my cheese hat, which my engineers would steal or pepper with obnoxious post-it notes whenever the Packers lost a game. There were the yellowing, unframed paper gag awards of appreciation or jest I had tacked to my corkboard, which meant more to me than their fancier etched glass counterparts marking years of service with the company. There was the third place ribbon I received during my 5K phase, the only physical fitness award I'd ever won in my life. And there was the fuzzy cotton snowball Doug had left with me as a parting gift when he'd pack up his things the week before. We had kept the silly snowball in our cube year-round for surprise attacks, randomly chucking it around the office to break up the monotony. Like there had ever been monotony when we were around.

Finally, when it was unavoidable, I reached onto the top of my metal 5-drawer filing cabinet to pack the last sentimental item: my Turd Finder hat. As I picked up the ridiculous-looking ball cap with the plastic poop glued to the brim, I was immediately transported back to my very first day on the job. I remembered with a rush how completely out of my element I had felt. I had been hired with zero engineering background, having previously worked as a language arts teacher, an executive secretary, and assistant to several high-ranking CEOs. Shocked that I had even gotten an interview, the manager who hired me had insisted I would fit the bill. He was looking for a self-starter with strong written communication skills, not worried about engineering or manufacturing experience, confident those would develop in time. So, he ran with his gut, gave me a shot, and there I was.

That first morning on the job nearly seven years ago, I remember I contemplated fleeing a hundred times. The Human Resource girl, who didn't even look old enough to drive, had unceremoniously dumped me off at a desk without any instructions, supplies, or information, and I had absolutely no idea what I was supposed to be doing. As I perched stiffly on the edge of my chair in the only suit I owned, my new boss, a tall, rail thin, nervous man, spied me as he sped past on his way to a meeting. Noticing me looking forlorn and abandoned, he took a step backward and stopped by my side.

"Oh, sorry, Colleen, I don't have any time this morning, but I'll get with you this afternoon to go over an action plan. Until then, I want you to go down to the TWS Conference Room and observe the ERB meeting."

I tried desperately to follow what New Boss was saying, but the man was speaking in tongues and I didn't have a notepad to write anything down. TWS? ERB? I had no clue what any of that meant. He may as well have been speaking Martian.

My blank look must have registered when New Boss finally met my panicked eyes, because he smiled and took on a softer tone. "Okay, I realize you won't know anybody or understand what's going on, but eventually you'll be attending these meetings regularly. So, for today, just try to absorb what you can. We'll go over it in more detail later, but for now I have to run." And with that, he was gone.

I looked around the office, desperate for some assistance, but every desk in the area was empty. Hesitantly, I wandered into the hallway looking for a warm body. Still not seeing anyone, I headed toward the main entrance, contemplating whether to leave and never come back. Glancing into one of the glass windows that lined the corridor, I saw workers garbed in white smocks, blue booties, and surgical hair caps peering into microscopes and using scientific equipment I'd only seen in movies. Behind another I glimpsed a team of three scientist-looking types peering into a darkened box lit with multi-colored laser beams. Behind a third I watched a massive industrial machine with a see-through drum cutting razor-sharp edges into a chunk of metal while it was sprayed with water. Engrossed in the spectacle at the last window, I was startled when a man's voice came out of nowhere, shattering the silence.

"Hello, can I help you find someone? You look lost," said a pleasant-looking, bearded gentleman with a smile.

Grateful for a friendly face, I introduced myself. "Hi, I'm Colleen," I said with an outstretched hand. "I'm the new Documentation Specialist. My boss said I'm supposed to go to the EMS conference room to attend a TRB meeting. Or something like that. Would you happen to know what he was talking about?"

The bearded gentleman laughed as he extended a hand in greeting and set me straight. "Hi, I'm George. Welcome aboard! I think you mean the Engineering Review Board meeting in the Thermal Weapon Sight area. That's where I'm going. C'mon, I'll show you." And without further ado, he pointed in the direction from where I had just come, and together we walked down the hallway.

"We call this the Green Mile," George informed me as we went. "They like to make sure we get our exercise." He chuckled and I felt like we were old friends. I was feeling better and more confident that things might work out after all. I hoped everyone would be as nice as George.

At the end of the hall, we passed through a set of double doors edged in rubber that looked like they belonged to a walk-in deep freezer.

"This is TWS," George said proudly, waving a palm-up hand across the expanse of a massive production floor. There were workbenches, hand tools, soldering materials, rack upon rack of machine parts, and a flurry of activity for as far as the eye could see. A veritable beehive of humanity. I had never seen anything like it before and had a hard time keeping my composure in check. This place was impressive!

"The yellow tape on the floor indicates the areas that are ESD sensitive. ESD stands for electrostatic discharge, which can damage the optics. You'll need to wear your blue smock when you go behind that yellow line," said George.

"Ah, I was wondering what the blue jackets were for." Every worker behind the yellow tape wore a thin blue smock with their name embroidered above the pocket. Was I going to get one of those? Cool!

Leading me away from "the line", as the production area was called, George guided me through a carpeted cube farm on the perimeter of the production area to a series of three conference rooms. Each room was identical with a white-topped elliptical table in the middle surrounded by eight mesh-back grey chairs with wheels. The south wall consisted of floor-to-ceiling windows with a view of the parking lot, the east wall was nothing but a giant white projector screen, and on the west wall hung a long white dry-erase board. Without so much as a nameplate on the door to indicate which room was which, I wondered how people knew where to go. I never would have found the right place on my own. Thank heavens for George.

Stopping at the wooden door of the nondescript meeting room in the middle, George gestured for me to go first with a gentlemanly wave. Four seats were already occupied by middle-aged men in various styles of casual/professional dress. George took a seat in the middle of the table's far side by the windows and motioned to the empty seat in the middle, which I gladly took. I looked at the bevy of unfamiliar faces and began introducing myself as George handed me a set of engineering drawings. I'd never seen an engineering drawing but tried not to show it. Fake it till you make it. Right?

Gazing at the odd renderings, I was grateful that at least I wouldn't give away my ignorance by looking at them upside down as I had the Hebrew prayer book when I visited a temple service with a friend during my childhood. I keenly watched George display his papers and placed mine before me likewise. Smiling, he leaned over and whispered, "We've been having issues with the fit of the O-ring." I nodded like I knew exactly what he was talking about. I hadn't a clue. The only other time I'd ever heard of an O-ring was when the news reported about problems with the space shuttle. I studied the schematic curiously, trying my best not to look stupid.

The energy of the room suddenly turned tense, everyone getting stone quiet when the last gentleman entered and closed the soundproof wooden door behind him. He carried the air of someone revered and looked like a mob boss. Though he wasn't excessively tall, he had a giant presence. His frame was broad, his mustache was thick, and his voice was deep. He looked like he would have played football back in the day and been a fierce competitor. With a head of thick salt-n-pepper hair, bushy eyebrows over intelligent brown eyes, dressed like a detective in a crisp white button-down shirt, black pants and loafers, he reminded me in every way of Tom Selleck in the role of Magnum P.I. He seated himself at the head of the table closest to the door, wasted no time bringing up a picture of the schematic drawing on the full-wall projector screen, and began the meeting in a booming baritone. He was clearly not happy.

"So, gentleman, can anyone tell me why we have yet to resolve this O-ring issue or how we are going to fix it before we have to halt production?"

Heads around the room bowed and butts squirmed in chairs. I wanted to ask George who this character was, but I didn't dare. And in the next second I didn't have to, because Magnum spied me in his midst, stopping mid-sentence to stare me down.

"Who on earth are you?" he blared.

"Colleen Pierce, sir. Your new Documentation Specialist!" I smiled brightly, belying my pounding heart, which was sending flee orders to my brain.

Magnum just grunted. He was obviously not impressed.

The meeting continued, as all stared up at the screen and tried to vanish into the woodwork. Struggling to make sense of the pieces and parts projected on the wall, I noticed it was rather like a puzzle, where the parts list, illustration, and series of numbered notes on the drawings came together as an instructional manual for assembly. Interesting. Looking at how the problem O-ring fit into the mix, I spied a set of numbers that were transposed, resulting in the part number for a circuit board referenced in the parts list to differ from its counterparts on the illustration and in the notes. I raised my hand.

"May I help you?" Magnum bellowed, looking at me indignantly. I realized at once that nobody raised their hand here; this wasn't seventh grade for crying out loud. I felt like a doof.

"Ummm, well, I was looking at item number eight on the parts list, and ...," I proceeded to blurt out the whole of my discovery as fast as I could, hoping speed would make it less painful. Like ripping off a band-aid.

The room grew even more silent when I finished, if that was possible, as all heads bowed over the drawings before them. Magnum's voice, now an octave higher, broke the silence. "Gentlemen, would you like to explain this to me?" His gaze then went to me again, and I slumped in my seat. Uh, oh.

"What's your name again?" Magnum demanded.

"Colleen Pierce, sir." I said with as much confidence as I could muster, which wasn't much. I would like to have died.

"Well, it may as well be Turd Finder, since you found the turd in our punchbowl!" Magnum exclaimed, his scowl relaxing as he finished his statement. "Good work, Ms. Pierce! I'm Gene and we've been looking for this issue for weeks. Get on it, gentlemen, and Ms. Pierce, I expect you at all my ERB's from this day forward." Needing to say nothing more, Gene arose from the table, grabbed his coffee and notebook, and left. Watching him go, I was in awe. The dude had swagger!

So began my career as the Turd Finder for the rest of my days with the company. Over the years I would find countless turds in the thousands of engineering meetings I was required to attend, ingratiating me to the intimidating Gene, who loved to shout, "Hey, Turd Finder!" when he spotted me on the Green Mile. I would burst out in giggles, sometimes shouting something back, while everyone around me would stare agog wondering how I'd broken through his gruff facade. And then one day the Turd Finder hat showed up on my desk and I proudly displayed it as a badge of honor from that day forward. Its roots and creator forever a mystery.

Now, on this my last day, I placed the hat lovingly in the box next to my favorite silver-framed photograph of Dani and me at her graduation from nursing school. Then I took a moment to take one last long look around the space I'd occupied for so many years. I'd had a good run here; it had been an adventure. But now it was time to move on.

Waxing sentimental, I put the cover on the banker box and readied myself to leave for my going away luncheon. Gene was hosting the gathering at my favorite Irish pub, and the time had come to head over. I was reaching for my car keys when my cell phone rang. The caller ID said: *Neil - lawn guy*. I looked at the ID perplexed. The only previous correspondence I'd ever had with Neil had been by text.

"Hello?" I said, thinking for sure Neil had butt-dialed.

"Uh, hi, Colleen. This is Neil, your lawn guy."

I couldn't for the life of me imagine why he'd be calling. "Yeah, hey, Neil. What's up?"

Neil took a deep breath before continuing. "Uh, okay, I'd first like you to know that everything is fine…" Everything is fine? No good conversation started that way! I froze like a statue and steeled myself for whatever came next. Good thing I did.

"So, the fire department just left your house, and my friend, the arborist, said your magnolia tree should fully recover in no time," Neil said in measured tones. Stunned, I removed my cell phone from my ear and stared at the screen before putting it back. "Colleen, are you there?"

Fire department? Magnolia tree? What the hell was going on at my house? I slumped blindly into my desk chair, dumbfounded. "Yeah, I'm here," I said slowly.

Neil continued, "Well, so, with all that has happened, I was hoping I could park my lawn mower in your carport until I can borrow a trailer, since mine burnt down to the frame."

I stood bolt upright again and shouted, "What?!" Everyone in the cube farm turned to look. Red-faced, I sat back down.

"I know, I know! But honestly, it all sounds worse than it is. Your house and everything are fine. My trailer and equipment took the brunt of it," Neil was talking fast now, trying to get everything in.

My mind raced as fast as Neil talked. Suddenly, a panicked, concerning thought came to mind, causing me to interrupt. "And what about you? Are you okay?" I shouted.

"Well, kind of. I have a bit of a burn on my arm that the paramedics said I should get checked. I'm headed to the ER as soon as the police leave. I just wanted to make sure it's okay to leave my mower here."

Jesus, of course it was okay.

"Alright, Neil, listen. You can leave your lawnmower wherever it is for as long as you need. Just please go get your arm looked at. You can give me all the details later. Tend to that burn!"

If anyone could sympathize about burns, it was me.

Neil thanked me and hung up. After he got home from the hospital a few hours later, arm bandaged with first and second degree burns, he called to fill me in on exactly what had happened. I was just finishing dessert at my farewell luncheon and excused myself to go outside and take the call.

Neil dished the whole scoop, and I listened enthralled. He said he and his lawn crew had been on a job earlier in the morning that involved substantial clean-up after the strong storm we'd had the previous evening. They had piled a huge mound of yard debris in the corner of the trailer with the intention of unloading it after mowing my yard, since my house was close to the dump. Not wanting to waste gas going to the dump and then backtracking, they headed straight to my house.

After mowing my yard and pulling the mower onto the trailer, Neil returned to my yard to blow off the clippings while the other guys finished edging. While their backs were turned, the lawnmower's hot engine ignited the pile of dried leaves and branches, and in seconds the whole trailer was engulfed in flames. The fire burned so fast and so hot that it consumed the wooden trailer down to its steel supports, creating ten-foot-tall flames that licked at my front yard's gorgeous magnolia tree.

Not wanting to wait for the fire department, whose sirens Neil said could be heard wailing in the distance (two fire engines and three police squads), Neil ran to my next-door neighbor's house to borrow their outdoor hose. He had attempted to use the two hoses at my house, but my water was off because my house was being replumbed. That's a whole other story.

Neil pounded frantically on my neighbor's door to ask if he could use the hose, waiting for what seemed like an eternity for them to answer. A dude came to the door, stoned out of his mind. A cloud of marijuana smoke billowed into the open air when the guy opened the door.

"Can I help you, man?" Stoned Dude asked Neil in sloth tongue, not noticing that there was a two-alarm fire just ten yards away.

"I need to borrow your hose! Can I borrow your hose?" Neil asked frantically, not thinking he needed to explain further. He said he could feel the heat of the fire from where he was standing.

"I don't know, man. I don't live here," said Stoned Dude, abruptly closing the door without another word.

Baffled by the exchange, which he would laugh at later, Neil gave up on the hose and dashed into the raging flame to save his bread-and-butter mower, scorching his arm. The fire trucks then arrived and set about extinguishing the inferno.

Neil said his arm was feeling better and the attending ER doctor told him he may not even have a scar. I hoped not; he was truly a good guy, always doing mission work with his family on the off season, and I felt sorry about all he'd gone through. I asked him to keep me updated and we said goodbye.

Back at my luncheon, I got to regale my comrades with one last outlandish story. They listened spellbound as I told them of Neil and the flaming lawnmower.

"Wow, Mrs. Pierce! You can start a fire without even being there! You're like a flame thrower!" Ryan said with a chuckle and look of awe. Everyone at the table laughed. They all knew my history with fire.

"Sounds like the perfect last *To-From*, Colleen," cried Gene. He loved my silly gift tags. "To: The Flame Thrower; From: We're going to miss ya, Turd Finder."

"Awwww, I'm going to miss you guys, too!" I said through tears. And then quietly to Gene, "And I'm going to miss you the most, scarecrow."

An understatement as large as the man himself.

****

To: LOL

From: For handling the sheets I'll handle your face

Phyllis handed me a gift certificate for one of her awesome facials with this gift tag. I'd helped her out the night before by doing a couple baskets of her spa laundry, because her washer had gone on the fritz. *LOL* stood for Lead of Laundress and had been a title Phyllis had originally bestowed upon one of her New York acquaintances who ran the laundry department of a large hotel. The LOL title had since passed to me when Phyllis discovered I absolutely loved doing laundry.

Doing the wash is the one household chore I enjoy above all the rest. I honestly don't know what it is about the light scent of fabric softener on a laundered t-shirt pulled warm from the dryer that brings joy to my soul, but it's something. And whatever that something is, it's a concept Phyllis can't wrap her head around. I nearly had to wrestle the spa laundry from her, as she was certain I must be lying about the pleasure I take in doing it. She says she'd have more fun having a mammogram or bathing her cats.

This is the same opinion shared by Dani when I try to confiscate her dirties just to fill a load. She eyes me warily looking for the catch, not believing I'm just looking to amass enough enjoyable folding to make it through the latest episode of *Married at First Sight Australia*. She makes me just about beg to get my hands on the goods to get my fix, unlike her FSU days when I got appreciative unsolicited deliveries. How I miss the Friday night calls she'd make driving home from college that started with, "Hi, Mommy! Wha'cha doin'?"

This was a laundry code from back in the day when I was in my glory. Dani knew doggone well Friday was my laundry night, so she would time her calls home accordingly.

"Just sorting colors from whites. Wanna join me for a grilled cheese?" I'd say, the customary reply in accordance with our tradition.

"Sounds great. I'm just exiting 95, so I'll see you in a few," she'd exclaim with too much enthusiasm for spending a Friday night home from college with Mom.

Twenty minutes later I would hear the rumble of Thomas, her beloved Ram 1500 pickup truck, in the driveway and into the house my child would bound and tilt her head for an obligatory hair kiss. She'd take a seat at the table and between bites of grilled cheese, she'd catch me up on the latest college drama, hardly missing a beat between sentences to ask, "Hey, do you have room in that load for a couple things? I have my laundry in the truck."

The question was just perfunctory. The answer would always be yes, and without further ado, out to Thomas she would bound to haul in 10 tons of laundry. Two loads in, my grilled cheese-filled youngster would flounce out to join her hometown pals, and I would happily finish her wash. On Sunday she would swing by for a snack, and I would send her back to school with all her clothes washed, fluffed, folded, and pressed. Ah, the good old days.

Now needing some comfort to calm the nerves of starting a new job on Monday, I called Dani to see if I could relive some of that joy. She answered on the first ring.

"Hi, Mom. What's up?"

"Just getting ready to do some laundry. Can I pick up some things to fill a load?" I stood stark still waiting for a reply, wondering how much of a fight she'd put up. She, like Phyllis, still didn't believe I liked doing laundry. Even after all these years.

"You know I always have tons," she said. "But really, Mom, you don't have to. I'm not going to make you clean up my mess."

This was the canned answer she always gave these days, as was my response that followed. It was our grilled cheese conversation 2.0.

"I know I don't have to; I want to. I'll see you in five!"

And out the door I went to collect some joy.

I finished Dani's laundry and collected a bonus load from Phyllis, able to spend my weekend laundering to my heart's content before starting my new job on Monday refreshed and invigorated.

The first few days on the new job were intense. I had to take a step back in time, like to the Cindy Lauper era, because some of the new company's processes were so extraordinarily antiquated, they were still being done on paper rather than via the computer. I felt like I may as well have been dipping a feathered quill in an inkwell. By Friday I was jonesing for laundry, but because there was none for me to fleece off family and friends so soon after my last binge, I had to find another way to combat the new job anxiety over the weekend. That's how I would come to find myself in one of the biggest pickles of all time and pull the most epic new job blunder of my employment career only five days in.

Knowing the embarrassing incident would get back to Glenn by the time Monday morning rolled around, I stopped by the liquor store on Sunday to buy him a bottle of Grand Marnier on which I placed this *To-From*:

> *TO: Should you get compensated after 90 days for getting me hired, it'll be a miracle*
>
> *FROM: Sorry, but I see an empty HR file, and I just can't help myself*

I prayed the combination of humor and hooch might soften the blow of my stupidity.

The whole hideous nightmare had started innocently, as my debacles usually do. Sitting on my back porch after work on Friday having a Jim Beam and ginger beer with no laundry to do, I had an epiphany. I would take a couple hours the next morning and get some backlogged paperwork filed at my new office, giving an unexpected gift to my overwrought trainer. My good deed would greet him Monday morning like a visit from the shoemaker's elf. Ta da! Nothing like a little initiative to make a good impression, mama always said. Or was that Murphy?

Excited with my plan, I popped out of bed early Saturday morning, pulled on my sweats, grabbed my badge, and skipped out of the house to my car. I had left my glasses on my desk in the main building the previous day, so I headed there first. There were no cars in the main lot and not a soul in sight when I arrived. I swiped my badge on the scantron pad and went in. The automatic lights overhead sprang to life as I tripped their sensors. Whistling a happy tune, I bopped through the halls, grabbed the glasses off my desk, badged out, and got back into my car to drive the two blocks to the warehouse building where the engineering files were kept. This was going to be great! I was all proud of myself.

When I arrived at the warehouse, there was one car in the opposite drive; a beat-up Nissan sedan was parked way down by the sister manufacturing building. I felt a momentary wash of relief knowing someone else was on the property, because the building where I needed to go looked to be dark. I contemplated finding the coworker who belonged to the car before going further but decided against it. Big mistake. Huge.

Peeking into the jet black abyss through the warehouse door's oblong window, all my warning radar went off. I ignored it. Why, oh why do I do that? Somewhere up in heaven my guardian angel must be beating her head against the wall just waiting to kick my ass.

Turning a deaf ear to my screaming intuition, I swiped my badge to enter the darkened building that held my files. I heard the inner mechanism of the door lock disengage, and when I yanked on the curved metal handle, the door easily opened. Stepping inside, I expected the overhead lights to come on as I walked into the darkness, but instead all hell broke loose. A tiny red light in the ceiling came on, a white strobe started flashing, and an alarm blared that was so loud you could have heard it in New Jersey. Scared senseless, the birds peeled off the roof, the squirrels fled from the trees, and I bolted back outside horrified. Ta da!

Slamming the door shut behind me, I bounced from one foot to another, then started running in circles like an exercising hamster. I reopened the warehouse door, shut it again, and swiped my badge across the sensor furiously trying anything to reverse the sequence. When that proved unsuccessful, I began screaming at the sensor box, "No! Shut off! Shut offfff!!!!!!!" Yeah, because that always works.

Picturing my image on a fuzzy green video on the evening news, I began freaking out. I ran for my car (reason unknown) and then fumbled with my cell phone, contemplating who to call. I settled on 911. The operator answered.

"911, what is your emergency?"

"Hello! Oh, thank God! I just set off the alarm at my new job and I can't get it to stop! It won't stop! Get it to stop!!!!" I cried like a mad woman. Then, as I was answering a battery of questions, the Nissan owner from the manufacturing building, a tall, thin, middle-aged guy with a scruffy beard in ballcap and jeans, came running down the driveway, pushed me aside and punched a code into the keypad, silencing the alarm. I was overjoyed. Him, not so much.

"Oh, never mind," I said to the 911 operator, like I was canceling a pizza. I'm sure she thought I was a complete idiot, but I didn't have time to care. I pocketed the phone and ran over to my coworker to offer up a kidney. I held out my hand and smiled brightly, introducing myself, having a flashback to my first encounter with Gene. But whereas that time I had a happy outcome, this held none of the same promise. Coworker Dude stood there stoic and scowling, before ordering me gruffly into the building next door.

Nearly grabbing me by the scruff of the neck, Grumpy Coworker had me follow him to his desk, where he silently dialed a number and punched the speaker button. Waiting for someone on the other end to answer, he eyed me disapprovingly.

A female answered the call on the second ring. "ABC Alarm Company. May I please have your password," she asked in monotone.

Grumpy Coworker grabbed up the receiver, supplied the information, and then stepped aside with the mouthpiece in hand, so I could take it and explain my side of the story. As I threw myself under the bus, Grumpy Coworker harrumphed and shook his head as I tried to disappear under my bangs.

When the call was over, Grumpy Coworker, whose name I still did not know, ordered me to go back to my desk in the main building and compose an email to our head of security. Obediently, I schlepped off to use my creative writing skills to plead ignorance and beg for mercy. After I was done, I headed out to my car to go home. Screw the filing. The road to unemployment was paved with good intentions.

Once in my car, I was just pulling out when two sheriff's department SUVs went flying down the street toward the warehouse. They stopped a half-block short of the building whose alarm I had just set off and began setting up SWAT style. Oh, Jesus. Would this never end?

Nope. A half-hour later, having used everything in my verbal negotiation toolbox to sweet-talk the Man into disbanding the army of law enforcement, media, and hierarchy en route to end my career before my first paycheck, I was finally on my way back home.

On the drive I got a call from Gene asking how my first week had gone. "Um, so, I may have done something kind of stupid," I started and then divulged the whole ugly truth. Gene's familiar baritone erupted in great guffaws of laughter that left him breathless.

"Hey, at least I didn't start anything on fire!" I shouted in my defense.

"Yet!" he replied with a laugh, as I nodded in silent agreement.

"Yeah, I guess the Turd Finder has become the Turd Maker," I conceded with chagrin.

I wonder if that title will come with a hat.

Chapter 8: AUGUST

August 4th is my nemesis. If danger is lurking, it will find me on this day. I dread the coming of August 4th as much as my annual trip to the cold, stirrup table of the OB/GYN.

The list of unfortunate things that have happened to me on August 4th seems endless. Here are just a few off the top of my head:

- I once drove 5 hours from Milwaukee to La Crosse on August 4th to surprise my college sweetheart, who was enrolled in summer school. He surprised me by being in bed with another girl when I arrived.

- Many years later, not realizing until afterward that this happened on August 4th, I broke up with the guy I had been dating because he kept going back to his ex-wife. I later learned that August 4th was also their wedding anniversary. A double whammy.

- In my early 20s, I had a gorgeous blue Chevelle SS that was my pride and joy. On August 4th I was driving her to work and got sideswiped by a Milwaukee city bus. I had the damages repaired, but she was never the same.

- Not wanting to tempt fate one year, I called in sick to work on August 4th, figuring I'd be safe just lounging around the house in my jammies. I wound up slipping on the bathroom throw rug and gashing my shin open on the sharp, tiled footer of the walk-in shower. My leg still bears the nasty scar.

- And then there was the Queen Mother of all August 4th catastrophes – when I found myself on a date with one of my former seventh grade students. Let me clarify that this incident took place twelve years after I quit teaching, and I didn't initiate the date. I knew the guy was somewhat younger than I, but to what extent I had no idea. Over drinks and conversation, I discovered the age difference was 23 years and he discovered I looked familiar not because of seeing me around the gym, but because I taught him how to write a 5-paragraph essay when he was 13. I was his first teacher crush. Flattery and tragedy wrapped up together in one ridiculous package.

So, given my history with the doomed date, I was not surprised to wake up this August 4th with a knot the size of a minivan in the pit of my stomach. Being that this was my Chariot Year, I was terrified to drive and tried to think of any excuse to stay home and cover myself in bubble wrap. Alas, I had a critical meeting at work I couldn't miss, plus I had promised my friend Betsy I'd collect her mail while she was vacationing. With both my office and Betsy's apartment too far away to walk or bicycle, my escape hatch was closed, leaving me no choice but to drive. A frightening prospect.

While I showered for the day, I talked myself off the ledge. I reasoned that as much as I didn't care for the Blood Clot, the National Highway Traffic Safety Administration had issued the Chevy Cobalt a good safety rating, so that was something. I also rationalized that I would much rather be surrounded by steel when I got into an accident, rather than be hit while walking or biking. Odds of not having my body parts rearranged were much better with air bags. Furthermore, if I did get into a crash, once they sewed all my appendages back on, I might get enough compensation to finally buy the shiny new Honda Civic I always wanted. All prospects that had me temporarily bolstered, but unfortunately didn't last. By the time I had applied my makeup and blown my hair dry, I had to down a handful of antacids to calm my nervous belly.

Feeling like I was walking to my execution, I schlepped out to my carport and slid reluctantly behind the wheel.

"We can do this, old girl," I said as much to myself as the car. I recited the Lord's Prayer and keyed the ignition. We were off!

I puttered along in the car at a snail's pace, opting to take side roads whenever possible. Twice I nearly got hit–once by someone not looking before they backed out of their drive, and again when a teenager on a crotch rocket whizzed around me, and then cut me off. What was normally a 20-minute drive took over a half-hour. But at least I arrived at the office intact.

After settling down and having my morning coffee, the workday went surprisingly smooth. I'd grown so confident by noon that I even went out to lunch. And by 5:00 PM when the workday was over, I was beginning to think I'd evaded the curse.

Only one item remained on my agenda before I could boogie home: the mail pickup at Betsy's apartment. Betsy was a friend I'd worked with at my last job and with whom I traded house watching duties. When I was out of town, she'd keep an eye on my house and bring in the mail, and vice versa, I'd do the same for her when she was away. She had watched over my place while I was away on my big, important business trip, so now it was my turn to repay her while she was on vacation in the Bahamas. An honorable girl code thing.

Betsy's apartment complex was nice and typically Floridian, a patchwork of two-story buildings interspersed with manmade grassy knolls sprinkled with palm trees and Azaleas. It wasn't anything particularly fancy, but it was well-manicured and safe, with mail delivered to banks of metal mailboxes located in the parking lot a short distance from her building.

Arriving at her complex, which was half-way between my office and home, I was on a mission. I wanted to get in, get out and get done. Pulling up in a visitor slot on the backside of the knoll that was directly behind Betsy's mailbox grouping, I threw my car in park and left the engine idle while I quickly jumped out. Figuring the collection would only take a few seconds, I didn't even bother closing my car door. I cut across the knoll to the front side of the mailboxes, slid the key into Betsy's mail slot, and then caught something moving in my peripheral vision. Glancing over my right shoulder, I was blinded by the evening sun reflecting off the metal mailboxes and could only make out a fuzzy white blob moving in my direction. The apparition was about 100 yards away. Leaning forward and squinting to get a better look, I observed what appeared to be an albino feathered creature sprinkled with brown patches of fur, taller than a chicken but with a longer neck, a cross between a vulture and a mini ostrich. Strange. And ugly.

Unrelenting in its scrawny-legged pursuit, the bird seemed to be angry and was closing in on me at an alarming rate. My internal radar went off and I became suddenly afraid. Looking over to my car in a panic, I realized there was no way for me to make it back to safety without crossing paths with the crazy bird. I needed another plan. And quick! Not knowing what else to do, I made the split-second decision to make a run for the management office about 50 yards to my left. Without wasting another second, I streaked across the blacktop shrieking in terror, *Frankenchicken* now just a few feet behind me. I'd never run so bloody fast in all my life!

Quickly losing steam with the horrid creature hot on my heels, it became apparent I wasn't going to reach the office before he caught me. So, I banked a hard left and bolted up the first staircase I came upon, taking the steps two at a time. In my wild ascent, my brain raced with what to do next and how I could defend myself when I got to the top. Mid-flight it came to me: my heels! I had on my 3-inch heels!

When I got to the landing, perspiration dripping from my forehead, my hair mussed, and my breath heaving in my chest from the sprint across the parking lot, I whipped off a bright orange pump and spun around brandishing the shoe like a ninja. Only then did I realize my foe was still on the sidewalk below, stalking and squawking, unable to manipulate the stairs. Awash with relief, I doubled over, half-shod, hands on knees, and struggled to catch my breath.

"I see you've met our wild Asian chicken!" came the shout of a man's voice.

Spinning around with wild eyes looking for the voice's source, I spotted a golf cart through the iron slats of the stair rail. Behind the cart's wheel sat a handsome, middle-aged guy dressed in a blue button-down shirt and khaki slacks. He was tan from the Florida sun and his hand was clasped over his mouth to hide his amusement. As I straightened and attempted to pull myself together, Golf Cart Dude succumbed to great guffaws of laughter that brought tears to his eyes.

"Sorry, but that was hilarious," he said, gulping for air and then struggling to sober himself the best he could. "I'm Tom from Management. Are you alright?"

"Jesus, I thought I was a goner!" I shouted back with a half-smile, feeling the twinges of attraction.

"I'm Colleen. I'm watching Betsy McKnight's apartment," I said, flirting a little harder than I should be after a life-threatening event. Then I noticed Tom was wearing a wedding band. Just my luck. Damn August 4th!

Not wasting anymore of my girlish charm on a married man, I said in a more serious tone, "Tom, could you please run off your feathered friend there so I can get back to my car?" I motioned to the Blood Clot idling in the distance with its door still open.

Giving me a thumbs-up, Tom spun the cart around and drove the awful bird back in the direction from which it had come. Wasting no time when the coast was clear, I sprinted down to the mailbox, grabbed Betsy's mail, beelined for my car, and launched myself into the seat so hard I bruised my hip on the center console. Throwing the mail on the seat next to me, I headed home without so much as a backward glance. It was home or bust for this chick!

On August 5th before collecting Betsy's mail, I stopped by Walmart and picked up two mini air horns. One of the horns I opened and carried with me for defending myself against the Frankenchicken, should he make another appearance, which of course he didn't. The other horn I left atop Betsy's mail pile with the following *To-From*:

> *TO: For days when you're wearing flats*
>
> *FROM: Faster than a speeding Frankenchicken*

To date neither Betsy nor Tom has heard of another sighting of *Frankenchicken*. Regardless, I carry the horn with me whenever I check Betsy's mail.

****

Not a week had passed after the incident at Betsy's apartment, when my friend and coworker Karla asked me to doggie-sit for her aging Jack Russell terrier, Bingo. Karla was flying to Ohio for her daughter's baby shower, and Bingo was too old to kennel because he had a bad heart and the kennel stressed him out. All Karla's relatives who'd normally doggie-sit were busy (or said they were), so she had grown desperate.

"Please, Colleen," Karla begged. "You're my last resort!"

The *You Are My Last Resort to Watch My Pet* is a common theme among my friends with pets, and that they come to me at all I find forever perplexing. Every one of my friends know I don't own pets by choice, I have a litany of animal allergies, and am accident prone. Yet I seem to be among the first they ask to watch over their furry family members while they are away. I guess I should be flattered that they entrust me with the care of their precious companions.

I waivered uncomfortably as Karla continued to plead her case. "I just can't put Bingo in the kennel, the anxiety will kill him, and it's only for the weekend. Pleeeeeease?" She was kneeling next to my desk now, hands clasped in prayer, batting long eyelashes, and smiling angelically.

"Uuuchhhh, you know I have a non-sitter rule!" I exclaimed, unable to meet her eyes. "I don't watch friends' children or animals. It's too much responsibility!" True, and true. With all the nonsense I get into, it just wasn't a good idea.

"It's only a couple days; what could happen? You'll be fine. Promise!" She'd obviously forgotten who she was dealing with.

"Karla," I continued, "Did I not just tell you about the Asian chicken? And that happened while I was just trying to bring in the mail! Bingo is 15 years old. If he dies on my watch from one of my freak accidents, I will never forgive myself! Nor will you!"

"Oh, for heaven's sake," she sighed wearily. "I'll sign a hold harmless waiver. C'mon, you'll have the whole house to yourself (it was a really nice house); you can eat and drink anything you want, swim in the pool, and relax. It'll be like a vacation! Please?" Her eyes filled with tears, and she looked downright pathetic.

I caved. God, I was such a softie.

"Alright, alright," I said with a sigh. "Only this once because it's for you to see your daughter!" She knew Dani was my Achilles and I'd do anything for a mom wanting to be with her kids.

"Great!" Karla shouted, grabbing me around the neck as I sat straight-backed in my chair not reciprocating. "Oh, gosh, I appreciate this! Come by the house on Friday and we'll go over everything. I owe you!"

"Yeah, yeah," I grumbled, shooing her back to her desk with my hand. "You can buy me a Ferrari."

On Friday after work, I went to Karla's house as instructed. She showed me where she kept Bingo's treats, told me when he got them, how often he should go out, where his leash was kept, what neighbors to stay away from, and his feeding regimen. All seemed simple enough.

"I think I should try taking him for a walk to see if he's good with me on the leash," I said when Karla had completed her instructions. I'd met Bingo several times and he was comfortable around me, but I still wanted to make sure he was okay with our new arrangement.

"Great idea," Karla agreed and stepped aside so I could get Bingo's leash. I grabbed the leather strip off the hook, snapped the end onto his collar, and then the three of us moseyed through the neighborhood. All went fine. We got back to the house, I unhooked him, hung up the leash and got ready to leave.

"Great! So, here's the house key, and I'll walk Bingo before I leave in the morning. If you're here by noon, that should be good. I'll be back Monday night by 7 and my flight info is on the counter. I really appreciate this!" Karla said, grasping me again in a bear hug as I stood there unmoving. When she released me, I fled out the door before I could change my mind.

The next day, Saturday, just before noon I arrived at Karla's with my overnight bag. I'd be staying for the duration of the weekend, as we'd agreed, so Bingo wouldn't get lonely. As soon as I put the key in the front door, a barrage of barks and growls ensued. Fighting the urge to flee, I let myself in and found Bingo standing there in the tiled entryway silently eyeing me up. Instinctively, I held the overnight bag in front of me for protection, seized by fear thinking of my recent encounter with Frankenchicken. I sized up my little 4-legged roommate as I stood there, and he did the same.

"Hey, buddy," I said sweetly, slowly kneeling to his level, but keeping my bag between us. "Looks like it's just you and me, kid." I held out a cautious hand over my bag and he considered it before giving a snort and showing me his backside. I replied with a sigh. "Awww, c'mon!"

"Wanna go for a walk, bud?" I asked enticingly, trying to force some excitement into my voice. He turned his head but not his body, and just stared me down. Lord, couldn't anything be easy?

"C'mon, let's get your leash," I said, trying a different approach. I stood up and walked into the kitchen but was the only one that moved. Bingo stood riveted to the spot in the entryway, still showing me his backside.

Not giving up, I went into the laundry room to retrieve the leash and found the collar was attached. Hmmm...I hadn't bargained on that. Would Bingo be cool with me putting on his collar? I had visions of pulling back a bloody stump where my hand once resided. When I was little, my Auntie Norm had vicious Chihuahuas that really packed a punch. More than once I'd come home bandaged and bleeding from random, unprovoked attacks. I suddenly wished I had one of those training gloves that the instructors wore when they worked with the K-9's. I grabbed the dish towel and wrapped it around my hand, just in case. The towel could double as protection while being useful for mopping up the blood.

Steeling my nerves, I went back to the foyer and bent down to Bingo with my wrapped hand and invited him to sniff. He just looked at me but didn't shy away or growl. Taking this as a good sign, I presented the collar, like I was parading a new refrigerator on the *Price is Right*. That got him; he took a step toward me and waited patiently while I buckled the little blue strip around his neck. I was victorious and overwhelmingly proud of myself. Hurrah!

With bolstered confidence, I stepped out of the house with Bingo on the leash. Down the street we went, but only got 50 feet before he stopped to take a poo in the only yard he wasn't supposed to. The property belonged to Karla's next-door neighbors, the "Mean People". Karla had told me the couple was so fanatical about their grass they had installed video cameras to record evidence of dogs doing their business on their property, which they presented at homeowner's association meetings for eliciting fines. Since Karla lived on a cul-de-sac with a drainage pond on the other side of the street, she had no alternative but to take Bingo past their house to go on a walk, and he just loved violating their lawn. As a result, Karla had been fined so many times she was considering setting up automatic payments.

Prepared with my baggie, I swiftly scooped up the little poop nuggets before anybody came out of the house to accost me. I looked around nervously and felt like I was trying to heist jewels before the cops arrived. "C'mon, Fingers, let's get outta here," I cried to Bingo, encouraging him to walk as fast as his little stubby legs would carry him.

When we got a safe distance away, I had a chat with him about his behavior. "You couldn't hold it until we at least got down the block? Rude!" I swear he was grinning with defiance when he looked up at me.

The rest of our walk thankfully went off without incident, and I made sure there wasn't even a drop of pee left in his tank for the Mean People's yard when we passed by the second time. Safely back inside Karla's house, I unleashed Bingo and gave him a bacon treat as instructed, which he unceremoniously gobbled down. When he was done, he stood in the kitchen looking at me. I don't know why, but I felt like I owed him an itinerary.

"Okay, so, I'm going to get settled in the guest room, check my email and then we'll have a cocktail by the pool. Are you good with that?" Like he was going to answer. I shook my head at my own ridiculousness, bent down to give him a pet, but he ran around the corner to the living room before I could touch him.

"Just like a man," I grumbled as I rose to go to the guest room to get my computer.

And not ten seconds later was the first time I heard it - the most gawdawful noise to ever hit my ears. I stopped dead in my tracks at the sound and listened.

Eeeeeee...awwwwwww!

HhhhEeeeee...owwwwwww!

Yeeeeehhhhhh...awlllllll!

Quiet as a mouse I stood frozen in the middle of the hallway outside the guest room. I waited to hear it again, and in a few seconds, I did…

Eeeeeee...awwwwwww!

HhhhEeeeee...owwwwwww!

Yeeeeehhhhhh...awlllllll!

The cry had the ear-piercing bray of a donkey combined with the caterwauling of a barn owl, the chorus growing deeper and longer as it went. As I stood stock-still there in the hall, it went off for a third time…

Eeeeeee...awwwwwww!

HhhhEeeeee...owwwwwww!

Yeeeeehhhhhh...awlllllll!

This time when the howl ended, I turned and went flying down the hall in my stocking feet to locate the source, slipped on the polished tile floor and damn near killed myself when I overshot the doorway and went crashing into the jam.

Gathering myself, I rushed into the living room and found Bingo sitting in the middle of the living room rug, looking indifferent and calm as ever.

"Hey, buddy, did you hear that donkey? Freaky, right?! I know your neighbor is an ass, but I didn't think Karla meant it literally!" I laughed at my own joke, snorting loudly.

"Awww, c'mon, Scoobie Snack, that was funny!" I cracked up again. Bingo showed me his backside and walked away. Dog had no sense of humor.

Thinking the sound was coming from the *Mean People*'s house as a revenge tactic to be annoying, I closed the open sliding glass doors to the pool before returning to the guest room. But I didn't even make it half-way there before I heard the hellish braying begin again, clear as day.

Eeeeeee…awwwwwww!

HhhhEeeeee…owwwwwwww!

Yeeeeehhhhhh…awllllllll!

This time I was sure the sound was coming from inside the house near the master bedroom. Thinking maybe Karla had left the television on in her room and there was a documentary playing, I strode across the house to turn the annoying thing off, mentally apologizing to the *Mean People* for having jumped to rash conclusions. Rounding the corner to Karla's bedroom, I saw Bingo, sitting in the middle of the master bedroom carpet, head tipped back like a highland wolf, howling from the deepest reaches of his belly.

Eeeeeee…awwwwwww!

HhhhEeeeee…owwwwwwww!

Yeeeeehhhhhh...awlllllll!

"That noise is you?" I cried, catching him in mid-*awlllllll*, making him jump.

"Uh-uh, no way, shorty!" I scolded. "We are not spending the weekend with that crap! Let's go outside to the pool and talk about this." When I had gotten a few steps out the door I realized I was alone, so I turned around and stalked back to the room. There he sat still in the same spot on the carpet.

"C'mon, son!" I said with more insistence. Reluctantly, this time he followed.

Out at the pool we had a heart-to-heart over a vodka tonic while playing fetch with Bingo's favorite ball. We came to an agreement about the wretched yowling, whereby I would enjoy two days of happy silence in exchange for a bacon treat.

"Okay, bud, let's shake on it," I said, leaning down with an open palm. Reluctantly, he offered a paw, eyes locked on mine, giving me the willies. It reminded me of guys that kiss with their eyes open. I hated that.

I should have known Bingo was not a man of his word. Either that, or he did not understand the terms of our negotiation, because he let rip with one long, ear-splitting howl that night at the precise moment I had drifted off to sleep. Like the bellow of a tornado siren from my childhood, the wail scared the beejeebus out of me, landing me on the floor when I bolted out of bed.

In the morning over coffee, Bingo and I had another discussion and renegotiated the sound of silence. After our walk we made nice, and he apologized, but then puked up his bacon treat onto the Oriental rug, bleaching the color out of the tapestry in a splash pattern. I probably would have fretted about that all weekend, had I not seen two older spots that matched.

At bedtime Sunday night, following a full day of peace and quiet, I went over our agreement just to be sure. Bingo agreed not to bray, yowl, or caterwaul in exchange for a long game of catch and a belly rub, but then retaliated by taking a pee on the tile right outside my bedroom door. When I stumbled out of bed for a midnight potty break, I slipped on the puddle, went down in a flurry of limbs and cursing, slicing open my right knee on the bottom corner of the linen closet. Splayed across the hallway tile bleeding, I looked up to see him sitting on the other end of the hallway watching. I swear the little shit was laughing.

Thankful it was the last night I had to spend with my spiteful canine companion, I spent the remainder of our time wordlessly agreeing to disagree. I bandaged my knee, lined the hallway with towels and shut the door to my room, ruining his fun and taking away further temptation. He was pissed and I didn't care. Three chances was my limit and more than he deserved.

Now, though Bingo may not have enjoyed my visit, I can't say the same for the Mean People Husband. On the last afternoon of my stay, I decided to forgo my damp bathing suit for a skinny dip, figuring I'd be safe behind Karla's 6-foot privacy fence. Now while this normally would have been true, my nude water frolicking on this day just happened to coincide with the exact moment the Mean People Husband chose to prune his tallest palm tree. Stepping onto the top rung of his ladder, Mean People Husband casually glanced over the privacy fence to Karla's pool and saw me getting out in all my naked glory. He went slack jawed and nearly took a header. Good thing his chainsaw wasn't on.

Not knowing what to do in this awkward moment, I decided it best to be neighborly. Smiling cheerfully, I gave a friendly wave, trying to come off undaunted. Caught completely off guard, Mean People Husband slowly raised his hand and did the same. When in Rome. I would have liked to have laughed about it with Bingo, but we weren't speaking.

A few days after Karla returned home from Ohio, she stopped by my desk with a beautiful plant as a gift of thanks. As she turned to leave, she was struck with a thought and whipped back around to ask me, "Did you say anything to my neighbors? You know, the mean ones?"

"Nope. Can't say that I did," I replied. It wasn't a lie. "I did give a friendly wave, though." I answered honestly. "Why?"

"Well, the husband was all smiles when he saw me this morning," Karla said. "Odd," she said, lost in her own thoughts.

"Yeah," I agreed. "People are weird." I added, smiling.

Eventually, I would tell on myself and share all the juicy tidbits of the weekend, but for now I was having too much fun giggling in the wings while Karla pondered how I won over her neighbor. With her Christmas gift, a bottle of her favorite vodka to replace the one I'd put a sizeable dent in during my stay, I included a bag of bacon treats and a bottle of carpet stain remover. The tag read:

TO: That's why I named him Bingoooooo!

FROM: Mean Neighbor Charmer

****

TO: Misplaced Affection

FROM: FOURTH seat in the third row!

The end of August marks one of my favorite times of year: the return of NFL football. Go Packers!

As such, the end of August also marks the rekindling of the Packers-Vikings bet I have with Mitch, a guy I've known since grade school. Mitch and I have had a friendly wager on the Packer-Vikings match-up for a couple years now, ever since our 30th high school class reunion. I, of course, go for the Pack, and he, now a native of Minnesota, backs the Vikings. Whomever's team loses the matchup is required to purchase the winner a gift costing no more than $10.

It has been a riot seeing what the loser will produce for the winner, as ten bucks forces you to be downright creative. The first year we started our friendly wager, Green Bay went down in flames, so I sent Mitch a hideous set of plastic pink flamingo lawn ornaments. I affixed them with the tag at the top of this story, which I will explain in a moment. The silly birds arrived in Minnesota during a raging blizzard, so Mitch displayed them proudly atop a three-foot snow drift in manner of a "major award" like the fishnet-hosed leg lamp from the classic *Christmas Story movie*. He sent me a picture. It was hilarious.

Another year when the Vikings lost, Mitch sent me a ridiculous sock monkey he had found at a craft fair, and so when the Packers lost, I sent him a sock monkey Kama Sutra calendar to carry forth the theme. I was proud of that one.

The favorite gift I ever received from Mitch was a green hand-held lime squeezer he bought while in Cuba. I love that thing and use it nearly every day for squeezing wedges of lemons and limes. It's fabulous.

But no matter how awesome the prize, it is the story of the night the wager came to be that is the real gift. The tale is also the reason why everyone should attend their high school class reunions. You never know what juicy tidbits you might learn. The possibilities are so worth the airfare.

Now, before I begin, let me say to all my high school friends who will wonder: yes, this is truly the way it went down, but no, these are not our classmates' real names. I had to change them to protect the guilty. I promised.

So, with that, here we go…the best reunion story of all time:

As I've stated before, to say I wasn't the most popular girl at Whitefish Bay High is an understatement. I had fewer friends than I have fingers on one hand and flew so far under the radar I was nearly subterranean. I kept to myself, made a few very close friends, and waited until I went off to college to tear the lid off. My mother used to say she felt like sending me to college was like sending me to a shady dry cleaner – she knows what she dropped off, but she doesn't recognize what she got back. The shy, introverted teen she raised returned from UW-La Crosse outgoing, outspoken, opinionated and up for an adventure. A wallflower no more!

So, given my tough early years at Whitefish Bay High struggling unsuccessfully to fit in, I wasn't exactly gung-ho about attending my high school's 30-year class reunion. I'd gone to the 10-year event and only had a mediocre experience, so I hadn't returned for the 20-year festivities. But, after some contemplation, I figured we'd all experienced enough life by our 30-year reunion to have leveled the playing field and forced maturation. And I was right. Most everybody had taken enough lumps and hard knocks to be more tenderized versions of their teenage selves.

Adding to my ease at the 30th was that so much time had passed, we no longer recognized one another. Such a weird, wonderful thing. People you'd been in school with for your entire childhood would come up and introduce themselves, and you would swear you'd never met them before. If it wasn't for the yearbook photo on everyone's name tags, we may well have been party crashers. I alone had changed so much I was mistaken by many as someone's wife before I found my nametag and affixed it to my chest!

The reunion dinner, held at the Harley Davidson Museum in downtown Milwaukee, was an especially good time. From the moment I checked in at the reception table, I found myself conversing with classmates I'd never dreamed of talking to when I was in high school – cheerleaders, prom court representatives, student government office holders, and lettered athletes. We were exchanging pictures of our kids, catching up on things we'd done over the years and wondering why we hadn't been friends in school. It was fabulous!

About half-way through the evening, I was laughing with a guy who used to sit behind me in study hall while we grazed at the hors d'oeuvres table, when Mitch approached me with a posse of three other guys and introduced himself.

"Hi, Colleen! How are you? It's Mitch Wunderlich," he said with an outstretched hand and smile. I searched his face after glancing at his nametag but struggled to connect the two. All I could think is my Lord he'd gotten tall!

"Wow, hi, Mitch!" I said, returning the smile. Mitch and I had attended school together since the second grade. "I'm fantastic. Just living the dream in Florida. How about you?"

"I'm good. I live in Minnesota now with my wife and boys," Mitch answered, pleasantly. I could tell by his demeanor he was happy and content, which was not surprising. He was always such a kind, quiet guy. A real gentleman, even back then. And smart. Ridiculously so.

What happened next will stick with me till the day I die. Our conversation took a pregnant pause, while Mitch grew a rosy blush and started switching his weight from one foot to the other, nervously. I saw one of his buddies elbow him in the side and throw his chin toward me in a motion of encouragement. Then Mitch, who prior to this exchange had never spoken a single word to me during all those years of school, said, "So, Colleen, why didn't you ever reply to the note I left in your desk in Mrs. Abrahamson's class?"

I let the words register, but they made no sense. The only Mrs. Abrahamson I knew had been my strict fourth grade teacher. "Mrs. Abrahamson's class? Like as in fourth grade Mrs. Abrahamson's?" I asked, bewildered. I couldn't even recall what I had for breakfast, much less anything from fourth grade!

"And did you say a note? What kind of a note?" I added, now really baffled. I searched his buddies' faces, wondering if this was a joke. Geeeez, hadn't these guys gotten this nonsense out of their system in high school?

Still blushing, Mitch searched for the words to fess up to the incident from so long ago. Evidently, he still was a better writer than an orator. "Umm, the *love* note I put in your desk," he finally said so quietly I could hardly hear him.

"*Love* note?!" I exclaimed, dumbfounded. My mind searched frantically through its files marked "Lydell Grade School: fourth grade; love note", but there was nothing. Nope. File was empty.

Mitch plowed on, bolstered by liquid encouragement. He confessed to having had a humongous crush on me back then. I apparently was quite the babe in my highwater pants and white earmuffs. But, as luck would have it, I was totally oblivious to being Mitch's heart's desire. So, one day, unable to carry the burden any longer and feeling the need to profess his affection, 9-year-old Mitch scripted his passion on a note. Then, cunningly, he waited in the shadows of the coat room until we went out for recess, at which time he secretly slipped the note into my desk. And waited 38 years for my reply.

Standing there in the middle of the Harley Davidson Museum, a speared shrimp hanging in mid-air while I tried to digest the information, I was open-mouthed and stunned. I'd always been a hopeless romantic, even back then, so there is no way a love note would have escaped my notice. No way. In fact, I'd only ever gotten one love note in my entire life and I'd married the man that wrote it!

"I'm sorry, Mitch, but I swear to you I don't remember getting a love note in Mrs. Abrahamson's class. Or in any other class, for that matter. Are you sure it was me?"

Just then, Jeremy Richardson, who had been standing behind me at the hors d'oeuvres table, joined our circle looking like he had seen a ghost. "Wait, Wundelich, did you say you put a love note in a desk in Mrs. Abrahamson's class?" His eyes went from Mitch's to mine, and back again.

"Hey, don't look at me," I said to Jeremy, stabbing my shrimp-laden fork in the direction of Mitch, the guilty party.

Jeremy went on, his voice growing octaves higher until I was worried only dogs would be able to hear it. "I got an unsigned love note in *my* desk in fourth grade, but I thought it was from Lana Bailey! Lana Bailey! No wonder she acted so weird when I asked her about it! Oh my God, that was from you, Wunderlich?!"

The color drained from Mitch's face as he realized what had happened. Jeremy had sat in the desk directly in front of mine back then, and Mitch had put the note in the wrong desk. As a result, embarrassed that his love was unrequited, Mitch had never mentioned the note to me until he got up his nerve nearly 40 years later just now at the reunion! Oh. My. God!

And the story doesn't end there. Jeremy explained that after he received the mysterious love note in his desk, assuming it to be from Lana Bailey, whom he had a huge crush on, he had sidled up to her on the playground, like bloody Casanova, to let her know he returned her affection, but was left crushed and confused when she rebuffed him. Shakespeare would have loved this stuff!

All of us crumpled with laughter there at the Harley Davidson, making a scene. When we finally got our wits about us, we discussed how Mitch's bad aim may have changed the course of history for us all, like the proverbial ripples of a pebble hitting a pond. Had Mitch landed his note in the right desk, I certainly would have returned his affection, likely dating him in later years and getting to go to prom, something I always regretted missing because I never got asked. Jeremy wouldn't have freaked out Lana, which may have been the reason her overprotective, devoutly religious family pulled her out for private school in the middle of fourth grade. For all we knew she told her parents Jeremy was a stalker, which may have been enough to spark the drastic move. All because of one misplaced fourth grade love note!

Alas, we're left to wonder what might have been. Luckily, what we do know is that life circled back around for each of us and in the end all was well. Mitch, Jeremy, and I (and hopefully Lana) went on to find love, marry and make beautiful children.

Before the end of that crazy evening at the Harley Museum, after things settled down, Mitch and I created the Packers-Vikings wager, which we have honored ever since. We also exchange birthday greetings and congratulatory notes when new grandchildren are announced. Though Mitch missed our 40_{th} reunion and I haven't seen him since that night of our 30th, I'm hoping he can make our next one, where perhaps some other unknown secrets may be revealed. I know for sure I'll be there. I won't be missing any of them for the world!

Chapter 9: September

To: Enjoy the nap and pancakes

From: Orange with envy

I gave this tag to a girlfriend of mine with a gift certificate to her favorite breakfast restaurant a week before her first colonoscopy. I was jealous of her appointment to my senna-stained core.

If I've learned anything about my colonoscopy experiences, it is if you ever want to get a lively conversation started with a group of middle-aged adults, simply make a comment about having a colonoscopy. When this girlfriend of mine who had scheduled her first one came to my Labor Day cookout and casually mentioned it while unfolding her canvas lawn chair at the fire pit, we older folks lit off storytelling about our innards faster than a bowel full of Moviprep colon cleanser.

"OMG, I'm so jealous!" I cried. The rest of the group looked at me in horror.

"Jealous?" One of the guys shouted, aghast. "Are you insane? Uchhhh, that gallon of power wash they make you drink!" Knowing heads bobbed in agreement.

"You can't tell me you honestly enjoy that stuff. It's disgusting!" said the guy's girlfriend.

"Oh God no, but the power nap?" I said with reverence. "Best sleep I've ever had! Plus, all the guilt-free pancakes you can eat afterwards. How can you not love that?" I was salivating just thinking about it.

Much to my surprise, I discovered I had a kindred spirit in the group. "I've got to agree with her," chimed one of the guys, a fellow nonsleeper. "Last time I begged the anesthesiologist to keep me under for another round. Told him I'd pay cash," he laughed. I nodded my assent while everyone else shook their heads at the two of us.

Another of my friends offered my girlfriend a word of caution. "Whatever you do, don't be doubting that the prep will take hold! And be darn sure you're close to the bathroom. Oh, and do not have a slowpoke drive you to your appointment!" he said, leveling his gaze at his wife, adding, "Putzing along at 15 mph while I'm dying in the seat…"

His wife laughed and then vehemently defended herself. "Oh my god, have you still not forgiven me? It's your own fault for not saying you had to go! I would have pulled into a 7-eleven or something!"

"I was too busy holding on and praying we'd pick up speed!" he cried.

The whole group was laughing now, tears rolling down some people's cheeks.

Everyone wanting to get their two cents in, another friend chimed in to continue counseling my girlfriend on her first appointment. "Be warned: the outpatient facilities are just as challenging once you get there. They put the bathroom about two hundred yards down the hallway. I'm convinced it's so the nurses can place bets on how far you'll make it before you crap yourself. That's why they have that yellow tape on the floor with the hash marks. 'Ten bucks says that old guy doesn't get to the third line…oops, only two – you win, Helen!'"

The stories kept coming. I was laughing so hard I nearly peed myself.

Just then my friend Phyllis came out of the house, after having disappeared over a half-hour earlier. "Oh, for crying out loud, are you people still talking about colonoscopies? Move on!" she begged. We tried but went right back to it. The stories were just too juicy. In five minutes, we were back on the subject howling with laughter. Every one of us had a tale to tell.

While I was recounting my own story, I was reminded again of how grateful I was to be currently single. At the time of my first colonoscopy, I was in a relationship with a guy that was a real jerk. My friend, the one who was about to undergo her first colonoscopy, used to call him "The Asshole" and could never understand what I saw in him. Thinking back, I can't remember either. Though he was good looking with dimples, hazel eyes, a smooth olive complexion and broad shoulders, he had not one drop of compassion running through his ice-cold veins. Having tried to overlook or rationalize this character flaw throughout our time together, his horrific lack of empathy became unbearable during my colonoscopy experience.

Start to finish, Asshole Boyfriend was a pill. During the fasting phase of my colonoscopy prep, he came home from work to our shared rental home with take-out from my favorite Thai restaurant. He knew full well I was in the middle of a 48-hour fast and was allowed nothing but clear liquids, but in keeping with his moniker, he couldn't have cared less.

Hungry enough to chew my own arm off and have it for dinner, I was standing at the microwave in the kitchen heating a cup of clear broth when he entered through the back door carrying the delicious-smelling food. Opening my mouth to greet him, Asshole Boyfriend cut me off before I could get out any words.

"Hi, hun. I'm starving, so I'm going to go ahead and eat," he said rushing by without bothering to look at me.

My eyes fell on the back of his Captain America t-shirt, and I grimaced. I hated that shirt. Grown men wearing superhero shirts looked ridiculous to me, even if the wearer was buff. And Asshole Boyfriend had become far from that. He'd gained so much weight over the previous year that the tee now failed to cover his protruding belly, hanging like a too-short tablecloth. Such a turn off. I preferred meat on my man's bones, but only if it was suitably wrapped!

Not stopping to even get a plate from the cabinet, Asshole Boyfriend headed straight to the dining room, and I heard the rustling of plastic bags. Barely taking time to sit, he tore into the takeout containers, and I could hear the grunts of satisfaction coming from the other side of the wall. I wondered for the millionth time how I could be in a relationship with this lout and his closet full of cartoon tees. I'd had at least a half-dozen opportunities to be done with him, but always took him back when he showed up begging after a breakup. Damn guilt. I really needed to work on that.

When my broth was heated, I took my cup to the table and sipped on the unsatisfying liquid as I watched Asshole Boyfriend polish off an entire container of broccoli and beef with pork-fried rice, wonton soup, and two egg rolls. To his credit, he did apologize. Swallowing the last shovelful, he said, "Sorry you couldn't have any, honey. It was exceptionally delicious today!"

Giving his fingers one final lick, he then retired to the couch, leaving the mess of containers sitting strewn across the dining room table. As I watched his retreating holey Captain

America shirt and daydreamed about launching myself from atop the dining room table and taking him down in a headlock like a WWF wrestler, the alarm on my phone went off signaling it was time to start drinking the first liter of Moviprep colon cleanser. I took his dinner mess and my soup cup to the kitchen, started the dishwasher, and pulled the Moviprep jug out of the fridge. The instructions from the doctor said I was to drink eight ounces of the mixture every fifteen minutes until the whole liter was gone, so I poured myself a glass full. The liquid was the color and consistency of lemon-lime Gatorade, and so my brain told me that's what it would taste like.

My brain was wrong.

Very, very wrong.

Lord Almighty. I cannot describe the flavor of Moviprep any better than journalist Dave Barry, who equated it to "a mixture of goat spit and urinal cleanser, with just a hint of lemon". On point, Dave. Standing there in the pass-through window of the kitchen after taking that first horrible swig, I swore like a sailor and twitched in disgust. My antics drew the attention of Asshole Boyfriend, who paused his show to watch.

After a few short minutes of witnessing my grimacing, gagging, retching, and foot stomping while trying to get through the first glass of the foul drink, Asshole Boyfriend exclaimed with a look of disgust, "Have fun with that. I'm going to go watch my show in the other room," following which he skipped off to our bedroom with his full round belly and closed the door behind him.

"What an asshole," I remember saying under my breath. My girlfriend was right.

Grabbing clean sheets and a beach towel from the linen closet, I headed for the guest room. The considerate person my boyfriend wasn't, I'd decided to spend the night in the other bed so as not to keep us both up. Though Asshole Boyfriend had taken the following day off from his job as a construction supervisor to shuttle me to and from my appointment, a procedure requirement I couldn't get out of, he needed his 8-10 hours of sleep or he was a beast. Not only was he an asshole, but he was also a prima donna.

Between swigs of Moviprep, I made up the guest bed and put the beach towel down as a pad for insurance. Finishing just in the nick of time, not a second after I tucked in the last sheet corner, I felt a little gas bubble that sent me running for the john. And from then it was on. All night long my innards were locked in battle with the Moviprep and there was no sleep to be had.

By the wee hours of the morning, I was exhausted and miserable. Besides feeling like someone had taken a belt sander to my exit door, my back was killing me. No matter how I propped a cheek, leaned, repositioned, or arched, it was impossible to maintain good posture on the commode for all those hours on end. Plus, no matter what I did, I couldn't stop my feet from falling asleep. More than once I had barely saved myself from taking a header into the sink when I got up to wash my hands. After the last close call, I decided it was safer to just remain sitting on the toilet with dead feet until I'd expelled every drop. So, for hours and hours and hours, I had sat. Like the sad, naked statue of the thinking man.

Finally, at 3 AM I experienced a full 20 minutes without any action. Wanting desperately to lay down, I danced my feet awake and dragged my weary body to the guest bed for a little shuteye. I snuggled beneath the fluffy down comforter and was out like a light. For about 15 seconds. That's how long it took for the gatekeeper of my lower colon to relax and allow a warm trickle to escape and ooze its way down my butt cheek. The sensation rousted me awake immediately, like one of those dreams about peeing when you're really peeing. I sprang up in the bed, groped for the beach towel I'd blessedly placed beneath me, fashioned the happy yellow terry cloth fabric with the pineapples around my bottom like a diaper, and poopy walked back to the bathroom to wait out the dawn. I shall never argue again with anyone accusing me of being full of crap. I must have been salting it away since the moment of birth.

Around 5:30 AM I grew brave enough to give leaving the confines of the bathroom another try. This time I felt it best to avoid lying down, a plan that proved successful. Without soiling myself, I miraculously got the sheets, towels, and mattress cover rinsed and into the washing machine. Unfortunately, my respite was short-lived, as no sooner had I pressed the washer's start button that my phone alarm signaled it was time to start the second liter of Moviprep. Back to the loo I went with the Moviprep jug and a cup for another two hours of sitting, aching, squirting and dribbling.

When the clock hit 8:00 AM, I was not supposed to ingest anything further. This was not a problem. I never wanted to consume anything ever again. Nothing in, nothing out. I ran myself a nice warm bubble bath and settled my weary war-torn sphincter into the glorious water. The soothing warmth felt wonderful, but I regretted not having my earplugs or some music to drown out the loud snoring of Asshole Boyfriend penetrating my sanctuary. He had slept soundly through the night, confirmed by the endless hours of nasal symphony I had endured for the whole of my confinement.

A half-hour into my bath the snoring finally stopped. Then I heard the plodding of heavy feet on the carpeting in the hallway outside the bathroom, followed by Asshole Boyfriend's voice shouting into the jam of the locked guest bathroom door.

"How's it going in there, honey?" he inquired.

"Just ducky," I replied in deadpan. "Good times."

"Did you get any rest?"

"Nope."

"Well, I slept great! Man, was I tired," he spouted with a smile in his voice.

"Bully for you," I replied crisply, thankful there was a locked door between us.

"Hey, getting my rest was important for taking care of you today," he said, like he was gearing up for the Ironman competition.

When I got out of the bath and ventured out into the hallway wrapped in a fresh towel, rosy and clean from the luxurious bath, I saw the door to our bedroom was again shut. This habit of his, of always shutting the bedroom door when he knew I'd be following shortly behind him, annoyed the crap out of me. I had let him know time and time again how much this practice offended me, but I shouldn't have wasted my breath. He seemed to do it more often, on purpose, and with relish after every time I brought it up.

Trying not to let the closed door irk me, I opened it wide, propped it with the rubber wedge and went in to get dressed. Asshole Boyfriend, resting on the bed in his boxer-briefs, half-asleep, watching cartoons, made no acknowledgement. Poor thing already looked exhausted from taking care of me.

Since my appointment at the outpatient center wasn't until 11:30 AM, I found three hours of erect things to do to stay awake and unsoiled. I leisurely dried and styled my hair. I put on a full face of makeup. I unloaded the dishwasher. I did three loads of laundry. I dusted. I swept the garage. I emptied all the waste baskets, then took out the trash. And for a grand finale I vacuumed every square inch of the house, including the porch.

Meanwhile, Asshole Boyfriend never left the confines of the bedroom. He played video games. He watched cartoons. He took cat naps. He scratched himself. And he intermittently announced he was hungry. Finally extracting himself from the bed, he schlepped out to the kitchen around 10:30 AM, looked in every cupboard, grumbled there wasn't anything in the house he wanted to eat, then fell suddenly quiet, having located the 4-piece cheesecake I was saving for after dinner to celebrate my colonoscopy survival. Standing in front of the open refrigerator, bare chested, he gobbled down all four pieces in uncivilized fashion, complaining the meager fare would have to hold him. I swallowed my own spit.

As soon as it was the appropriate time to leave the house, I sprinted out to Asshole Boyfriend's truck, leapt in, and waited to go. Normally late for everything, I was Johnny on the Spot today. Just the thought of being rid of this man for at least an hour had me giddy with joy. Unfortunately, I wasn't going anywhere for a while. Asshole Boyfriend took his sweet time, left me waiting in the cab for 20 minutes, then bitched the whole length of the ride about what an inconvenience the whole thing was, stating taking care of me was really an ordeal.

Once in the waiting room, over 45 minutes passed without my name being called. In that short amount of time Asshole Boyfriend had been busy. He'd managed to piss off the receptionist, the sweet elderly volunteer lady who helped patients to their cars, and every other individual in the waiting room. He was worse than an unfiltered, ego-driven, hyperactive 5-year-old.

> "Can that lady talk any louder on her phone?" he shouted for all to hear. The woman, who was not talking loudly at all, was discussing her husband's test results with her son. I looked at her with an apologetic blush. She harumphed and went outside.
>
> "Why did they take that guy in before you? We got here first!" he exclaimed, causing the very pleasant girl behind the intake counter to slam shut the glass window.
>
> "Kids should be seen and not heard. All that shrieking is giving me a headache!" he cried, looking menacingly at the adorable child playing with blocks in the corner. I looked at his mother apologetically, and she looked back at me more so.
>
> "Oh my God, I'm so freaking hungry. Can you just reschedule?" Everyone in the waiting room looked at me with pleading eyes as I seriously contemplated whether I could endure another round of Moviprep to put us all out of our misery. It was fast becoming an option.
>
> "Can these chairs be any more uncomfortable?" *Yep, they could be toilets.*

"Why didn't you tell me we'd be here so long?" *I did, you just weren't listening.*

"I don't even have anything to drink. They must have juice or something back there. I need some juice." *No, buddy, you need Moviprep. Hey, that gives me an idea...Nurse!*

Growing more and more impatient as each minute clocked by, Asshole Boyfriend announced at last, "I'm going to march up to that desk and demand that they take you next! I don't have time for this!" Like he had an appointment with Congress to discuss the deficit.

As he stood and prepared to head for the reception desk, I panicked. I grabbed his arm, forced him back into his seat and spoke to him in calm, measured tones. "Babe, why don't you go on home, and I'll call you when I'm done. I'll be fine. Really!" Lord almighty, man; these people are about to stick a 487-yard hose up my butt, and you want to piss them off? Oh, hell no!

In compliance, much to everyone's delight, Asshole Boyfriend stood up and headed for the exit. He was nearly there when the unit nurse opened the surgical bay door and called my name. Hearing it, Asshole Boyfriend turned around, the waiting room occupants let out an audible gasp of disgust, and he backtracked in a huff to retake his seat. Blowing past him, I ran as fast as my depleted body would carry me, nearly plowing over an elderly woman in my haste to get to the nurse holding my file. When the grey double doors of the procedure area shut behind me, I tapped the kind-looking, middle-aged RN on the shoulder and pled frantically.

"Whatever happens, do not let the guy in the Bart Simpson t-shirt back here. Under no circumstances! If there's an emergency, call my daughter!" I was half-crazed from lack of food and sleep deprivation.

Alarmed, the nurse stopped to look me square in the eye and asked gently, "Has he harmed you? Are you in danger?" Her eyes searched my face with concern. Hmmm, I had to think about that one for a moment.

"No, he's just been a giant pain in my ass, and I need a freaking break," I said at last. Pain in my ass. I laughed at the phrase considering the circumstances.

"Ah, I understand," said the nurse with a knowing nod and smile. Pains in the ass were her forte. "I got you," she added.

And she did. From then on, life was grand, and we were buds. Once in a gown, I was settled into a bed and given warm blankets and comfy slipper socks. Everyone was super nice and if it wasn't for the clinical surroundings, I would have thought I was at a spa. Both of my nurses were named Helen and were delightful humans. Helen #1 started my IV with such finesse I didn't feel a thing. Then as a bonus, she injected some happy juice, and I got all warm and fuzzy.

"How are you feeling, m'lady?" Helen #1 asked, while simultaneously checking my pulse and blood pressure, making equipment adjustments, and noting this and that. She seemed to have more hands than an octopus.

"Like I've just had great sex without the effort or sweat!" I replied with a giggle, wriggling my head deeper into the fluffy pillow, enjoying my buzz. Helen #1 fell out laughing with a contagious, trilling sound that made me smile.

After a few more equipment checks, Helen #1 seemed satisfied and informed me we were ready to get started. She released the breaks on my bed and wheeled me a short distance into the procedure room, where I was introduced to Helen #2. Helen #2 provided a brief explanation of what would be happening next, then gave the floor to the anesthesiologist, who asked me to count backwards from 100. I remember getting to 99.

What seemed like two seconds later, I awoke to the sound of both Helens singing in unison to "Smoke on the Water" by Deep Purple as they wheeled me back into the hallway. Groggily, I choked out a raspy, "Fire in the sky!" (the next line in the song, which was one of my all-time favorites) and both Helens roared with laughter.

"I told you this one was a firecracker," Helen #1 exclaimed to Helen #2 as they parked my gurney in a recovery slot and pulled a privacy curtain around my bed.

While I stretched and yawned blissfully, Helen #1 left to go get me a nice cold cup of cranberry juice while Helen #2 delivered my stellar test results. I'd passed with flying colors - no polyps, no irregularities, all was well.

"And, honey, were you clean!" Helen #2 exclaimed with a wink, giving me a thumbs up. I returned the gesture with pride.

The doctor came in along with Helen #1 and the juice. He was looking at my chart and getting ready to relay what I assumed was the same report I'd just gotten from Helen #2, so before he could say anything I cried, "Hey, doc, I hear I'm a perfect asshole! Or, wait, maybe the Helens were talking about my boyfriend!" I found my own humor delightfully funny and cracked up. Everything was hilarious to me, and I couldn't remember the last time I felt so rested. I asked the Helens if I could make a reservation to stay the week.

"I'm glad you've enjoyed your time with us," my doctor said, amused. He was short and small-framed with an unruly head of light brown hair that made him look no more than 12 years old. If it wasn't for the white lab coat with his name embroidered over the pocket, I would have thought he was there because one of his parents had taken him to work, unable to find a sitter.

"But I do have one question for you, Mrs. Pierce. Do you take a senna supplement?" he asked.

Suddenly sober with concern, I sat up and answered, "Two Senokot every night. Why? Is that not okay?" I was trying my best not to panic.

"No, no, there's no harm in continuing," chuckled the young doc. "It just makes for a colorful exam, is all. See," he said, holding up the colored photos taken during the procedure.

Well, I'd be damned. A section of shiny bright orange colon was pictured in the center of the page with a separate photo of what looked to be a pumpkin spice wax tart with a hole in the middle. "Holy cow, I'm ass tart orange!" I exclaimed. Both Helens at my bedside rolled with laughter. The doctor turned away and I could tell he was laughing behind his mask. His shoulders shook and when he turned back his eyes were watering. Wordlessly, he parted with a wave, still unable to speak.

Relishing the last drops of liquid nirvana in my veins, I sipped another cup of juice and took my time getting dressed. Neither Helen rushed me. When things in the ward started getting busy though, I knew it was time for me to go. Having enjoyed me as a patient, the Helens begrudgingly called for the sweet transport lady, who wheeled me out to "Asshole Boyfriend". The Helens waved goodbye from the grey surgical unit doors with much fanfare, and I felt like a departing rock star. I blew kisses and thanked them for the wonderful visit.

"They were awesome," I said to Asshole Boyfriend as I ambled slowly out to the car. "What lovely humans!"

"I didn't like them. Any of them," he grumped. "And those awful people in the waiting room. Everyone talking on their phones, kids running everywhere, no common courtesy…" He went on and on until I was ready to beg the Helens to let me back in. It would be worth chugging another two liters of Moviprep!

When we arrived in the driveway at home, Asshole Boyfriend turned off the car and announced, "I'm exhausted, I have a headache, and I can't wait to lie down!" Then, without waiting for me, he trotted into the house, closed the blinds, cranked the A/C, and disappeared into the bedroom, shutting the door behind him. In 30 seconds, I could hear him snoring away. I opened the door of the bedroom and leaned against the doorway for a moment just watching him. It was then and there I decided I deserved better for myself and packed a bag. When I was done, I closed the door to the bedroom behind me, went out to the garage, and called my girlfriend to pick me up and take me out for pancakes. It was the same girlfriend that had nicknamed my boyfriend The Asshole. She was delighted to oblige.

We went to my favorite diner, and I ordered a full stack of flapjacks with the works. They were the best damn pancakes I'd ever eaten. Then I ordered a patty melt to go and had my girlfriend drop me off at my mother's house, where I could rest in peace. Which I did.

Relaxed and refreshed the following day, I called in sick to work and moved my stuff out of Asshole Boyfriend's house. This time I stuck to my guns, told guilt to take a hike, and that was the end of that. Thank Heavens (or perhaps Helens). The experience had taught me I only had room for one asshole in my life – the one that was ass tart orange.

****

TO: Running with My Nipple

FROM: The Fatted Sow

September is my birthday month. Birthdays are a big deal in our family, and we always try to do something fun and different to celebrate. This year, Dani surprised me on my big day with reservations for a private mother-daughter tea at an adorable boutique cafe in downtown Melbourne. We had just recently discovered the café and its delectable offerings while shopping for a baby shower gift for one of her friends. The cafe was a great find. The owner, pastry chef Lily Jensen, made the most mouthwatering macarons and butter cookies we had ever eaten, and her cucumber sandwiches...to die for! Even her blend of tea tasted like it was sprinkled with magic.

The delectables weren't the only things to enjoy in Lily's tea house. The café's décor was just as delicious as her pastries. Quaint, white lacquer tete-a-tete tables with curvy, clear acrylic chairs dotted the room, the walls adorned with giant white and gold paper flowers. In the sitting area she had a luxurious Victorian velvet couch in the lightest shade of pink, accompanied by white bunny chairs that were irresistible to grownups and kids alike. Little tasteful touches were everywhere, unassuming, and delightful.

Lily's work area was equally adorable. Surrounded by gorgeous antique white Victorian dressers, Lily would plate her homemade goodies like art on three-tiered gold plate stands before wheeling them to the table on a cart that resembled a gold bicycle. From an old-fashioned, 2-handle, pastel blue Smeg refrigerator, she'd bring out flutes of ice-cold champagne, which she would offer alongside her own delicious blend of herbal tea, poured from golden pots with long, thin, curving spouts into gold-trimmed pastel pink tea cups shaped like hearts on matching plates. Everything in Lily's Cafe was kissed with gold and utterly divine.

Going all out for such a girly affair, Dani and I dressed to the nines for our fancy tea date. Since Dani's car was toddlerfied and we wished not to walk into Lily's with stray Cheerios hanging off our butts, we decided to take my car. And because my darling daughter always gave me a ration about my driving, I let her chauffeur.

"I'm driving Miss Daisy," she snickered as we got in the car. Smartass thirty-something had no respect.

Pulling out of the driveway, *Pedestal* by Fergie came on my car radio. The Blood Clot was too old to have a video console or any fancy technology, so my only option for music was the car radio. A Hair Band girl from way back, the radio was usually tuned to what Dani considered "the Oldies station", though they played a mixture of both old and new songs.

Song titles and artists are like historical events to me—none of them stick in my head. Likewise with lyrics, though I sing along anyway, inserting whatever I believe the artist might be saying. So this is what I did when *Pedestal* came on. The song had a catchy tune that I liked, though I didn't know the title was "Pedestal", since "Fatted Sow" was what I heard when it played. In my defense, though ridiculous, the words made sense to me because I thought Fergie was using a metaphor for being led to slaughter, since the song's story was about people thinking they are better than her. Creative types are prone to use poetic license, so far be it me to question these things.

So, there Dani and I were, stopped at a traffic light on our way to tea, Fergie playing on the radio, and me in the passenger's seat belting out the chorus:

> "...But have you walked in my shoes?
> **The fatted sow**
> **You put incense on...**"

Immediately, I felt my daughter's eyes on me. "The fatted sow you put incense on?" she asked, looking at me over the top of her sunglasses with the *Oh My God This Is Not My Mother Please Tell Me I Was Adopted* look. You mothers know the one.

"Ummm, I take it that's wrong, huh?" I asked, breaking out in a doofy grin.

In reply I got an eye roll and a lyric correction "The pedestal you put yourself on", followed by a lecture about how I should stick to music from "my own" era. Ironically, the next song to come on the radio was a modern remix of a song from "my" era, the elderly 1980s. I pointed to the car radio and stuck out my tongue at Dani. "See, Mommy is listening to 'her' music. Ha!" I exclaimed.

At the café we had a wonderful time enjoying two luxurious hours of sipping champagne and devouring every goodie placed before us. Chef Lily had even made chocolate covered strawberries decorated with pieces of edible gold leaf. She was really something.

Getting back into the car feeling like the fatted sow I'd been singing about, I offered to tune the radio to a station Dani preferred, but she declined.

"No, it's your day, mother. I'll tolerate your 'old people' station," she said wryly. I shot her my "Mom Look" in reply. You mothers know the one.

As we pulled out of the parking spot on the street outside the café, *Running with the Devil* by Van Halen came across the radio airwaves. In a jovial mood, my beautiful red-headed girl began singing along. I was about to do the same, until I heard her sing:

"Oooh, yeah, I'm runnin' with my nipple…ah-haaaa, woo-hoo-oo, I'm runnin' with my nipple…"

Amused to my core, I looked over to see her just bopping away in the passenger seat, long ponytail flying, letting the world know that she runs with her nipples. I collapsed in the seat with laughter, and she stopped mid-chorus, wondering what had me so tickled.

"Running with your nipple?" I inquired, chuckling, and Dani knew immediately she may have mistaken the words.

"Yeah, I always thought those were weird lyrics," she replied with a grin. "But hey, you can't run without them!" Valid point.

"How about 'running with the devil'?" I said, putting air quotes around the correct lyrics, to which I received an enlightened, "Ohhhh!"

"Looks like perhaps we should both stick to 'our own' music, huh?" I chided her.

We laughed, knowing neither one of us would ever sing the correct lyrics to "Running with the Devil" again.

And we never have.

****

While in the waiting room at the dentist's office today, I read an interesting article on menopause that caused me to reflect. We women really got the short end of the stick. It's bad enough to battle 30+ years of debilitating monthly cramps accompanied by uncontrollable, embarrassing outbursts of PMS, but then we have to endure another 5-10 years on the roller coaster of menopause, only to find our sex drive has left the building by the end of it all. Not to sound juvenile, but it's just not fair.

The more I read the article, which, like so many other articles about menopause, was detailing ways for women to control their hormonal outbursts for the sake of their precious, thin-skinned men, the angrier I got. When I was in the thick of my midlife transition, I wasn't even aware I was experiencing a behavioral change, so how was I supposed to fix something I didn't even know I had? Sure, I felt a little grumpy now and then, but not so much that I thought others were noticing. Although they were. Everyone was just too afraid to call me out on it.

During the time I transitioned from PMS to menopause, I was rooming with my buddy Geo in a beautiful condo right on the Indian River in Port St. John, Florida. The condo was my first residence after getting separated, a time in my life when nothing felt stable, including my body.

Before signing the lease with Geo, I had been living with my mother and was desperate to get out. My husband Rick and I had agreed when we split that he would stay in the house with Dani, because I could go stay with Mom. But after three months of this arrangement, I had reached my limit. I needed my own pantry.

Right on time, the Universe delivered. A girlfriend from work and her husband had decided to put their beautiful 3-bedroom Florida riverfront condo up for rent. I'd always adored their place, having visited it often for dinner on their terrace with jumping river mullet and dolphins to entertain us, or for late-night cocktails with the moon shining a prism across the quiet water, or for a rocket launch, since their place was directly across the water from Kennedy Space Center. The place was a slice of heaven. I even loved the smell of it, a mix of bergamot, sandalwood, and lavender.

Knowing I would treat their home with all the tenderness and care it deserved, my girlfriend made sure I was the first person to find out the condo was available to lease. Unfortunately, the timing couldn't have been worse, as I had just started a new job as the Executive Assistant to the President of the Chamber of Commerce, and the pay wasn't enough to sustain such luxury. I turned down the offer to lease the condo, as much as it pained me to do so.

The following day I had to host the monthly meeting and luncheon for the Chamber of Commerce Board of Directors in the headquarters' boardroom. After the festivities had concluded, I was in the office kitchen cleaning up when Geo came in looking for a refill on coffee. Geo was a member of the Chamber Board, serving as the Chair of Government Affairs. He was just a few years younger than me in his mid-forties at the time, a tall, handsome, muscular guy who oozed charisma by the bucketload. Geo always smelled fantastic, his clothes were impeccable, and his thick brownish-blonde hair was styled to perfection.

Tag the Present

I smiled when I saw him enter the kitchen, though only half-heartedly, and he noticed.

"What has you so down in the mouth, princess?" Geo asked, filling his cup from the urn on the counter next to me.

I could smell his cologne and it made my head spin. *My God he is handsome*, I thought, his crystal blue eyes locking on mine. An uncontrollable blush rose to my cheeks, and I was embarrassed thinking he could surely read my thoughts. How I hated that stupid, unruly blush of mine. It had betrayed me my whole life.

"Oh, it's nothing," I sighed, refocusing my thoughts on the serving platter in the sink so my face color would normalize.

I'd just about succeeded in quelling the blush when Geo fished my soapy hand out of the water, grabbed the dish towel, and led me to the little round table in the corner of the kitchen. My heart nearly ceased to beat, and I felt once again fevered with color. I was flushing so hard my ears were on fire!

"Now, it's obvious something," Geo said, azure blue eyes boring into mine as he continued to hold my hand in his giant paw.

"C'mon, you can tell me," Geo continued with sincerity. *Look at those shoulders*, the little voice in my head screamed, as I tried with every fiber of my being to concentrate on the conversation.

The details of what next transpired are foggy. I was certain for days I had dreamt it, for by the time I knew what had happened, Geo, Brevard County's most eligible bachelor, was moving into the condo with me as my roommate!

The smitten kitten that I was, I was convinced our roommate status wouldn't last. Or, more accurately, I was hoping it wouldn't. Accustomed to getting my way with males of the species, I gave myself a month to win Geo over and begin our journey as a couple. Unfortunately, my womanly wiles had met their match. One month stretched into two, and then into three without progress. We'd have moments of promise, but they would be immediately followed by an act of Geo sabotage. A romantic dinner and canoodling would be followed by Geo going out on a date with another woman, thus sticking me firmly back into the friend zone. Then, contrarily, Geo would fume with jealousy for days should I then go out on a date. The double standard was very confusing and what I blamed for my uncontrollable mood swings. By the end of our third month of cohabitating, this roller coaster had me beside myself, so I took a bull by the horns (Geo was a Taurus) and sat him down for a heart-to-heart.

Over a dinner of slow-cooked short ribs over egg noodles, a Geo favorite, I dove in.

"So, G, I have a confession," I said, unable to meet his eyes. I suddenly understood the design of church confessionals, where one could be heard but not seen.

"When we moved in together, I thought we would eventually become a couple," I divulged. "Well, I hoped we would be, at least."

Geo stared at me without eating, a piece of French bread in his right hand and a butter knife in the other, hanging in mid-air. He was a lefty.

Plowing forward before I lost my nerve, I went on.

"I think I'm getting the message that we're not going to get there from here, but then sometimes I feel like we might. I get a lot of mixed signals that I don't know how to read. Like when I went out with John last week, you gave me the silent treatment for days."

Setting down the bread but not the knife, Geo's jaw flinched at the mention of my date. The outing with John had been set up by Stephanie, who knew John from work, and the whole thing had been a disaster. For starters, I had worn a miniskirt and John had arrived on a motorcycle, prompting me to have to change. I invited him into the condo while I slipped into jeans, and there he encountered Geo, who despised motorcycles. The tension was so thick in the room I could have cut it with a knife. Then, the guy wound up being so full of himself he tried to make a move on me at the restaurant before our appetizer even arrived, so I ducked out the back door and called Stephanie to pick me up and take me home.

"Well, that guy was an asshole!" Geo exclaimed. He was so upset at the thought he was red-faced.

"Okay, I agree, but why do you care so much? Is it like a brotherly thing, or something else? 'Cuz you wouldn't talk to me for days."

Geo looked away as he contemplated. Then calming, he turned back, and his beautiful blue eyes met mine with sincerity.

"I don't know myself sometimes, sweetheart. I care for you deeply, and I really hate the idea of losing you to another man, but a full-time commitment? I just don't think I am capable of that. If I was, believe me, I would have chosen that with you long ago."

I looked away with tears in my eyes, knowing the truth before he spoke it. Tough love was the worst. When I could meet his eyes, there were tears in Geo's, too.

"I hate that I hurt you," he said.

"No, I would rather know. The wondering was torture. But you can't get jealous when I go out, okay. If I can't have my cake and eat it, too, neither can you," I smiled, a single tear streaking down my face.

"I will try," he said, kissing my cheek. "Now can we dig into these ribs before they get cold?"

"P'shhh, yeah!" I agreed, though there was a lump in my throat and my appetite was gone.

Setting aside those feelings was difficult for both of us at first, but we slowly adjusted and fell into a comfortable routine. People looking at us from the outside undoubtedly assumed we were a couple. We went to the gym together every morning, had cocktails on the terrace most evenings, cleaned house together on Saturdays, and had a standing Sunday night dinner date at home that became a ritual. Tradition for Sundays was to splurge, at least once a month having ribeye steak with sweet potatoes and spinach, and always setting the table with folded cloth napkins and a vase of fresh flowers. Over a delicious home cooked meal we would chat about our week, talk about anything and everything, gossip, laugh, and confess our sins. Then we'd have a scrumptious dessert, do the dishes, and wind down to prepare for another Monday, knowing any negativity that transpired during the upcoming week would be washed away over dinner on Sunday. We had achieved a healthy balance.

For months I thought Geo chose ribeye so often for our Sunday dinner because steak was his favorite food. Then one day shortly before Christmas, I discovered the real reason.

The steak revelation came on a Tuesday. A conversation was sparked when I spied the day had been circled boldly in red on our shared wall calendar at the condo. I was in our spare room paying bills at the time I noticed the red circle and asked Geo about it when he passed through the hall on his way to the kitchen.

"Hey, G, what's going on today that has it circled in red on the calendar? Am I forgetting about something?" I asked innocuously, staring at the calendar with knitted brows. The date didn't appear to correspond to anyone's birthday, a meeting, doctor's appointment, or any other significant event that I could pinpoint.

Geo didn't answer, so thinking he didn't hear me, I went out to the kitchen to ask my question again. This time I know he heard me, but his only response was to blush and look uncomfortable. Averting my eyes, he attempted to flee the room, but I stood firm in his way. This was very uncharacteristic behavior for the bold, self-confident Geo. He never acted this way.

Blocking the doorway with my arms, I kept him trapped until he came up with an answer. He squirmed uneasily, and realizing I wasn't going to let him go, he struggled for a reply.

"Ummm, I, well, it's ..." he stuttered.

"Oh my God, what?" I pushed. I didn't know whether to be irritated or concerned.

"Ummm, it's to mark...Evil Tuesday," he blurted.

Then, without even stopping to take a breath, he asked, "So, did you want spinach or broccoli with our steak on Sunday, sweetheart?" His voice was overly bright, and I didn't know what to make of this Evil Tuesday comment.

"Spinach, please. Evil Tuesday? What in God's name is that?" I said, reaching for my phone to Google it. I'd never heard of such a thing as Evil Tuesday. Odd name for something to memorialize. It sounded cultish!

"Oh, hun, no, it's not something official or anything. It's just something silly I do. Hey, have you seen my green folder? I was going to work on the proposal for the Chamber rebranding tonight. I think they're really onto something with the spacesuit idea," Geo said, rambling as he darted around the condo picking up random things under the pretense of looking for a green folder.

Unmoving, I stood rooted to my spot in the kitchen, staring at him while I waited for him to notice. I wasn't done with this Evil Tuesday issue, and he knew it. When he finally glanced over at me, he knew his gig was up.

Halting his concocted green folder search, he stood in the middle of the living room, closed his eyes, and let out a tortured sigh as his perfectly coiffed head drop to his chest. Bringing his eyes up to meet mine he quietly confessed, "Okay, so. There's a Tuesday every month when your, you know, *womanly stuff* might have you a little, ah…out of sorts."

Out of sorts? *Womanly stuff*? I was so confused. I stared at him, puzzled, not knowing what he was trying to get at. He rambled on, mortified.

"Yeah, so, I began keeping track just to make sure I was prepared. For the sake of us both, you know? Really, that's all it is. Not a big deal, I swear." Finishing his declaration, he wore a sheepish look, and suddenly I grasped what he was trying to communicate.

"Oh my God, you track my periods?!" I cried. Hiding my face in my hands, I thought I would die of embarrassment.

When I looked up, Geo was blushing, too. He threw up his hands in surrender, and suddenly the whole thing struck me as outrageously funny. I broke out in crippling giggles, eliciting a relieved half-smile from my embarrassed roommate.

"Okay, if you say it's nothing," I said when I recovered. "But you'll tell me if it isn't, right?" I asked before heading back to the spare room to continue paying my bills.

"Yep," Geo replied quickly, busying himself with the Jim Beam and Coke. "Now, I'm having a drink. Would you like one?" And without waiting for my reply, he pulled two glasses from the cupboard.

A couple weeks later when I flipped the den calendar to the next month, I saw the now familiar red circle two weeks down the road. With the next "Evil Tuesday" safely in the future, I brought up the subject nonchalantly over Sunday dinner. It had been eating at me.

"Okay, G, about this Evil Tuesday business. I need you to give it to me straight. Am I really that bad?"

"No, sweetheart. Absolutely not. I never should have said anything about it," he said, trying to avert the subject. But I could tell he was holding back, and I really wanted to know.

"Seriously, I want to know the truth, G. I can take it. I asked Dani and she says I've been really crabby. I realize an eighteen-year-old is always going to say her mother is crabby, but still. C'mon, stop sugar coating it."

I truly wanted to know. I had sensed my fuse growing short more often in the past year, but I thought I had been managing without anyone noticing. According to my brutally honest daughter, that was totally not the case. I needed Geo to speak frankly about my behavior because I knew he would and the thought of running around acting like a shrew horrified me.

Geo put down his fork and looked me in the eyes. He registered the panic that was setting in as I felt tears beginning to well. "No, no, listen, sweetie. It's just your hormones, and you can't help that. Here's how it goes, for real: on Monday during one week every month, you complain you're tired and you turn in early. That Tuesday you can sometimes be touchy, so I tread lightly at first to test the waters. I know you need extra iron, so I make sure we eat steak that week."

"Oh my God," I exclaimed, hiding my face in my napkin. Once a month this poor guy had to come home to an irritable woman that wasn't even his, gently open the door to the she-devil's cage and toss in a piece of raw meat, hoping to escape without getting his nuts handed to him. He deserved a medal!

"Then Wednesday," Geo continued with a boyish smile, "I know you're going to be weepy, so I avoid anything sentimental on TV, usually tuning to a funny movie for us to watch. That brings me to Thursday, when you're in pain and crampy, so I make sure the heating pad is out."

OMG, he sure did. The damn heating pad was forever right there on the back of the couch on crampy days when I needed it!

"I always assumed the heating pad was out because you had been using it on your bad shoulder!" I exclaimed, aghast.

"You've been doing that for me?" I cried with awe.

Geo smiled and nodded, obviously pleased. Then he continued, "By Friday it's over and we're home free. We go to happy hour with the gang, and all is well. Come Saturday you're back to your fun-loving self and we're done for another month. So, see, it's nothing to get worked up about. We're good!"

I looked at the beautiful man sitting next to me at the dining room table in wonder. His humble explanation was about the sweetest thing I'd ever heard! This big ole softie knew more about me than I knew about myself. I leaned over and gave him a huge, heartfelt hug.

"You're really one hell of a guy, G. I love you!" I cried. And I meant it. He was my bud.

"I love you, too, sweetheart," he said, blushing as he returned my hug. "But don't you dare let any of this get out; you'll ruin my reputation!"

True, that. He relished his aloof, narcissistic persona.

"I pinky promise," I said, holding out my little finger. He locked his giant pinky in mine, and we exchanged a grin.

I tried to go easier on the G-man after that, keeping my eye on the little red circles. I was fascinated he had so perfectly nailed my internal calendar, while I had been so oblivious to the cues of my own body. Sure enough, once a month on red circle week I was tired on Monday, wicked on Tuesday, weepy on Wednesday, crampy on Thursday, and by Friday I was back at home plate. Just like clockwork.

Figuring I owed Geo a little something for putting up with my ritualistic abuse, I also began picking up his Happy Hour tab on the Friday of Evil Tuesday week. It was the least I could do. In addition, for Christmas, I bought him a calendar so he could continue flagging red circle Tuesdays. I also included a gift card for Publix, so he could stock up on red meat. The *To-From* on the package read:

To: And his hair was perfect

From: Evil on Tuesday

And with a giant helping of compassion sprinkled with iron, all was well.

Chapter 10: October

I sat on the thinly padded seat of the walnut pub chair at my kitchen table and moved aside the burlap placemat to have a smooth surface for writing. The time had come to craft a tag for my daughter and son-in-law's third wedding anniversary present: a matching set of fawn leather dopp kits embossed with their names. I had chosen the toiletry bags because the Guide to Anniversary Gifts by Year, a laminated business card I had picked up at Hallmark years ago, said "leather" was the traditional gift for a third wedding anniversary. Selecting the gift had been easy. As for the *To-From*, I found myself struggling.

Rhythmically clicking the blue ballpoint in my fist, I pondered unsuccessfully, absently examining the walls and ceiling for clues. When nothing came to mind, I consulted my cellphone notes for ideas. Forever paranoid about exhibiting the early signs of dementia that my mother had displayed, these moments when I was unable to instantly and organically create a *To-From* troubled me deeply.

Grabbing my ancient Samsung from the side table where I'd left it earlier, I awoke the sleeping phone with a press of a button and waited while the screen pulled up the picture of Dani and me on her wedding day. Three years had passed since that glorious day, but the wallpaper photo still made me smile. My freshly highlighted blonde hair was swept into a loose interwoven design secured in the back with a rose gold comb that perfectly complemented the elegant lace sleeves of my blush pink mother-of-the-bride gown. My arm was wrapped around Dani, who was standing on my left. She was a vision with cascading ginger curls that fell to her waist in a waterfall, with a braided band of hair that wove across the crown of her head to the back where it edged a small bun for securing her veil. Her backless white satin Maggie

Sottero dress, the second of the two dresses I'd promised to buy her so long ago, was inlaid with panels of the most delicate lace that matched the filigree which adorned the soft v-neckline and thin straps. The gown curved around her perfect figure and was fitted to a tee. She held a spectacular bouquet of white roses in full bloom with peonies, ranunculus, viburnum, framed by sprays of eucalyptus, as fragrant as it was beautiful, but paling in comparison to the radiant bride that held it.

After a brief moment of reflection, I swiped past the wedding photo and scrolled through the phone's apps to find my archived notes. Locating the *To-From* file I was looking for, I swiped up and down through the names to find something I could use for the anniversary tag. But then, as always happens, I got lost in thought and swept off-track the minute I happened upon the first interesting morsel I stumbled upon. Today it was a decade-old text from Dani sharing one of Shawn's hand-crafted haikus:

> *POOH ... by Shawn*
>
> *My hands clench the seat*
>
> *The dank aroma like death*
>
> *Fertilizing waste*

Sitting at the kitchen table reading the prose, I chuckled. My son-in-law was a piece of work. He attacked life systematically, like it was a mathematical equation to be solved, yet had all these other unexpected sides, like haiku writing, that he only occasionally let creep out. He was more in his element when things were methodical, specific, rational, and defined, one of those guys that read instruction manuals before assembling parts and researched consumer reports before making big purchases. We joked that by the time he settled on the diamond for Dani's engagement ring, the jeweler in Winter Park where he bought it could have hired him as a gemologist.

Yet somehow, this discerning, methodical, logical guy had chosen my spirited, spunky, whirlwind of a daughter to be his forever. Dani would rather have teeth extracted than consult Consumer Reports about buying anything. She marched to the beat of her own drum, preferred to fly by the seat of her pants, and to love her was to accept her as is. And love her Shawn did. With his quiet, conscientious, analytical ways, he was the perfect counterbalance to her Herculean independent streak. In turn, Dani forced Shawn outside the comfortable four walls of his flawlessly measured 90° angled box, getting him to relax and live a little. They truly were perfect together. But it sure had taken them a long time to get there.

Though barely into their 30s and only celebrating their third wedding anniversary, Shawn and Dani had been a couple for 15 years and friends for six years beyond that. Theirs was a love story that started in seventh grade, though for many years everyone saw the spark except for the two of them.

For nearly two decades I had erroneously told their story wrong, portraying their tale as love at first sight, my favorite genre of romance. Mistakenly thinking it had been Shawn who had deposited Dani in a trash can on her first day of seventh grade as a young man's way of showing affection, I would eventually get informed it hadn't been Shawn at all. A different boy entirely had been responsible for Dani coming home that day in her beloved Ramones t-shirt, distressed jeans, and black Converse, spitting nails, declaring: "My first day of junior high was stupid! A boy picked me up, doubled me in half and threw me in the trash can! The trash can! I've never been so humiliated. Never!" Her voice shrieked so high it could have broken glass.

Trying to soothe our enraged middle-schooler, I remember Rick and me sitting across from her at the dinner table attempting to explain this was a pre-teen boy's clumsy way of showing affection. To our rationalization, Dani had rolled her eyes in disgust, angrily shoveled a load of meatloaf and potatoes into her mouth and railed, "Well, that's just stupid!" And we hadn't disagreed.

Shortly after the trash can incident, I first met Shawn, and seeing how close he and Dani had become in such a short time, I automatically assumed he was Trash Can Boy. However, recently I was informed that's not how he captured Dani's interest at all. The correct version of Shawn and Dani's story, as I was schooled, started a few weeks after school was in session during a band rehearsal. Their saga opens on a day when Shawn entered the band room in a particularly grumpy mood after having had extensive dental work performed to install a Herbst Device. As uncomfortable as it sounds, a Herbst Device is a metal hinged contraption affixed with brackets to the top and bottom molars for moving the top jaw back and the bottom jaw forward. It works in conjunction with a palate expander, which is an equally Spartan custom-made appliance designed to stretch the upper jaw using incremental turns of a key. Being that Shawn was a trombone player, the hardware on his teeth was not only painful, but it made it extraordinarily difficult for him to play his instrument.

Between the discomfort of his poor aching teeth and the frustration of struggling to play his trombone, Shawn wasn't in the mood to be messed with on this particular day, a message he couldn't get through to his buddy Richie. Richie was a ballbuster, and this scenario was too tempting for him to leave alone. Richie relentlessly pestered Shawn throughout band class, reaching through the slide of Shawn's trombone whenever he attempted to play, causing Shawn's mouthpiece to bump his tender teeth, sending bolts of pain rippling all the way to his toes.

When Shawn couldn't take the harassment anymore, he lost his temper and shouted "Fuck off!" into Richie's face. The sound bounced off every wall of the acoustically enhanced band room, drawing gaping looks from the entire class, who were momentarily stunned into silence. Dani, who was passing out sheet music to the clarinet section at the time, froze in the aisle and took notice. Shawn's outburst, though resulting in a rebuke from the band teacher, stole Dani's heart and captured her affection.

Throughout middle school and high school, Shawn and Dani were inseparable, though not a couple. They were instead each other's best friends, support systems, and safety nets, always there in the wings with a strong shoulder. Through thick and thin Dani had Shawn's back and Shawn had Dani's. And though they both dated others and had relationships over the years, there was always something undeniable about the way they were together–a look, a smile, a jab, or just a wrap on the shoulder–that made everyone wonder. Everyone, that is, except for the two of them.

Time flew by and high school graduation arrived. Commencement was held on the gleaming polished floors of the Florida Institute of Technology's auditorium, the only space large enough to house the massive graduating class plus family and friends. Over 400 students clad in royal blue satin robes sat restlessly in rows of metal folding chairs as happy spectators looked on from the risers. Fourteen years of hard work and persistence had led to this hallmark moment, and it was hard to tell which group was more elated. Or proud.

I watched through happy tears as my beautiful daughter and her many friends crossed the stage to accept their diplomas.

So many bittersweet emotions. We'd been through a lot on this adolescent rollercoaster, and times were about to monumentally change for us all. There would be no more hot chocolate study group sleepovers to cram for finals, no more hunts for prom dresses, no more dirty soccer socks to sniff out of the garage. Gone were the days of high school football games, watching the band on the field at half-time, and selling candy bars for fundraisers. It gave me a lump in my throat the size of a basketball.

After the ceremony, I rushed down to the graduates and gave a tearful hug to every familiar face I could find. In the midst of the chaos, I spotted my gorgeous girl's shining copper tresses near the farthest corner, gathered with the same group of kids that had once sat at my dining room table eating pot roast the first time I'd met them in seventh grade. How grown up they all had become!

In typical fashion, Dani and Shawn were standing off to the side of their friends, locked in conversation that was peppered with laughter. Both kids, decked out in their commencement garb, so tall and tan with gleaming straight-toothed smiles, they were beaming. Shawn with his signature blonde-brown curls and Dani with her sheath of auburn mane could have been models for a graduation brochure. Seizing the moment, I asked them to pose for a picture, and for once neither of them balked. Joined arm in arm wearing matching knee-length sapphire blue gowns, they looked happy and radiant. The photo was perfect, filled with young love and promise.

Yet even then, standing there like the embodiment of the picture-perfect couple, Shawn and Dani were still just friends. And throughout that whole summer after graduation nothing changed.

At the end of August, Dani started her freshman year at Florida State University. She roomed in the dorms with a high school friend and got immersed in college life while Shawn remained in Melbourne and attended the local college. They would see each other only when Dani came home for the weekend or over the holidays.

The summer after Dani's freshman year, she returned home to Melbourne to work and enjoy the comforts of home. She picked up with Shawn exactly where they had left off, joined at the hip, the best of friends. All their non-working time was spent together like the summers before, hanging out and catching up with their old crew who had also returned home for the summer break.

The carefree, enjoyable days of summer passed quickly and before it seemed possible, the fourth of July rolled around. Due to family obligations, work schedules, or previously planned events, all Dani and Shawn's friends were busy, so the two found themselves alone at the beach to watch the fireworks. And there, under the night sky exploding in a kaleidoscope of colors, the spark between Dani and Shawn, which everyone else had seen for years, finally ignited.

****

As for how I came to know Dani and Shawn had officially become "a couple", the story picks up the next day on July 5, a Saturday. Having been separated from Rick for over two years by then and living in an apartment, I was in the middle of making pancakes after a rare leisurely morning in bed when I got a phone call from Dani.

"Hi, Mom. Can you meet me at Dad's house Monday night at 6? Shawn and I have something we want to talk to you guys about."

Staring at my phone, which I had placed on speaker and sat on the counter so I could simultaneously cook breakfast, I was immediately jarred. Dani sounded fine, upbeat even, but a family meeting? Those were reserved for only big stuff.

"Yeah, I'm open Monday night. Everything okay?" I asked, trying desperately to sound nonchalant. My brain was afire with panic, my mind whirling with what could be so serious to require a family huddle. As with most mothers, my mind irrationally brought up only catastrophic scenarios, so no possibilities I landed on were good. They ranged from court to pregnancy.

"Yep, everything is fine. We'll talk about it Monday. Love you! Bye," Dani replied and hung up. I couldn't decipher anything from her tone, good or bad. She had sounded…normal.

After the call ended, I stood frozen in the middle of the kitchen with a spatula in my hand. My mind traveled further and further down the rabbit hole of doom, and I became more and more frantic. I was about to dial Rick when my cell rang again. The caller ID said it was Rick. His parental radar was apparently pinging, too.

"Hey, did Dani call you about a meeting at the house on Monday?" Rick asked, barely waiting for me to get out a hello.

Rick's voice was laced with concern. I could envision his jaw clenching and unclenching in spasms, like it always did when he was upset.

"Yeah, I just hung up with her and was going to call you. Any clue what this could be about?" I cried.

"No, nothing! You?" He asked.

"No!" I exclaimed. Still in robe, I was pacing circles in the middle of the kitchen, my pancakes burning on the stove. Smoke rose from the pan and got my attention. The contents were charred black around the edges.

Throwing the pancakes, pan and all, into the sink, I shut off the stove and sat at the kitchen table to kvetch with Rick. We discussed the possibilities. None were good. They again ranged from court to pregnancy.

After a sleepless weekend and distracted Monday, at 5:45 PM Monday night, I pulled up in the cracked cement driveway of the putty-colored house I'd lived in for 18 years. It was a strange feeling being a visitor there, as I nostalgically recognized every dish and piece of décor I had picked out during my tenure. There was comfort in the familiarity. The place still felt like a home.

Dani and Shawn hadn't yet arrived, so Rick and I went to the kitchen and took our usual seats at the only table in the room, a wood and wrought iron highboy with three tapestry cushioned chairs in beige and burgundy brocade. I'd picked out the set when we'd redecorated after the hurricanes of 2005, and since the kitchen was too small to fit a fourth chair, I had only purchased three. Since there were only three of us, it had worked out.

Rick's jaw was spasming violently, the muscles clenching and unclenching rhythmically. They'd probably been in action nonstop since Saturday. We launched into an exchange of frantic thoughts about what the pending conversation might entail, until we were interrupted by Dani and Shawn entering through the garage. The air grew heavy with nerves as I heard the familiar click of the kitchen door as it closed.

Dani gravitated automatically to her usual seat, the one between Rick and me, and Shawn stood next to her looking like he was going to address a jury. It was so quiet in the room you could have heard a pin drop. Shawn and Dani glanced at each other and then at the two of us, looking nervous. I felt like I was going to jump out of my skin.

Taking a deep breath, Shawn began.

"Okay, so we called you here because we wanted you both to know…," and there he stopped to glance at Dani.

Oh God, here it comes, I thought.

"…we've decided that we'd like to date," he finished in a giant exhale, looking from Rick to me for acknowledgement.

He got nothing; not even a hair on our bodies moved.

Rick and I both just sat there ramrod stiff in our seats, waiting for more. Finally, Rick broke the silence, saying what we were both thinking.

"And?" Rick asked with a rolling hand gesture.

"And what?" Dani said, looking at the both of us, confused, brows knitted.

"We want to date, as in 'being a couple'," she clarified, as if she was explaining the concept to third graders, growing increasingly irritated at our lack of response.

"That's it?" I asked, unsure whether I was relieved or befuddled.

"Well, yeah," Dani exclaimed, now clearly upset with our reactions or lack thereof.

"Oh! Well, congratulations!" I said, looking around with relief from Rick to Shawn to Dani, as the concept of them dating began to register as truly being the bottom line.

"So, that's it, really?" Rick said, jaw finally relaxing.

"Yes, really. Geez, you guys. Not exactly the response I was hoping for. Talk about sucking the joy out of it!" Dani said, peeved.

"Well, it's not like we haven't seen it coming for years!" Rick blurted, immediately realizing his mistake. Dani's emerald eyes burned into him like lasers.

"Down, Cujo!" Rick said, grabbing her shoulder in a fatherly side hug, extending the other hand to Shawn for a congratulatory shake.

On the borderline of collapsing with relief that this was the extent of the big family meeting, a short happy celebration took place. I shook Shawn's hand, gave Dani a hair kiss, and after several rounds of laughter and congratulations, all parties departed. I stopped off on the way home for a bottle of wine. My nerves were spent. These kids were going to be the death of me!

****

A lot of ups and downs would follow through the years as Dani and Shawn ventured forth as a couple. Shawn went on to complete a degree in accounting and finance, and Dani took a path that led to nursing. Their educational and employment pursuits had them crisscrossing the state for several years, but then landed them back home in

Melbourne, two homegrown natives happy in their own backyard.

Along the way, as we grew together as a family, we marked our progress with dozens upon dozens of hilarious and heartwarming *To-Froms*. Shawn wasted no time picking up our tag tradition, going head-to-head with Dani, who, with her sharp wit and quick-thinking, had long ago dethroned me in the creation of clever tags.

That's not to say Shawn was any slouch at gift tagging and couldn't keep pace. What I find most enjoyable about Shawn's creations is their simplicity, which makes them both brilliant and hilarious. To provide an example, this one ranks as one of my all-time favorites:

> *To: She who makes Dani mad*
>
> *From: He who makes Dani mad*

Something about the honesty of that one tickles me. At any one given time, my darling daughter is guaranteed to have either Shawn or me in the doghouse, and on the birthday when I received this tag from Shawn, we had both screwed up and found ourselves sharing adjoining rooms in the kennel.

Fortunately, Shawn and I eventually manage to make our way back into Dani's good graces. Husband Pastry and Little Spoon, as they call each other, married in 2019 at Waterford Castle in Ireland. It was a glorious, breathtaking event that the many friends who attended talk about to everyone that joins their coterie. Apparently, their Ireland wedding has become their moniker for introductions to any new people in their sphere, their friends presenting them as, "That couple that got married in Ireland!" And the new friends gasp, leaving Shawn and Dani feeling like rock stars.

Back at the kitchen table with the blank anniversary tag in my hand, I reminisced again about their incredible wedding day and my favorite moment of it. The beautiful ceremony had just taken place in front of the Portland Stone fireplace in the castle's Great Hall. The setting had been as magical as it sounds. Beneath the massive carved Fitzgerald Coat of Arms Crest, a roaring fire had snapped in the hearth, cutting through the damp and drizzle of the Irish fall. Elizabethan oak paneling, cathedral arches, embellished 16th century plastered ceilings, and thick wool tapestries awed guests as they arrived at the enchanting location, an island surrounded by the River Suir only accessible by ferry.

The day had been typically Irish, misty and crisp, which only added to the ambiance and made the crackling fire more welcoming. Not a dry eye was left after Dani had made her way down the rich tawny carpet on Rick's arm to where Shawn waited in his exquisitely tailored navy tux, grey plaid vest and wine tie. As was his norm, Shawn had spent more time laboring over his ensemble than Dani had on her dress. But his efforts had been worth it, eliciting an enormous smile from her when she saw him, matching his first glance of her, sending a wave of emotion through the room that brought tears. The joy and admiration they felt for one another was palpable.

The celebrant, looking wise and grandmotherly with coiffed brown hair and spectacles, gave a wonderful homily on what it took to pave a jubilant future together. Delivered in a rich Irish brogue, the message was riddled with funny quips and sound advice. When she finished, the ceremony moved through lighting of a unity candle and on to a traditional Celtic hand-fasting, the meaningful history of which was explained to the mesmerized room. Hands bound together with a braid of wedding colors – navy, burgundy, and ivory — a 3-strand cord that cannot easily be broken, Shawn and

Dani recited their vows, faces radiating ethereally in the unity candle's soft glow.

Tears rolling down my cheeks, I reached blindly for a tissue on the small table next to my seat. Not wanting to miss a single second of the precious sacrament, I didn't take my eyes from the front of the room until I felt something hot lick at my forearm. There was a candle on the table with the tissue box that I hadn't noticed. I'd nearly set my dress on fire!

Whipping my arm back to my side, I caught the attention of Dani's friend Elizabeth, sitting next to me.

"Really?" Elizabeth admonished, smiling with teary eyes. She knew of my history with fire.

I shrugged in reply, a tear escaping and falling onto the front of my dress.

After the ceremony concluded and the happy couple joined the kindly celebrant to complete paperwork and take photos in the magnificent castle gardens, guests retired to the Fitzgerald Room Bar. There, award-winning concoctions and mouth-watering tapas were served under Waterford Crystal chandeliers in a cozy space filled with ornate antiques, wide velveteen-cushioned armchairs and caramel leather sofas. I was enjoying my second champagne cocktail and forty-second smoked salmon cracker when I was called to go to the Conservatory for family pictures.

Slipping on my silver pumps, which I'd discretely discarded under my chair the first chance I'd gotten, I made my way through the luxe paneled hallways of the castle's interior. Passing through the dining room's splendid décor, with its massive windows cloaked in thick gold damask, centuries-old dark millwork paneling and ancestral portraits in gilt frames, I found Shawn standing alone in the Conservatory doorway, hands in pockets, looking captivated. Quietly, I came up beside him and stared in the direction of what had him so mesmerized. It was Dani. The photographer was posing her in the Conservatory Room for pictures.

Positioned in the center of the small circular entryway below the Conservatory's massive glass domed ceiling, Dani had her back to us. In front of her was a backdrop of nothing but dozens of lead-encased square panes of gleaming glass that comprised a picturesque curving box bay window housed in buttery ancient stone. The mist outside had subsided, giving way to the soft rays of pre-dusk sunlight, which created a thousand diamond prisms where the light met each corner of beveled crystal. The train of Dani's dress had been spread in a scalloped circle behind her, and she was looking over her right shoulder at it admiringly, her bouquet held low against her waist. Her shining russet hair fell softly against her left cheek, alluringly hiding the left side of her face, the rest of her hair hanging like decorative vines down her back. The Swarovski crystals along the edge of her veil twinkled in the light, adding to the mystical effect, which could never be captured on film. She looked breathtaking. Like a goddess.

"Just look at my wife," Shawn whispered into the air, never breaking his gaze. His eyes were misty, as were mine.

Of all the wonderful, extraordinary, happy moments of that day, this was my very favorite. This man would love my exquisite girl in every way I dreamed someone would. What could be better than that?

The kids have often said they intend to return to Waterford Castle for their tenth wedding anniversary to do the ceremony all over again in exactly the same way. I hope they do and that I'm here to enjoy it with them. Sitting there daydreaming about that possibility, I finally shook loose the *To-From* I'd been groping for:

To: That Couple That Got Married in Ireland

From: Leather for your 3rd to be used in Ireland for your 10th

Whomever said fairy tales don't come true is full of "shite", as the Irish would say. I've watched it happen.

Erin go bragh!

****

My Wisconsin childhood girlfriend Abbie finally came to visit me in Florida this year. It was about damn time; I'd only been inviting her for more than 30 years.

We had a wonderful time while she was here walking the beach every morning, exploring local sites every afternoon, and finding vegetarian restaurants for dinner every night. Abbie is a vegetarian. She has been one since our grade school days, a truly radical notion back then, but that's Abbie. It's one of the things I admire about her.

Abbie and I came to be friends in the 2nd grade when I was the painfully shy new kid. Our teacher, the sweet Mrs. Hannah, sat me at the desk next to Abbie's, knowing exactly what she was doing. The bold, confident Abbie wasted no time reaching her hand across the aisle to introduce herself, and we were inseparable from that day forward.

From the outside, Abbie and I looked opposite as could be. I was a pale blond, from a strict Catholic family, asthmatic, allergic to everything, and afraid of my own shadow. I was an analyzer with opinions I was taught not to voice, terrified of rejection and ridicule with abandonment issues. Meanwhile, Abbie was an olive-complected brunette, Jewish, and from a politically active household with a mother whose thumb was planted squarely on the pulse of Washington. Abbie was afraid of nothing, especially when it came to standing up against inequality and injustices. She'd call out anyone, teachers included, and could smell bullshit from a mile away. Compared to my world, she may as well have been from Mars.

But the one thing that bonded Abbie and me tight as sisters was our mutual family dynamic. Our mothers were divorced, working, single heads of household at a time when they may as well have been lepers. It was the 60s and moms were supposed to be at home in crisply ironed dresses donning aprons and awaiting their children's arrival home from school with warm cookies. That was most certainly not our reality.

But our upbringing made us strong and resilient. As Abbie's friend, not only did I get an insider's look at the customs and traditions of the Jewish culture, which I found fascinating, but Abbie taught me by example to set aside my fear and embrace diversity in all its forms. My mother had taught me to be kind to everyone, but Abbie taught me how to see and hear them. How grateful I am to dear Mrs. Hannah for seating me at that desk across the aisle from her so long ago. I received a beautiful gift.

The only reservation I have about any of my past is that there was a lapse of over 10 years where Abbie and I lost touch. We got busy raising families and wrapped up in our own worlds. But I never once stopped thinking about my oldest, dearest friend and one day randomly decided to reach out.

During those 10 or so years that Abbie and I were out of touch, a lot of life transpired. We had long, heartfelt chats in subsequent years to cover all the lost ground. Abbie had gotten married, and so had I. Abbie had birthed a son, and I a daughter. Abbie had survived breast cancer but lost her beloved husband to cancer several years later. I had gotten divorced. And in 1996 while Abbie was making a name for herself as a teacher and mentor in the Milwaukee Public School System, I was crowned and titled Mrs. Melbourne, a mail order beauty queen.

Now, I could have sworn I had shared that last tidbit with my lifelong friend somewhere over the years, but apparently not. For, while we were taking a leisurely stroll through Manatee Park while she was visiting, I made an offhand reference to my crown and sash that stopped Abbie in her tracks.

"What do you mean you have a crown and sash?" Abbie exclaimed, staring at me aghast with those familiar brown eyes. "You never told me about that!"

"Oh, I did, too!" I rebutted. "It was that whole ridiculous Mrs. Melbourne thing." I brushed away the conversation with a hand and kept walking.

"What Mrs. Melbourne thing? You have a title, too?!" Abbie cried, sounding honestly impressed. She shouldn't have been. I wasn't. I'd never gotten so much attention for doing nothing. The whole works - sash, crown, title and all — had just shown up at my front door in a 6 ½" x 9 ½" Betty Crocker Gel Food Color box.

"C'mon, I really never told you that story?" I asked, heading back to the car since we hadn't spotted any manatees, or "floating potatoes", as she called them.

"No, but you're going to tell me now!" Abbie exclaimed, all ears.

"Uch, fine. So, it was April 1996," I began and launched into the tale I'd told at least a thousand times…

I was working for the Florida Today newspaper in the circulation accounting department as an accounts receivable clerk and having a hellacious day. The department had just gone to a new Lotus program, and I had been trying in vain for hours to get my dot matrix printer to spit out my report. (I laughed when I wrote that, thinking of all the Millennials having to Google every word in that sentence.)

Tired of battling with the perforated green and white printer sheets, I called it a night and punched out. Arriving home over two hours late, exhausted, I grabbed the mail out of the mailbox and was surprised to find a note from the mailman stating he had left a package at our front door. How strange, I thought. I wasn't expecting anything.

Depositing my purse and mail on the kitchen counter, I greeted Rick and went to the front door to retrieve this mysterious package. Sure enough, I found a Betty Crocker Gel Food Colors box wedged between the screen and storm doors. Gel Food Colors? I flipped the box over to read the label. The return address said it was from the Mrs. Florida Pageant at a P.O. Box in Loxahatchee, Florida.

Mrs. Florida Pageant?

Thinking surely this was a mistake, I glanced at the delivery address, which read in big capital letters:

TO: MRS. MELBOURNE.

Mrs. Melbourne! I laughed out loud toting the box through the front hall to the kitchen.

"What's so funny?" Rick hollered from the kitchen.

"They think I'm Mrs. Melbourne! Check this out," I said, walking into the kitchen and holding up the box so he could see. "It's from the Mrs. Florida Pageant!"

Rick blanched.

"Oh my God, you won," he said. The knife he was using to chop vegetables hung motionless as he looked up with wide eyes.

"I won? I won what?" I asked, the smile fading from my face. Something fishy was going on, and it wasn't dinner.

I shot Rick *The Look*, and in reply he told me maybe I should open the box. So, never taking my eyes from his, I felt for the tape and tore it across the top. Then I opened the flaps and looked inside. And gasped.

Nothing prepares a woman for finding a rhinestone encrusted crown and a purple satin sash embroidered with "MRS. MELBOURNE 1996" in a Betty Crocker box on her doorstep. I just stood there for a moment and stared at the contents, stunned.

Part of me was horrified, thinking Mother of God, what are the ramifications, while the other half was rejoicing like Amy Farrah Fowler on Big Bang Theory when Sheldon gets her a tiara. "It's a tiara… a tiara! I'm a princess! Put it on me, put it on me, put it on me!"

Vacillating between conflicting emotions, Amy Farrah Fowler soon won out. I snatched the crown out of the box, scurried to the bathroom mirror and lowered the blingy thing onto my head. I stood back and took in the reflection and couldn't help but smile. Yep, nothing says you're the shit like a crown! I put my hair up, took it down, fluffed it out, looked at it from the back, and then saw an envelope peeking out from the corner of the box. Doggonit! There it was. The pound of flesh.

Tearing open the envelope, I began reading the words printed on the thick, ivory stationery below a gilded crest:

"CONGRATULATIONS! You have been selected by our judges to represent Mrs. Melbourne in the 1996 Mrs. Florida International Pageant in Orlando, Florida! On July…"

I had to participate in a beauty pageant!? Me, the woman that slaps her makeup on in the rear-view mirror enroute to work and hopes her dress isn't shoved into the back of her pantyhose? I couldn't participate in a beauty pageant!

"…participants will be judged in the Evening Gown and Fitness Wear competition…"

Evening Gown? Fitness Wear?? Just the day before I'd worn Rick's Fruit of the Loom tighty-whities to the gym under my sweats because all my underwear were in the wash!

"…we will be contacting you at the address provided on your application …"

My application? What application?? I didn't…and then came a recollection.

"Rick!" I shouted, and he took off running for the bedroom.

"It was your mother's idea! I only mailed it!" He screamed over his shoulder.

"You didn't!" I shouted, suddenly recalling a scene from my mother's car several weeks previous, when Mom had mentioned the pageant to us while we were going to dinner.

"I read in the Brevard Business News that they're looking for Mrs. Melbourne," Mom chirped happily. "Colleen, I think you should apply!"

God love mothers; they really do see their daughters through rose-colored glasses. You'll be in your sweats, unshowered for days, hair matted to your head with a zit in the middle of your forehead and your mother will say to you, "You look gorgeous!"

"Beauty queen? Seriously?!" I had said in the car that day. "Not in a million!"

Rick then agreed with my mother.

"Yeah, you should do it. That would make me Mr. Melbourne! Has a nice ring to it: *Mr. Melbourne*. I like it!"

Refusing to listen to another word of such nonsense, I'd changed the subject and thought that was the end of it. Obviously, it had been only the beginning. Now looking at the sparkling bits of crystal and strip of embellished satin, I let out a sigh and contemplated what to do.

Considering the crown and sash were really baller…and what was done was done…how bad could being in a beauty pageant be, right?

The answer: Bad.

Very, very bad.

A nightmare.

For starters, in 1996 my wardrobe was terrible. Our shoestring household budget raising a 2nd grader did not allow for evening gowns or fancy workout wear. Hell, I couldn't even afford a new bra! Getting creative was my only option, and I hadn't a clue how I was going to pull it off.

Searching the recesses of my closet, I located the only thing that would suffice for evening wear: a floor-length black pencil dress with a sleeveless white portrait-collared jacket I had bought at an after-Prom sale for $19.99. I'd used it as an Ivana Trump costume for Halloween in the early 90s. I slipped the form-fitting gown from the hanger to see if it still fit, and it did! I then paired it with long white satin gloves and swept my hair into an updo with a sparkly barrette. When I spun around and looked at myself in the bedroom mirror, I felt surprisingly pretty. Like Maria in West Side Story. This would do!

Athletic wear was another conundrum. My sweats looked moth-eaten, and my gym sneakers, though freshly washed, were still gross. I stood back from my open dresser drawer and brainstormed. Then out to the garage I went to dig through a box I'd carried over from my single days. In there I located what I was looking for: a black and pink leotard outfit I had hung onto from my Flash dance phase. It still looked to be in good shape, as did the white scrunchie socks and high-top baby pink Reeboks sitting in the box next to it. A little out of date but still do-able for '96. I threw on the ensemble right there in the garage and ran back to the bedroom mirror. Turning this way and that, I was shocked to find it was really flattering. I had workout wear!

Last up was the interview outfit. Nothing in my closet or garage was going to work for that, so I called in a favor. I phoned a girlfriend that had suckered me into doing some volunteer modeling for one of the high-end ladies' shops in Cocoa Village to see if she could talk them into lending me something. They agreed, allowing me to borrow a gorgeous peach minidress with matching bolero jacket that I swear was originally designed as a wetsuit. With that, I was set!

In no time, it was July, and the day of the pageant was here. I admit, I was pretty excited. Unfortunately, my excitement wouldn't last. No sooner had Mr. Melbourne and I checked into Orlando's Caribe Resort with the intention of heading out to enjoy the amenities then the pageant police called me on our hotel room phone. They were not happy. Apparently, I was supposed to be following some sort of crazy agenda that I swear I never got. There were briefings, and rehearsals, and meetings, and photos, and meet-and-greets, and on, and on, and on. It was ridiculous! But, vowing I would be a good sport, I begrudgingly sent Mr. Melbourne to have drinks by the pool with the other Misters, while I joined the sprayed, nipped, tucked, taped, and lifted rank-and-file. I fit in like a branch of goldenrod at an allergy convention.

I was a hot mess and couldn't do anything right.

At rehearsal for the opening number, I was so engrossed in conversation with my new friends Mrs. Mims and Mrs. Miami that I missed my entrance cue, so I got yelled at.

During the fitness workshop when I was asked what I did to stay fit and I answered that I vacuumed, I got yelled at.

When I asked when we were going to break for lunch, I got yelled at.

When we were practicing our answers to final interview questions and I was too hungry to pay attention and got caught daydreaming, I got yelled at.

When I snuck into the ballroom next door to scarf down a left-over club sandwich from the buffet because I was freaking starving, which made me late for the final opening number rehearsal, I got yelled at.

Tired of being yelled at, I hauled ass up to my room when we at last got a break, changed into my swimsuit, and joined the Misters at the pool. Finally enjoying myself, I was happily tanning my basal cells while sipping on a margarita when I was spotted by the pageant police. Big surprise: I got yelled at. According to their stupid timeline I was supposed to be getting ready for my judges' interview. So, with a harrumph, I took my beverage in a plastic cup and sashayed up to my room to change.

I will admit for this portion I was overconfident. I love interviewing. I've always loved interviewing. And having experienced 100% success rate on every job interview I've ever been through; I was a teensy bit cocky. Rookie mistake. It was a disaster. Every one of my cheeky quips fell flat, and except for one lovely woman judge that thought I was hilarious, the rest of the stodgy, stone-faced, party poopers hated me.

Later that evening I had to go to the prejudging of the evening gowns. I was certain I'd gain some ground there. Nope, wrong again. As luck would have it, they lined me up next to the girl who would take runner-up in her $7,000 custom-made gown. It was encrusted with emerald Swarovski crystals and looked to weigh as much as a refrigerator. I thought it looked ridiculous, like a green disco ball, and choked back church giggles every time I looked at her. But evidently, that's what the judges were looking for in lieu of an Ivana Trump knock-off purchased from a teen store sale rack. On my rating sheets, judges commented that I looked like Cinderella, which I took as a huge compliment. It was not. Getting disqualified would have netted me more points.

By the time we got around to the athletic wear judging, I had given up. I was sure I'd be crucified for my garage box throwback, but lo and behold, the judges loved it. I even scored higher than Mrs. Runner Up, who wore a monochromatic aqua latex number. She nearly had to grease up to get into it, a spectacle that was wildly entertaining to watch backstage. And don't even get me started on everything else I witnessed back there. There was double-sided tape and petroleum jelly put in places it should never go. Ever.

So, you don't have to be a rocket scientist to guess the outcome of that whole misadventure. Let's just say I didn't get a rose bouquet and no need to use the cup-hand parade float wave they taught us. On the flip side, I did get through the ordeal with my dignity intact, Mr. Melbourne got his fancy title, Dani and my mom got to sit in the audience and watch Rick and me sashay about the stage dressed up like Ken and Barbie, and I have a Halloween costume that never gets old.

I finished telling Abbie the story just as we pulled into the carport at my house. She was looking at me with equal portions of awe and disbelief.

"What, you don't believe me? C'mere, I'll prove it," I said, opening the door to the house and heading down the tiled hallway.

With her following at my heels, I headed to my bedroom where I extracted a Betty Crocker box from my teak TV stand. It was the same box that had showed up at my front door 26 years ago. I keep it just as I received it, the postal stamp faded but still readable, so I can prove to any doubters I can't make this stuff up.

I handed the box to Abbie, and she extracted the crystal crown and purple trimmed sash. Holding up the crown, she looked honestly impressed.

"Go ahead, try it on if you want. It's wildly uncomfortable," I told her with a laugh.

"No, that's okay, Mrs. Melbourne. You're queen enough for the both of us," she replied with a smile. True that.

A couple weeks after Abbie got back home to Wisconsin, she sent me a thank you card and gift for my hospitality. The *To-From* on the package read:

To: Mrs. Melbourne '96

From: Preserved in Ice

We now rarely have a conversation where Abbie fails to squeeze in a Mrs. Melbourne comment and enjoys addressing me by title when we are in the company of mutual friends. I'm thinking perhaps now I know the reason I may have neglected to tell her that story in the first place. Unfortunately, once the crown is out of the box, there's hell to pay.

Chapter 11: November

When I think of November, I think of my grandpa. His birthday was November 2nd. And when I think of Grandpa, I envision being wrapped in a cozy cocoon of red plaid flannel lightly scented with tobacco, his signature shirt.

Grandpa was my mother's dad. He was my babysitter, my protector, my chef, my teddy bear, my nurse, and my hero. He had the patience of a saint, was as big as Zeus, could instantly heal any ailment with the touch of his massive hand on my forehead, and I absolutely adored him. He was my angel on earth. My O.G.

In the 24 years he blessed my world, I never once heard Grandpa raise his voice. He was a gentle, quiet soul who was headed to the priesthood until he met my grandmother and fell head over heels in love. That's not to say Grandpa couldn't be forthright when he needed to. I've been told he once put a man up against a wall with one hand, the man's feet dangling two feet off the ground while Grandpa ushered him a warning that the dude's treatment of women needed to improve. And I doubt even at that moment Grandpa raised his voice.

Grandma, my mother's mother, was meek and soft spoken. Another kind, selfless spirit, she also originally had her sights set on serving God. She was preparing to enter a nunnery in 1916 when she met Grandpa and did a 180, equally smitten.

Grandpa and Grandma's piety and gentle dispositions were not the only qualities that made them nearly mirrored images. Both were chestnut-haired and considered tall, Grandpa at 6'1" and Grandma at 5'7", both were of pure German descent, and each was a first-generation American living in Wisconsin. But while Grandpa was broad-shouldered and muscular with a firm, square jaw, Grandma was as fine-boned and delicate as a china doll, with a softness that infused everything from the curve of her nose to the smooth gentle waves of her smartly bobbed hair. These subtle differences captivated my grandfather, who thought Grandma was the most beautiful creature that ever graced the earth. Theirs was a love so enchanting it is the likely reason I am such a hopeless romantic.

One of the things I regret most from not taking more interest in my heritage before my mother's dementia robbed her of her memory is that now so many of the family's priceless anecdotes are gone with no one left to tell them to me. As a storyteller, I don't care nearly as much about the names of who married whom or when, which can be uncovered through ancestry research, as how the couple came to be together, which is not contained in the archives. The stories are what I relish. To me, without the narratives, the rest feels a bit empty.

I long to know the details of the very moment my grandparents met. What was Grandma wearing? Where was she standing when Grandpa first caught sight of her, and her him? What were the first words spoken? And by whom? I vaguely remember being told they first saw each other at a harvest time barn dance. That may not be exactly right, but the one ingredient I do know for sure is that it was love at first sight. Of that, I am positive. Every tiny morsel of their tale I've ever gleaned, which hasn't been much, has started with that. I am equally positive that they were the light of each other's life. That piece I witnessed for myself.

No matter what their intentions had been before that magical first meeting, any thoughts of celibacy by both parties were thereafter vanquished. Grandpa said they were unable to think of a life without the other, and when neither family would consent to their marriage, they eloped. I have their fading sepia wedding photo sitting in a ceramic flower-trimmed frame in my living room and it's priceless to me. Though demure, Grandma's face has the faintest hint of a smile half-hidden beneath her fabulous Edwardian hat. What a great hat. It sits on her soft walnut waves cocked stylishly to the right, the visible side laden with elaborate folds of thick ribbon resembling an ornate bow so full that it touches the top of her shoulder. Her skin looks milky and flawless, and I imagine her tasteful, modest dress was the loveliest shade of dusty rose.

In the photo Grandpa is holding her close in an embrace that seems almost protective, looking positively dashing in a black jacket and vest with crisp white collared-shirt and wide white tie knotted at the neck. His hair, just as full as I remember, looks dark as ebony and thick, not white and fluffy as snow as I'd only seen it. The way his head tilts toward her, as near as he could get without crushing the brim of her hat, speaks volumes. Frozen in that moment they are the embodiment of respect, adoration, and joy. They represent what I wish for everyone to find in this life, including myself.

Both of my grandparent's families would eventually forgive them for running off together, unable to compete with their wills and happiness. Grandpa would go on to become a fireman for the City of Milwaukee, an occupation he loved. Saving souls and protecting those in need had always been his calling, so being a fireman was a perfect fit. The fire departments used horse-drawn wagons to transport tankards of water to the fires back then, eventually replacing them with massive, hinged hook-and-ladder engines that were as long as a city blocks. When Milwaukee got its first motorized truck, Grandpa was assigned to be the driver that steered the back end. The position required great strength and was known to be the most difficult and dangerous job the fire department had. Grandpa soon mastered the position and became known for being the best hook and ladder driver in the county.

Over the 32 years of fighting fires, my grandfather had incredible tales of heroism, but he would only tell them if relentlessly coaxed and cajoled. He had fallen through burning roofs and floors, landing hard on his back in basements, and gotten covered in flaming embers. He had carried countless men, women, and children down the fire truck's long ladders, rescuing them from the windows of burning buildings as flames licked into the air behind him. And he once got attacked by a huge swarm of angry hornets when their nest fell on his head during a house fire, knocking him off his ladder and landing him square on his back on the home's cement doorstep. He always said of all the injuries he'd endured, that one had been the worst. The wasps stings had been painful and made him deathly ill, while the fall had left his back permanently damaged.

By the time my mother came along, the last of their three children, Grandpa had relinquished his position on the hook-and-ladder truck to take a less hazardous job as a fire inspector. Firefighting had taken a toll on his body, and I imagine he welcomed the chance to get off the front line. By the time I came along, Grandpa had long been completely retired, for which I am ever so grateful. His retirement afforded him the time and energy to be my loving caretaker when my mother became a single, working parent, while he also provided compassionate care for Grandma, who was suffering from later-stage dementia.

Grandpa gave me the peace and serenity I so craved in my young life. My grandparents' white stone Milwaukee bungalow was my shelter in the storm and where I loved being, especially when the weather was warm, and we could play in the yard. That glorious, lush green yard. And garden.

Grandpa's garden was magnificent. He could grow anything. And did. After a brutal Wisconsin winter, at the first hint of spring Grandpa would turn the rock-hard earth of the rectangular plot in the corner of their yard into rows and lay atop them a thick, black layer of topsoil. Then, he would set long planks of wood between each one, so he and I could walk among the seedlings without disturbing the germination. I can remember gleefully working beside him before I wasn't even big enough to ride a two-wheeled bicycle. He would poke perfect, round holes into the earth with his giant finger, and I would follow behind hanging onto his pant leg, dropping one or two little seeds into the freshly sculpted divots. When we were through, together we would gently cover the recesses, water our work, and rest on the old, weathered metal lawn chairs, admiring our efforts. He would quietly put his enormous, flannel-covered arm around my wee shoulders, and I would feel like St. Michael himself had engulfed me in wings of warmth and protection. He'd stroke my blonde ringlets with his huge hand, and all was right with the world. Simple. Wonderful. Heaven.

After a fortnight or two, Mother Earth would perform her magic and Eden would arise from our tended rows with a spectacular array of colors. Line after neat line of green onions, radishes, carrots, and sweet peas would be there for our taking alongside the most luscious tomatoes in all the world. By mid-summer the enormous tomato plants would bow under the weight of colossal, tasty Beefsteaks, wearing coats in hues redder than orange, large as grapefruit. My tiny little hand in Grandpa's great paw, I'd skip down the aluminum-rimmed linoleum stairs of the back hallway of the house beside him, and out to the blossoming garden we'd go to pick one of the giant tomatoes, the wooden screen door slamming shut behind us. He'd carry a small glass aluminum-topped saltshaker with him, and after instructing me which ripe delicacy to pluck from its grateful vine, I'd hold the tomato with both hands and devour the whole thing between little shakes of salt. He'd roar with laughter as seeds and juice ran down my face and onto my little pink seersucker jumper. It was a sound I heard so rarely that even as a toddler I knew to relish it. It was God's music.

Then, when the marigolds would spring from the rich, black earth and don their glorious fluffy blooms, the Monarchs would come. That was my favorite part. I would wait impatiently for my bright orange-winged friends from the day the marigold seeds were planted. Every single day of spring and summer I would run out to the back yard, stand upon the wooden plank of the row that was designated for flowers, and cry disappointingly, "Grandpa, when are the butterflies gonna come?"

He would lay a gentle palm on the back of my head as I looked up at his mighty form beside me and say, "After we are still for a while. We must be patient. Be still and they will come!"

And just as he promised, they would. The marigold plants would sprout and grow bushy pom-poms of yellow and orange blooms, and the monarchs would descend until early September. I would yip and dance among them, as we played in the summer sun. It was such a happy, happy time. Cherished, simple innocence. An incredible blessing.

In the early 1970s Grandpa sold the white stone bungalow and moved into a house a few blocks away from my Auntie Norm, my grandma's sister, on the south side of Milwaukee. Grandpa needed to be closer to family because Grandma had grown so sick that he needed help caring for her. She passed quietly into heaven in 1974 when I was thirteen and I saw Grandpa cry for the first time. It was a moment when I thought my heart would shatter and the first time I'd ever experienced grief.

In the early 80s, Grandpa moved out to California to live with my Uncle Vern for the remainder of his days. The few times I got out there to visit him, his smiles were few, so I cherished them all the more. I have a picture somewhere that was taken on my last visit on November 2, 1984, just after I had given him a new plaid flannel shirt for his 86th birthday. The tag on the box had read:

To: My Forever Hero

From: Your Little Shadow who Dances with Butterflies

The snapshot captures the two of us sitting on the glider bench of my Uncle Vern's front porch, my head resting on Grandpa's shoulder. He's wearing a gray zip-front jacket over his signature flannel shirt, and I'm in jeans and Kelly-green ski jacket, my arm locked in his as we gently sway back and forth, reminiscing. We had been sharing memories of the white porcelain wringer washer in his basement in Milwaukee, talking about the old ham radio on his workbench that had a real morse code clicker, recalling how we used to test TV vacuum tubes on his monitoring device, how he used to take apart the pink blossoms from the bush in his yard into seven separate pieces to Sean and my delight (the baby's bottle and the slipper are the only two my brother Sean and I can remember), and how I used to be fascinated with the little log cabin penny bank with the metal trap door on the bottom. This would be the last time I saw Grandpa, and from the forced smiles on both our faces in that photo, I think we both knew. He passed four months later of emphysema. Grandpa had been a lifelong smoker.

Several months after his death, I received a small package in the mail from my Uncle Vern, executor of Grandpa's estate. The package contained a little yellowing jewelry box and a note from Uncle Vern that said its contents had been earmarked just for me. I sat with the unopened box for a long while, waiting until the tears had cleared enough to see before removing the top. I couldn't imagine what was in it. When I was able to pull off the lid and remove the little square of yellowed cotton inside, I found Grandpa's miniature copper fireman's helmet, a pendant he had received from the fire department when he retired. I used to play with the tiny helmet when I was little, fascinated by it.

Admiring the miniature hat in my hand, I was immediately transported back to toddlerhood. I remembered the spot on the lowest shelf of the built-in cabinets in the living room where Grandpa used to keep the little copper helmet so I could reach it whenever I wanted to play with it. Delighted with the privilege, my routine whenever I visited was to burst through his sun porch door, hug Grandpa around the legs, and then head straight for the cabinets to retrieve the charm. I used it as jewelry on my Barbie to impress Ken and the neighbors. It always worked.

To date, the little charm is one of my most valued possessions. I wear it on a chain around my neck or keep it in my pocket when I feel I need a little extra strength or encouragement. Or, more so, I rely on its power to remind me to just be still for a while and wait for the fruits of my labor. Feeling Grandpa's calming presence close to me always does the trick. Angels tend to do that.

****

"Blonde One, come get your phone. It's driving me crazy!" Glenn hollered to me from his patio door.

I had just gotten out of his hot tub and was sitting on his screened back porch discussing chick flicks with Paul. The forecasters were predicting a nasty storm was moving in, so Paul and I were coordinating our storm preparation priorities: movies and munchies.

I got up from my comfortable brightly pillowed porch chair and left Paul's jungle of plants behind me to retrieve my phone and save Glenn. I entered their family room, which doubled as Glenn's office, sliding the patio door behind me. Picking up my phone from the coffee table directly across from where Glenn was sitting, I saw I had two missed calls and a voice message from a 617 number. The only phone number in the 617 area code belonged to my adopted family from Boston, Pamie and Brian. Awesome!

Punching the voicemail button, I listened to the message. Out of the speakers came Pamie's voice, unmistakable with its New England accent.

"Colleeeeeen! Okay, so I had to call and tell on myself. You know how I said all the stupid stuff only happens to you? Well, you're rubbin' off, girl. Give me a call! Love ya, hun. Bye!"

Smiling, I clicked off the voicemail, thrilled to have a fun story awaiting me. It was about time the Universe made someone else the butt of its jokes. Packing up my wet bathing suit and thanking Glenn and Paul for a wonderful afternoon of snacking and splashing in their hot tub, I headed home, anxious to call Pamie back and get the scoop.

Brian and Pam, or Uncle Brian and Auntie Pamie as I still called them, had come with my marriage. Brian was the brother of Rick's stepmother, a simple, dependable, pint-sized muscular guy, who would find something he liked and stick to it. Forever. A plain white t-shirt, khakis, sneakers, glasses, and a smile was his go-to uniform. At 65 years-old, he had worked at the same job for 43 years, the head maintenance guru for some large Boston outfit. For work he donned a suit, likely the same color and brand he had worn for his entire career, and used words like boiler, breaker, coupling, and steam valve. Brian was known to be called out of the house at every odd hour of the day or night, through every kind of despicable weather, because he was the guy that could always be counted on. That's the kind of man Brian was. A good one.

With Brian came Pam. A few years younger and a few inches shorter, she could have been Brian's female twin, glasses and all. They were a matched set and had been together as a couple for like 135 years. When I think of Pamie, I imagine someone I would have invited to junior high sleepovers, spilling secrets in comfy jammies, giggling, and dunking Oreos in milk. Pam's the kind of person to whom you could hand a winning Lotto ticket for safe-keeping and know she would take it to the grave uncashed, pristine, and probably ironed. People are on a waiting list to have her watch their kids. They know that while they're at work, Pamie is running through the house dodging blocks, wiping mouths, kissing boo-boos, singing nursery rhymes, and clutching crayoned drawings of stick figures to her heart like she'd just been given a Picasso. She's the most selfless, giving, nurturing, kind-hearted person I know, and the mother we all want to be. The caregiver and the peacemaker. That's Pamie.

Back in the day, Brian and Pamie's families had bets that Brian and Pam would never get married, but they did. In the early 1990s they had a big, fat, Greek wedding where they served huge bowls of comfort foods and I learned to do the handkerchief dance in my lace anklets and heels ala Madonna. Their wedding was a blast. And a few years later against all odds, as they entered their forties, a miracle happened. They had Beth-Anne, an exquisitely beautiful girl with flowing light brown hair and the sweet, selfless disposition of her parents. She was the cherry on the sundae of their life.

Every year since I met Brian and Pamie in 1987, they have driven a minivan down to Florida from Boston for one fun-filled week of vacation in the sun. They stop on the way down at the exact same midway point they've used every year, they rent the exact same condo in Indian Harbor Beach while they're here, and then they use the exact same return midway point on the way back. They leave Boston on the Thursday before Memorial Day, arrive on that Friday, stay until the following Friday, and have me over for a fried Spam and fettuccine alfredo dinner one night while they are here, with lemon meringue pie and coffee for dessert on the balcony. It's tradition. A tradition that I adore with these salt-of-the-earth folks that make me feel like a better person just for knowing them.

Not even waiting to get into my house, I dialed Pamie's number from my carport, cradling the phone on my shoulder while trying to get the key in the lock of my back door. She answered on the second ring.

"Hi!" she exclaimed, breathless. "Sorry, I just got in from shoveling."

I grimaced as I walked through my laundry room. How people could continue to live in those northern climates was baffling to me.

"Sounds fun. I was just at Paul and Glenn's in the hot tub," I replied with a grin.

A resentful grumble was all I got in return. Satisfied, I continued.

"So, do tell. What did Auntie Pamie do that was cringeworthy? C'mon, did you make me proud?" I encouraged, fishing through my cupboards and fridge for a snack to munch while I listened. How I loved a good story!

"Ugh, okay. So, you know how I have this elderly neighbor Mary that I check on?" Pamie began.

"I do. Yep. Go on," I said, stuffing a Wheat Thin into my mouth.

And then out poured the whole sordid tale…

Boston had just been hit with another nor'easter and having already suffered through record-setting snows for November, the city was once again buried. For the length of the most recent storm, Pamie hadn't gotten a call from her elderly neighbor Mary, whom she looked out for, so she had grown concerned. Mary had recently fallen, so Pamie was worried she might have done so again. Unable to wait any longer, Pamie decided to brave the massive snow drifts and pop next door to check on her friend.

"Wait, why didn't you just try calling?" I asked, washing down another cracker with some lemonade.

"Well, I don't know!" Pamie shouted in defense. "I guess I didn't think of it!" And she continued with her saga before I could get in another word.

While Pamie suited up in her snow gear, Brian was already outside trying to carve a path down the walk using their temperamental snow blower. When the snow was exceptionally wet, which this snow was, the blower would only run intermittently, conking out every couple of feet and demanding to be unclogged. Fortunately (or unfortunately, however you looked at it), the wind was working in Brian's favor that day, blowing great plumes of the fluffy snow that was falling onto the top of the soggy lower layer from previous storms.

"Wait, why didn't you just ask Brian to check on Mary since he was out there anyway?" I asked through another mouth full of Wheat Thin.

"Well, I don't know!" Pamie shouted again, exasperated. "I didn't think of that!" And again, she continued with her story before I could interject. I had to mute the phone to let out a giggle, thrilled to be on the listening end of the conversation, something that rarely happened.

To her credit, Pamie did have a plan for checking on Mary that day. Although it wasn't exactly a good one. A good one would have been to pick up the phone and call Mary or have Brian do her bidding. Instead, Pamie's idea was to leap her way, gazelle-style, through the giant snow drifts from her back door to Mary's and then shovel a wider path through her preformed tracks on the way back. Apparently, this sounded rational at the time. In retrospect, not so much.

Plan formulated, 5-foot-nothing Pam, outfitted in a black overcoat and mid-calf snow boots, headed out through the back door into the elements. From the back stoop of her house, she grabbed a snow shovel and took a giant leap into the snow-covered yard towards Mary's house. The result was more moose than gazelle. Pamie sunk up to her waist in a drift and snow packed into the tops of her boots and began to melt, soaking her socks. She decided perhaps hers wasn't the best strategy after all. Best laid plans of mice and men. And moose.

Debating whether she should retreat, Pam bullheadedly decided to trudge ahead through the massive drifts. In about three steps, she would regret this decision. Breathless and flailing, she lost her balance and fell through the fluffy snow onto her back. She landed more than two feet down, outlined like a cartoon character, the only thing visible being the bright red plastic handle of the snow shovel. It poked straight up into the air from where she landed, like an X marking the spot.

At this point of her story, I had collapsed on my couch holding my sides and crying with great guffaws of laughter with my phone muted. I could just envision the whole scene.

Looking up into the sky and discovering she was helpless as an overturned turtle laying in the bottom of the snow drift, Pamie started hollering for help.

"Help! HELP! H-E-L-P!" She cried. But the usually uncooperative snow blower had decided this was the day it was going to show up for work. It droned on and on with no signs of letting up. Pamie feared Brian wouldn't find her till spring!

Out on her porch, Pamie's neighbor on the opposite side of the house from Mary had heard Pamie's shouts, but only as a strange distant sound and opened her back door to listen. Disgusted, the neighbor decided the muffled cries were only the loud rambunctious kids down the block teasing each other outside in the snow. She harrumphed, returned inside, and slammed the door. So much for Pamie's rescue party.

As Pamie pondered whether the soggy lining of her boot held enough nutrition to sustain her until help arrived, she suddenly heard the snow blower turn off. Jabbing the snow shovel's red handle as high into the air as she could, she commenced her desperate cries for help. And thank heavens, it worked; Brian's face peeked over the side of the drift and stared down at her.

"Luv, what the hell are you doing?" Brian exclaimed with a chuckle.

"I was going to check on Mary. Never mind! Just get me up, will ya?!"

Brian told me he knew better than to reply. After 135 years, Brian was a smart man.

Turns out Mary was just fine. She'd gone into her back room and taken a long nap. When Pamie finally made it over to her house and knocked on her door, Mary let her into the foyer and looked at Pamie perplexed. Pamie was flushed and dripping. Mary asked, "Why didn't you just call?"

I laughed so hard at this point it honestly hurt.

"So, there you have it," Pamie said, finishing her anecdote with a harrumph.

Still trying to recover from my uncontrollable laughter, I asked her to hang on while I ran to get my notebook.

"Oh, no," I heard her shout at the other end of the phone, realizing she'd just made her tag for Christmas. She was right. The tag would read:

> TO: *I've fallen, and I can't get up*
>
> FROM: *You made me proud, snow dweller*

I wrote the *To-From* on the back of a Winn-Dixie gift card, thinking it could be used to buy Spam, fettuccini alfredo, and lemon meringue pie for our dinner in May. Only I knew it wouldn't get used for Spam, fettuccini alfredo, and lemon meringue pie, because Pamie always took her Boston groceries on vacation with her. Evidently she thought Florida's Spam, fettuccini alfredo, and lemon meringue pie weren't as good as the items of the same brand she purchased at home, or that maybe her groceries needed some sun after the long Massachusetts winters, too. Regardless of the reason, Pamie toting tins of Spam and packages of dry pasta 1300 miles across the country had become just another part of our tradition. And I wouldn't have it, or her, or them any other way.

****

When Shawn and Dani moved into their house seven years ago, they took over hosting holiday dinners. Dani is an incredible cook, so she always prepares the turkey and mashed potatoes, assigning the other attending members of the family the fixings and beverages.

Likewise, Shawn enjoys making the standing prime rib roast for Christmas, proudly carving it up like the Grinch with roast beast in Whoville, while the rest of us supply the rest of the meal. I'm always put in charge of the broccoli cheese casserole and the sweet potatoes for both Thanksgiving and Christmas, as Dani insists I make them better than she can. This is absolutely not the truth, as my daughter is a wonder in the kitchen; however, me providing these two dishes has everything to do with tradition. And Dani, like me, is all about tradition. Besides providing the casseroles, I always bring a little extra something to the feast, because that, too, is part of my tradition. This extra offering allows me to use a piece of my Auntie Normie's gold-rimmed Noritake china. The china has been in my family since decades before I was born, and was to be brought out only on the holidays.

The beautifully crafted Noritake set is nearly as dear to me as the fire helmet charm I inherited from Grandpa. As much of a surprise as the helmet, Normie's china arrived in very much the same way, in an unexpected box from Uncle Vern. He was executor of Auntie Normie's estate, too. Why he never gave me a heads-up that either treasure was coming my way before I received them, I never asked. I guess he just enjoyed doling out surprises. Like Santa Claus.

Normie never had children of her own, but she didn't have to; she had my cousin LeeAnn and me. Even in our teen years, LeeAnn and I were never too busy for a weekend sleepover at Auntie Norm's. We would play with her Chihuahua Twinkie, watch Jeopardy and the Wheel of Fortune, feast on her homemade goodies, and play cards till bedtime. It was good, old-fashioned balm for the heart, and I absolutely loved it.

All that said, and despite the undeniable bond I had with Normie, which was nearly as tight as the one I shared with Grandpa, when Normie's exquisite china was bestowed upon me, it baffled the rest of the family. The delicate pieces and I had a history, and it wasn't good. Being the family tomboy, I had always been more interested in sneaking off with my cousin Dale after holiday dinners to watch my Green Bay Packers play football on TV, than joining with the rest of the female clan in the kitchen to wash, wipe, and gossip. The single time I did follow suit to do my ladylike service (Green Bay had played the early game), Uncle Vern's wife, my Auntie Ann, had to dive across the kitchen like a wide receiver to save the first cup I washed before it hit the floor. Subsequently, I was banned from partaking in holiday kitchen duty from that day forward, which was fine with me.

I, however, knew perfectly well why I was the recipient of such an enormous gift as the china. What Normie alone understood that the family did not, was that nothing could have been dearer to me than those precious dishes. That Noritake china held a beautiful secret, a wonderful message, and my favorite Auntie Norm story. She would tell me all her stories, but the one with the china was my favorite. Every time I slept over, I would gaze at the delicate cups in the china closet and ask her to tell me the tale again. It was like my very own Aesop's fable.

When I took a Writer's Workshop a decade after I received the china from my Uncle Vern and was tasked to write a short story about a possession that had a special meaning, crafting the legend of the china was a no-brainer. I could hardly type the words fast enough, as they erupted from my past and poured from my soul. I wrote the story for Normie, and it came from my heart. I received the highest grade in the class and promised the workshop's teacher I would include it in my book if I ever got around to publishing one.

In keeping with my promise, here is that story for you to enjoy…

Cherished Pieces

I was six years old, sitting cross-legged and content on that old, pink sofa with the prickly cushions. Auntie Norm and I shared a sweet and a memory, her faded blue eyes twinkling as she gazed at the china in her cabinet. Her thoughts retreated into the past as she told me the story for the hundredth time. I never got tired of hearing it.

The year was 1920, and Norma was a plucky, young woman, working as a secretary in the city to earn money for her ailing mother. Every Friday, she would collect her meager pay, stop by the post office, and glance in the shop windows along the way. Every week it was the same–she would stop to linger through the clear glass panes of one particular shop, whose window boasted the most beautiful, gold-rimmed china she had ever seen. She would marvel at the detail on every piece and dream of being an elegant woman, proudly serving Christmas dinner to a large family on those incredible plates.

Unable to think of anything else, one Friday afternoon she ventured into the shop to ask the salesclerk the price of that treasured set. It was $25, imported Noritake, a service for twelve. That was a fortune for Norma. Crestfallen, she left the shop with a heavy heart.

That evening at home, Norma told her mother of the china in the shop's window. She couldn't have been more surprised at her mother's reaction. Katherine encouraged Norma to save for the collection, even purchase it one precious piece at a time. "Always reach for your dreams, Norma," Katherine had said. "It's the only way you'll ever touch Heaven."

It would take Norma five years, the set long since retired to the back shelves of the store, when she proudly walked in to purchase the complete set of her beloved china. She told me she could still remember the sound of the bell as it clanged against the store's front door that day, the smell of sawdust and linens scenting the air that greeted her, and the clerk's look of appreciation at Normie's smartly tailored gray wool suit with the long jacket and tie belt that accentuated her tiny waist. Norma had dressed especially for the day, selecting her finest white blouse, ironing it twice for the occasion. She always told the story with so much feeling I could picture the scene perfectly and smell it, too, snuggled up close next to her on those overstuffed cushions.

Decades later, Normie long since passed, her voice still whispers to me every time I use a piece of her cherished Noritake. "Always reach for your dreams, child, always reach for your dreams." I picture her standing in the china shop, dressed in her finest wool suit with the perfectly pressed white blouse, and I can't help but smile.

"What thought is making you so happy, sweetheart," my husband asks as he comes up behind me and plants a kiss on my cheek in the kitchen.

"I'm just recalling a secret," I tell him as I carefully dry the last gold-rimmed saucer and place it lovingly in my cupboard after another beautiful family dinner. This family I always dreamed of having to serve, just like Normie.

Grandma Katherine was right. If you reach for your dreams, you will land among the stars, and it will feel like Heaven.

Just ask Normie.

Or me.

I never wrote Normie any funny *To-Froms* because she wouldn't have understood them. Like her sister, my grandma, and now my mother, Normie was stricken with dementia in her later years.

Had I gotten the chance, I would have placed this tag on a gift to her:

> TO: *My favorite storyteller*
>
> FROM: *Keeper of all things priceless*

Inside the package I would have placed the first copy of my book, not only because it is an accomplished dream, or because it was Normie who taught me how to weave a tale, but because my book houses something more valuable than china or little copper fire helmets. It contains our family's stories.

One's family stories are the most precious belongings one can have. They are priceless because they are too easily lost, from no fault of our own, just rotten genetics. Like the females in my family before me, I might turn around one day, and my stories may have vanished along with my memory. Gone forever. Like dust in the wind.

So, at least now through my book I will be able to leave behind these precious few anecdotes for generations to treasure. They are like little pieces of Heaven.

Chapter 12: December

Listen, I find nothing wrong with being a thrifty frugalista. In today's economy when most everyone is struggling just to get by, a gal's gotta do what a gal's gotta do to make her dollar stretch till it screams. My pals Beth and Phyllis wholeheartedly agree, so long as my penny-pinching ways don't interfere with my footwear or my face. According to my girls, those two categories hold irrefutable exemption status when it comes to scrimping.

Beth is the advocate for shoes. With her perfect little fairy feet, she plants a well-manicured foot on her glitter bedazzled soapbox to argue that a lady, especially one about to become "a world-famous author", should never, under any circumstances, step out in shoes that are not impeccably kept and HDC (the Highest Degree of Cuteness). Even if donning sneakers, Beth purports that a woman's foot dressing is to be clean and possess interest, a fun color at the bare minimum. If shod for a formal occasion, she expects the interest quotient of the shoe be quadrupled, as well as the maintenance level. This is the Gospel of Beth.

Beth is so devoted to the presentation of my feet that I believe if she caught me stepping onto a stage with a frayed heel, it would sever our friendship. I have tried to find loopholes in her legislation and enact exceptions concerning designs I find unacceptable for my unspeakably ugly feet, but so far, all arguments have been vetoed. For instance, Beth contends that having long, knobby-ended, finger-like toes such as mine is no excuse to snub open-toed sandals. As long as my toes don't hang over the front end, I conceded on thongs and most strappy styles; however, Beth and I have agreed to disagree on peep-toes. On those I will not waver, for I have never found a pair that can keep my second and third toes from working their way through the hole, resembling zombie fingers trying to claw their way from the grave. Something to which Ms. Perfect Fairy Feet cannot relate.

On the opposite end of the body, Phyllis, the esthetician, is the advocate for the face. Hearing that I've strayed from the Eminence line to try something less costly or new, consequently paying the price with a complexion breakout resembling the surface of the moon, throws Phyllis into apocalyptic conniption fits. While she has me captive on her facial table, my face wrapped like a mummy with the steamer blowing full blast to counteract the blemishes and rosacea, she'll deliver me a blistering sermon laced with *I told you so*s and *for crying out loud*s. Her lectures are brutal.

Now, I'm not saying either one of my friends is wrong. They are not. A woman should always put her best foot and face forward. What I am saying, however, is that a lady must learn how to filter sage advice through her gut and apply only the select bits the inner wee voice tells her she should. Trusting the omnipotent gut is a crucial life skill and one I wonder if I will ever learn. Ignoring my intuition, running roughshod in the opposite direction, and landing square on my face seems to be my greatest superpower.

Lucky for me, the Universe is patient with us gut deaf types and continues to provide ample opportunities for growth and learning. My most recent opportunity came with getting headshots for this book jacket, something I absolutely did not want to do. I suck at posing for headshots. It's as though I have a communication disability in following the instructions of a photographer, causing frustration for all parties and pictures that are even more disappointing than the session.

This conundrum has been with me since kindergarten and my very first Picture Day at school. Unlike the adorable photos of my 5-year-old classmates, I'm shown hunched forward in my seat wearing a constipated smile that's anything but endearing. I wish I could report my snapshots got better over the years, but that's just not the case. In every single school photo my expression looks tortured, my hair is a mess, and my outfits are awful. The worst of the lot is the one I took for eighth grade, where immediately after the picture was snapped, I heaved my breakfast into the trash can at the photographer's feet. I had a fever and the onset of the flu. I had tried to tell the curmudgeonly photographer that I didn't feel well, but he refused to believe me. I guess I showed him.

Probably because I got vomit splatter on the photographer's loafers, my request for retakes was refused, so that gem of a picture with my sweaty hair and red rimmed eyes is immortalized on the eighth grade class composite photograph. Every time someone at one of our school reunions pulls out that print, I want to curl up and die. Worst picture ever.

Because of this lifelong history of abhorrent class photos, it should come as no surprise that I will do anything to avoid photo sessions that cull me from the herd. When I was Mrs. Melbourne and had to submit a picture for the pageant catalog, I gave them the "after" photo that had been taken when I had a free Mary Kay makeover. It was the one and only decent headshot I'd ever taken. Had the picture not been so dated, I'd have used it again for this book jacket. Unfortunately, Bianca, my sage and talented writing coach, insisted I get something more current than a photo from 1995. So, I succumbed. Begrudgingly.

Beth was the first one to whom I mentioned the headshots when she called that evening.

"Hey, girlfriend! What's new with our soon-to-be-famous author?" Beth chirped in her energetic way.

"Well, Bianca just tasked me with getting headshots. I'd rather prep for a colonoscopy," I grumbled.

On the other end of the line Beth laughed in her tinkling fairy way. "Oh my gosh, how exciting! Who's doing your makeup?" Beth asked excitedly.

My makeup? Was that a thing now?

"Am I supposed to have someone do my makeup? I was just going to do it myself," I said, bewildered. Having somebody else do my face hadn't even occurred to me.

On Beth's end there was silence.

A full minute passed without sound.

"Hello?" I cried, looking at the still-engaged screen to see if my phone had dropped the call.

"I'm here," Beth replied with some hesitation. "So, you're going to do your *own* makeup?"

Realizing there was something I was missing here, it suddenly occurred to me Beth was trying to tell me my makeup skills sucked. Had I been running around all these years looking like a buffoon?

"Is my makeup that bad? Oh my God, why have you never told me?!" I exclaimed, horrified.

"No, no! Your makeup always looks wonderful," she cried. "It's just…"

Then I was struck by another thought. *She* wanted to do my makeup. Oh, that was a great idea! As with all things, Beth never looked anything but flawless.

"Would *you* like to do my makeup?" I asked, excitedly.

"Oh, heck no!" Beth shouted immediately, sounding like she'd just touched a hot burner. "You need a professional for that!" Then, sounding as though she had caught herself overstepping, she quickly added, "or maybe get it done for your second book. A New York Times bestselling author deserves to be spoiled, you know! And even though it's headshots, you better not be slacking on the shoes. You know my rule!"

"It's a headshot; nobody is going to see my feet!" I laughed. "But now I'm thinking maybe I should get my makeup professionally done...," I said more to myself than into the phone. "Okay, I'll give a call to the place that used to do my lashes. Thanks!"

"Fabulous! Keep me informed!" Beth exclaimed happily as we hung up.

In my phone contacts I found the number for the lash salon I used to frequent back in the day when I used to pamper myself with such things. Since I began working full-time from home, I had dispensed with trivialities as lashes and nails except for when special occasions arose.

My call to the lash salon was answered on the first ring by Crystal, the salon's vivacious owner. She must have had Caller ID because she greeted me by name.

"Hey, Colleen, long time no hear!" Crystal announced.

"Hi, Crystal! Yeah, it's been a while. Listen, I need my makeup done for some headshots for the book I'm writing. Do you do that?"

"Wow, you're writing a book? That's so exciting! Yep, makeup is kind of what makeup artists do," Crystal said, laughing.

"Oh, yeah, I guess so, huh?" I giggled, feeling totally stupid. "Well, when do you have an opening?" I asked, trying to compensate for my foolishness by being accommodating.

"When is your photo shoot?" Crystal countered.

Silence.

Damn. I hadn't yet made the appointment. D'uh!

Not wanting to appear any more idiotic than I had already, I told Crystal I had an urgent call coming in and would have to call her back. I said goodbye as fast as I could and hung up. What a freaking project this was!

Scrolling through my phone's contact list I found the name and number of the photographer Dani and Shawn used for their holiday photos and dialed her. She picked up before I even heard the phone ring.

"Hello?" came a woman's voice from my phone's speaker before I was ready.

"Oh, hi! I'm Colleen Pierce, Dani's mom. I know you've done a lot of her family pictures, but do you do headshot photos? I need one for a book cover."

"Oh, hi, Colleen! Yeah, I just saw Dani and Shawn last week. Yes, I do headshots. Most photographers do," she said with the same laugh and tone as Crystal had used.

Feeling once again like I'd asked the Queen Mother of stupid questions, I quickly scheduled my session and got off the phone while I still had a shred of dignity. Then I called Crystal back to coordinate a makeup appointment. Relieved I was done with all the nonsense, I relaxed. Sadly, my peace only lasted a mere four hours.

Phyllis phoned that evening wanting to know if I could come see her at the spa the following Friday for a facial.

"So, I was thinking that if you took the appointment after Beth, the three of us could have a little girl time. We haven't been able to get together for weeks!" Phyllis proclaimed. True that—we girls had been so busy in recent days I felt like we hadn't seen each other in a year.

"I know; I miss you guys! But I can't next Friday. I have to do a photo shoot to get headshots for the book." I whined.

"Headshots? How exciting!" Phyllis exclaimed with glee. "Who's doing your makeup?"

I rolled my eyes to the ceiling before answering in monotone, "Crystal, the one who used to do my lashes. Have you been talking to Beth?!"

"Beth? No, why? Is Crystal also doing your hair?" Phyllis asked.

"No, I'm doing my hair!" I shouted. "What's wrong with the way I do my hair?"

"Nothing is wrong with your hair! They just usually do both. Have you decided on what you're wearing?"

Silence.

Damn. Here we go again. What was I wearing?

"Ugh. I don't know. What do authors wear?" I asked.

I hadn't a clue what authors typically wore. I'd never noticed. Picking up the book I was currently reading from the end table, *The Weight of Ink* by Rachel Kadish, I turned to the inside of the jacket to look at Rachel's photo. Dressed in a scoop-necked black t-shirt under an unzipped lavender chenille sweater jacket, she stood smiling in front of a lush green hedge looking relaxed and pretty. The chances of me obtaining something similar? Slim to none.

Placing the book back on the end table, I headed down the hallway to my closet to find similar clothing options. Black was out of the question. Though I was a natural blonde and supposed to look good in black, I always felt the contrast was too stark against my white Irish skin and washed me out. Putting Phyllis on speaker, I laid the phone on my dresser while I pulled my best white blouse from its hanger. Holding the blouse against my chest, I looked at my reflection in the full-length mirror. White, too, made me look pale and lifeless.

"Do you have anything in royal blue?" Phyllis's voice blared from my cellphone's speaker. "Blue will be nice with your blonde hair. Definitely go with something bright. Lots of color," Phyllis suggested.

Rejecting the plain white blouse and throwing it onto my bed, I returned to my closet and rifled through every blouse, sweater, top and jacket I had. Nothing seemed right. So, I begged off the call and sloughed out to the kitchen to make dinner. This headshot business was giving me a headache.

The following day my girlfriend Sandy came to visit me for the weekend. I told her about the photo shoot.

"That's so exciting!" she exclaimed with far more enthusiasm than I had. "What are you wearing?"

"I have no earthly idea," I said with disgust. "Wanna go to Ross with me tomorrow?"

"Sure!" Sandy said agreeably. Everybody was way more enthused about this whole ordeal than I was.

The following afternoon, Sandy and I trekked to Ross, and I combed through bushels upon bushels of clothing options. Every fabric and color of blouse, jacket, dress, and sweater adorned the pile in my dressing room until finally, with the room's narrow bench resembling a casbah table after a riotous sale, I settled on a thin knit, open front, amber yellow cardigan over a white and navy color-blocked Ralph Lauren tee. Deeming it the best of the lot, I modeled the ensemble for Sandy, and she approved. At long last, my preparations were done!

The day of the photo shoot was chaotic. Having gotten out of the habit of doing my hair, which had been second nature in the days before I started working from home, the unruly waves took over an hour to style. As a result, I was late for my makeup appointment, arriving sweaty and disheveled.

"There she is!" Crystal cried when I walked through the door. "Come sit down, Miss Author!" Yet another person more enthused about the day than I was.

Wasting no time, Crystal began the transformation of my face, which was quite a production. First, she applied a foundation, which was expertly mixed on the heel of her hand before being stroked on my skin artfully with a painter's brush.

Next, false lashes were applied, after which a short analysis took place Crystal stepped back and contemplated me like an artist studying a blank canvas. She tilted my head this way and that, and I half expected her to close one eye and focus on me over a raised thumb. Finally, after a confident nod, she dove in.

With an impressive array of brushes, varying from small and round-nibbed to flat and wide with bristles like oriental fans, Crystal dabbed purposefully into palettes of eyeshadow and blush. Each compact she opened held a dozen or more quarter-sized divots of pressed pigment, favorites with the metal exposed in the middle, like pie-bald heads. After she would apply a few touches of color, she would stand back and review her work with a furrowed brow. Then she would go back with more of the same color or choose something different, dab, dollop, study, and repeat.

After what felt like an eternity, Crystal's face finally relaxed, and the brushes were set down. Pleased, she spun me around so I could view my image in the mirror. Stunned, I honestly didn't recognize myself at first. Staring back at me was a face that was expertly done, but definitely not the one I was used to seeing. My reflection looked...foreign.

In the deepest reaches of my belly a rebellion began. The still, small voice was screaming that this was not the way I wanted to appear on my book cover. This face in the mirror looked too glamorous and felt like a lie. A betrayal to my authenticity. I thanked Crystal, paid my bill, and rushed home to change into my "author's clothes." At every traffic light or stop sign, I turned my car's oblong rearview mirror toward my face so I could stare at my reflection. Who was that person looking back at me? Trying to ascertain what made my appearance look so unfamiliar, I thought perhaps it was because eyeliner and mascara was missing from my lower lashes. Assuming this omission must be a headshot "thing," I decided not to fix it. Gut check blunder two.

Once home, I decided maybe adding more curl to my upper lashes would compensate for what was lacking on the bottom. I rushed to the bathroom and extracted my eyelash curler from the makeup drawer in my bathroom vanity. I opened the jaws of the curler wide, leaned into the mirror to gently capture the newly glued lashes of one eye in its gaping mouth, but stopped when the curler's rubber gasket fell into the sink.

"Dammit, always at the worst possible time!" I cried, losing my patience. I didn't need this aggravation today.

Eyelash curlers throwing their aging gaskets overboard was not an unusual or unexpected occurrence. As curlers aged the gaskets wore out, which is why most manufacturers included one or two replacement gaskets in the packaging. What the manufacturer fails to include, however, is the key to getting the replacement rubber to fit so it is functional. The replacements never fit. And I have yet to meet a woman who has been successful in making one do so.

Even more frustrating than eyelash curlers' useless replacement gaskets, is that originals die out at the most inopportune moment. For this exact reason, I normally buy two curlers at a time, so as not to get caught in a lurch feeling unfinished and frumpy with uncurled lashes. Like now, moments before I needed to leave for a professional photoshoot.

Unfortunately, the gasketless curler I was holding in my hand was the only one I had. With my new working-from-home frugality, I hadn't seen the need to buy two. Staring at the worn gasket from the only curler I had lying in the sink, thereby rendering the appliance useless, my gut begged me to give up and move on. Regrettably, as character traits go, Frugality and Stubbornness occupy the same cubicle in my personality workspace, serving as each other's backup. So now that I found myself in a Frugality-induced pickle, Stubbornness stepped in to save the day. Gut check blunder number three.

Thrashing through the contents of the drawer I used for spare cosmetics, I hunted down a single, unpackaged replacement gasket, determined to make it work. The small, curved piece of white rubber had been in the drawer so long it was dusted with taupe eyeshadow residue. Stubbornness concluded that the mere fact I had retained the piece of rubber was a sign that today would be the day the replacement process would go off without a hitch. Easy as changing a light bulb. Wrong!

Grabbing the gasketless curler by the mouth and sliding the jaws open wide, I stuffed one end of the little dusty strip into the lower jaw's groove, pushing the rubber as close to the slide bar as possible. My intention was to work the piece all the way down the canal from one end to the other. This was a good plan had the gasket not been too long, leaving a tail hanging over the end. To remedy this, I jammed the rubber into the groove the best I could, then cut off the excess. Success! Proud of myself, I lifted the curler to my lashes, squeezed the handles together, and plop…the replacement rubber gasket fell out into the sink beside the other one.

"Gimme a break!" I shouted, tossing the curler handle into the sink beside the two gaskets before stomping out to the kitchen to fetch the Super Glue. Stubbornness was large and in charge.

At this point I should probably divulge that my relationship with Super Glue is much the same as my relationship with candles. With the exception of being able to stick my fingers together, things never turn out well. Today in the bathroom would prove no different. In an attempt to glue either gasket into the channel of the curler at the behest of Stubbornness, I managed to glue one to my left thumb, a Kleenex to the side of the sink, and the curler's metal slide permanently in the open position, rendering it forever unusable. I also somehow broke the cap to the tube of Super Glue, leaving me to balance the vial upright against the soap dish, where it dried up and had to be thrown out. A saving grace in the long run. Turns out, Stubbornness was right. Replacing the rubber strip was exactly like changing a light bulb–the one I changed in Texas during my very important business trip. No blood, but all the aggravation.

Frustrated, I emerged from the bathroom with uncurled lashes, dressed in a frenzy, and raced to my photo shoot, now very late. And sure enough, when the photos came back, I hated them.

To bystanders the headshots were fine, pretty even, and all my friends loved them. But for me, all I could see in every shot was that the face didn't look like me. The same awkward, uncomfortable emotions I'd felt the day of the shoot, with my unadorned lower lids and unsatisfactory curled lashes, seemed to leap off the page. Feeling I was obligated to use them, especially after all the effort and fuss, I identified the headshot I disliked least before forwarding the whole batch to Bianca.

"I love them!" Bianca cried. She had only ever met me through Zoom, where I was always clad in my writer's uniform of worn t-shirt and sweats, hair in a ponytail, with no makeup. Compared to that, of course the photos looked great.

"Yeah, thanks," I replied unenthusiastically.

"Oh, no. What's wrong?"

"It just doesn't look like me," I griped. "It's not how I envisioned my readers seeing me. But whatever. I'll get over it."

"No, no, you need to love the pic. I think the photos are beautiful, but I want you to think so, too, otherwise every time you see the jacket, you will be bothered. Can you ask for a reshoot?" Bianca asked.

"Yeah, no. I'm not going through that again and I'd be too embarrassed to ask. It's okay."

"Well, please just think on it. We have time," Bianca added consolingly. I really adored this woman. She not only understood my craft, editing in a way that never interfered with my writing style or voice, but she understood the photo's importance to my vision.

I contemplated scheduling a reshoot but, in the end, even Stubbornness couldn't justify the ask. I had brought this pain onto myself by not speaking up and trusting my intuition. Looking over each picture for the twentieth time, I suddenly remembered my friend Jill having mentioned to me her daughter did photography on the side. I telephoned her for details.

"Hey, Jill. Does your daughter do headshots?"

Tag the Present

"Hi, Colleen! Umm, yeah, she's a photographer. They take pictures of people," Jill replied, chuckling in that now familiar, discernible tone.

Rolling my eyes at my continued blunder, I asked shyly, "Do you think she'd have time to schedule me a shoot? Nothing fancy. Just a quick shot or two." I held my breath while I waited for the answer.

"Absolutely! I'll contact Lauren right now and have her call you." she said. I could always count on Jill to be as good as her word.

"Awesome! Thank you!" Finally, I, too, was excited about headshots.

By the end of the week, I had a session booked with Jill's daughter, Lauren. After I explained my situation, she requested I meet her in the park in the morning before the day became too hot, do my own makeup, wear my hair as I typically would, and put on something comfortable. All things that would make me feel like myself. She got me.

On the day of the retake shoot with Lauren, the gods, my gut, and the cosmos smiled. The weather, which had threatened rain, turned out to be glorious, mid 70s, with partly sunny skies supplying ideal lighting. My hair styled with little effort, and my makeup looked like it typically would on any given day I was meeting friends. I had purchased a new eyelash curler to ensure there would be no gasket issues, and the little appliance worked like a dream. As Lauren began to snap pictures, a light breeze blew my hair into its usual state of imperfection, and the result was a picture that I love. It captures me slightly windblown (my natural state), with bottom eyeliner and mascara (my usual look), wearing a thrifted secondhand shirt (in blue for Phyllis), and sporting my comfy but impeccably clean Converse (name brand for

Beth). My gut rejoiced and the Universe gave me a high-five sixty years in the making, rewarding me with a perfect author headshot.

Phyllis and Beth were thrilled when I reported with glee that the shoot had gone well and fully agreed when we got the proofs that the retake picture looked much more like my authentic self than the more glamorous ones of the original shoot. When we were finally able to get together for a spa day, Phyllis and Beth presented me with a gift bag that contained a new Revlon eyelash curler. The tag read:

> *TO: The Devil might wear Prada, but frugal authors wear Goodwill*
>
> *FROM: Here's something new and name-brand, for crying out loud!*

I was tickled to death with their thoughtfulness and spectacular *To-From*, which had me howling with laughter. I loved my girlies!

When I got home after lunch, I opened the curler box, threw out the enclosed replacement rubber gasket, and slid open the vanity drawer that housed my makeup spares. Reorganizing packages and jars to make room for the new curler, I spied the old, gasketless one that I thought I had thrown out. When I tried to grab it, I found it was super glued to the drawer's side wall. The rubber replacement gasket was cemented to its back.

****

A frugality practice I have found more successful than trying to replace eyelash curler rubber is to delay annual medical and dental appointments until after I have fulfilled my insurance deductible. Further, if I can book several of these routine appointments back-to-back on the same day, I only have to take a single day off from work to wipe them all out in one fell swoop.

This year, thanks to twelve months of extraordinarily good health, my deductible wasn't fulfilled until December. Regardless, I still managed to fit in a mammogram, a dental cleaning, and an annual physical all into one day before the end of the year. By 2 PM on the 8th of December I was done for another year and skipped out to my car a happy camper.

As I got settled behind the wheel to go home, I saw I had a missed call from Sean. He had also left me a text, which I clicked on to read before I pulled out of the lot:

Did you hear that Geo passed away?

I stared at the words and couldn't breathe.

The good vibes I had felt just seconds before vaporized into thin air and were gone. Switching immediately into denial, I was certain my brother had made a typo. Or had a different friend also named Geo. Sean's text couldn't be referring to *my* Geo, The *His Hair Was Perfect* Geo. Geo wasn't sick. I had just spoken to him the previous week and he had sounded fine.

Irritated, I phoned Sean to see what was going on. He picked up immediately.

"Did you get my text?" Sean asked without bothering to say hello.

"Yes, but who was it that passed away? You had me scared thinking it was Geo!" I scolded.

"It *was* Geo. Can you believe it? I just did his podcast on Thursday!" Sean exclaimed.

Again, came the vacuum in my lungs. I had begun pulling out of the doctor's parking lot but pulled back into a spot to gather myself.

Sean confirmed that there had been no warning for Geo's death, so I hadn't been wrong about that. He wasn't ill that anyone knew, and there hadn't been anything to outwardly indicate the sucker punch that was coming. Geo had suffered a massive heart attack, the one they called The Widow Maker. The Widow Maker had taken down my stepfather Ron nearly thirty years ago in exactly the same way, making my mother a widow. Boom. Gone in a split second.

Over the next few days, I gleaned whatever information I could from friends and acquaintances about the circumstances of Geo's death. As it turns out, there wasn't much to learn. Private as he was, Geo's exact time of passing was undetermined. He had last been seen in the gym on Saturday, and then on Tuesday a concerned neighbor had called the police because Geo's garage door had been sitting open for days. When the police arrived, they found Geo in his favorite chair long gone. I wasn't quite sure how I felt about that. On one hand I was glad his passing was quick, but on the other hand I was heartbroken he had died alone.

What did offer me solace about Geo's passing was that like a last gift, I had gotten to chat with him on the phone the Wednesday before he died. He had called me asking for Sean's number, hoping Sean would fill a gap on his podcast with some local police chat. Fortunately for them both, that would happen. Sean would be the guest on Geo's last recording, and they would get a chance for one last friendly jaw when the interview was over.

The series of events also afforded me one final conversation with my dear friend to hold in my heart like a rare jewel. During our time on the phone when Geo had called for Sean's number, we had belly-laughed over my most recent catastrophes, shared what was currently happening in our lives, and Geo had gotten to hear me say, "*Love ya!*" as I always did, one last time before we hung up. In turn, I had gotten to hear Geo say, "*Love you, too, sweetheart!*" as he always did, in his deep, rich, radio voice. We had gone out on a high. He'd like that. I certainly did.

On the evening of the day I got the shocking news of Geo's death, I sat quietly for hours on the floor of my living room, accompanied only by the lights of my Christmas tree and a bottle of cabernet. There, in the warm glow of the tree's lights, I contemplated my sweet friend, whom I had assumed would always be there. I tried to force myself to accept the fact that he was gone, but I just couldn't wrap my head around the loss. Nor my heart. It was too painful.

I chose instead to replay the times we had spent together as roommates in the beautiful condo on the river. Funny memories lined up in a queue as I sat there by the tree, and I entertained each one for as long as it wanted to visit. I thought about the time we had smoked an ancient joint Geo had found in one of his boxes while unpacking. Afterward we were stricken with a wicked case of the munchies, so we had ordered a pizza but were both too high to answer the door when it came. We turned off all the lights and hid in the dark, giggling, then regretted not having the pizza, so we ordered one from a different pizzeria and taped the money to the front door so we wouldn't chicken out when it was delivered. We wolfed down the pie laughing till we cried, then followed it with a half-gallon of vanilla ice cream for dessert, feeling like overstuffed puppies when we were done. Ridiculous.

I thought about the time Geo came home from golfing to find me scrubbing the floors on my hands and knees while absentmindedly singing "A Dream Is a Wish Your Heart Makes" from Disney's *Cinderella*. He found it delightfully ironic that I had chosen to sing that particular song while scrubbing the floor on my hands and knees Cinderella-style. When I told him I wasn't even aware I was singing, he said he had often caught me humming that same tune when I appeared content. After our conversation, sure enough, I caught myself humming or singing it dozens upon dozens of times, always when I was happy, and when he noticed he would say with a smile, "Cinderella, are we happy today?". He called it my happiness litmus test.

As I sat staring unseeingly at the lights on my tree, one of the tiniest ornaments suddenly vied for my attention. The bauble was a wee Radio Flyer sled with my name painted on the slats. Geo had given it to me during our first Christmas together, or, more accurately, the sled had appeared out of nowhere on our Christmas tree. The memory had me laughing through tears because the mere fact that we even had a tree had been a miracle unto itself. Geo had grumbled a litany of humbugs about getting a real tree weeks and weeks in advance of Christmas, every day grousing a different complaint, each one more amusing than the last.

"You're not messing up my new Camry with all that mess! Uh-uh, no way."

"Not to mention the fire hazard. We all know your tendency to start a fire!"

"And needles everywhere! For months! Years!"

"And what are we supposed to use for lights? Ornaments? Garland? I don't want some hokey-pokey, hodge-podge, sorry-looking eyesore cluttering up our living room!"

"And where are we gonna put it?! Oh, hell no. Nope. Not havin' it!"

And then as soon as the first tree lot opened, we got a tree. And though he'd be loath to admit it, Geo loved that damn tree. I had hardly plugged in the first strand of lights to see if all the bulbs were lit before I was ousted from my position so he could take over. He painstakingly placed every bulb into position on every branch to make sure they were balanced to his satisfaction, bitching and kvetching through the whole process. When he was done, he plopped onto the couch to watch golf. I hummed Christmas carols between renditions of *Cinderella* as I cheerfully hung the ornaments and trimmings, while he tried not to watch and acted disinterested. He was anything but, and we both knew it. I would catch him sneaking glances out of the corner of his eye and he'd reach over slyly to make adjustments whenever he thought I wasn't looking.

Over the next couple weeks leading up to Christmas, ornaments began mysteriously appearing on the tree, among them the little sled with my name on it, and decorations sprang up in every corner of the condo. I even came home from work one day to find my Packer ornament displaced by a gawdawful Michigan bobble in maize and blue. Geo was a proud University of Michigan graduate. I promptly restored my Packer ornament to its rightful place and buried his Michigan atrocity way in the back, signaling war. In the ensuing days, those two ornaments visited every branch, nook, and cranny of that tree. It was such good-hearted fun.

When that memory left, I refilled my wine glass and found myself thankful it was Christmastime, with its homey smells, soft lights, and creature comforts. I needed all of those things after having received the heart-wrenching news about my beloved G. When my eyes fell on the gifts below the tree with their quirky, ridiculous tags, it dawned on me that I had a treasure stashed away in my guest bedroom closet. I ran down the hall to find it: a small, tattered box that I could never seem to throw away. Now I knew why. Holding the package tightly to my chest, I carried it out to the living room, and sat down with it on the floor. The box still wore a Christmas label that read:

TO: Grasshopp'ah

FROM: Sensei

It had been my Christmas gift from Geo the year we lived together in the condo. Then, as now, the box contained only tissue and a printed poem on a sheet of holiday paper. When I felt ready, I opened the flaps of the aging box, lifted out the single page framed in holly, carefully unfolded it, and slowly read the scripted message:

It's not quite a shoebox

But the closest I could find,

And shoes won't fit in it,

But this note does just fine.

We will head to the sports store

Whichever you choose,

To buy you new foot gear,

Those eight-and-a-half size shoes.

'Cause that's what you wanted

But no one would buy,

So, I'm taking you shopping,

In the Camry we'll fly.

We can go out next weekend

Or on a weekday, you pick,
We'll get the cool sneakers,
The ones the kids say are sick.
Merry Christmas to you!
~ Geo

I smiled as the tears streamed down my cheeks remembering how touched I had felt when I had opened the box that year. I had told everyone that the only gift I wanted for Christmas was new gym shoes, because in coaching me from a lumpy couch potato into a lean, mean, iron-pumping machine, Geo had totally worn out my sneakers. Yet, nobody had gotten me new sneaks.

When I returned home from my family gift exchange without any new shoes, I was sure there wasn't any hope of outfitting my poor, tired fitness feet that year. The only gift I had left to open was Geo's, and he openly admitted he didn't listen to 99.9% of my babble. So, the chances of getting new sneakers from Geo? Not happening. I was sure of it.

I was even more convinced I had no sneakers to open when Geo presented me with a package that didn't even remotely resemble a shoe box. The parcel was small and flat, 11 x 6 x 4", not big enough to accommodate one shoe, much less two. Teasing him, I had held the wrapped box up to one of my feet before opening it and razzed him about purchasing the wrong size. He had scolded me to never judge a book by its cover. And that's when I opened the box and found the poem.

We did take his Camry to Sports Authority the weekend after that Christmas. There, I picked out a bright pink pair of Nike's that I subsequently wore down to the treads. How I had loved those pink shoes and the sentimentality that came with them. Because they were so dear to me, I had worn them well past their prime and never discarded the box that held their poem.

Several years later, when Geo and I met for lunch to touch base as we did every so often, I was once again bellyaching about needing new workout shoes.

"Don't tell me you're still in those awful pink things," Geo had cried, disgusted.

"Hell, yes! In fact, I still have their box and poem," I had told him proudly, puffing out my chest. "And don't call them awful; you'll hurt their feelings."

"Geez, throw them out and I'll buy you new ones before you go lame," I remembered him saying with a laugh. "And I'll have you know I kept your thank you poem, too. So there!" he had added, playfully.

Thinking back to that conversation, I found the thank you poem I had written to him in my computer's archive and printed out a copy to put in the keepsake box next to his letter. It reads:

> *TO: He who actually listens to my psycho babble*
>
> *FROM: Did you catch the part about my need for a new car?*
>
> *There weren't shoes in the box,*
> *But it was even better,*
> *For I will treasure for all my days,*
> *My sneakers in a letter.*

It touches my chick heart,
All the little things you do,
From spoiling me with dinners,
To spot cleaning the loo.
So, I will take a minute,
To find some time to say,
You are so sweet, my handsome friend,
You made my holiday!
~Love ya! C

When all my tears were done and I could cry no more, I closed the sneaker box and put it under the tree until I cleaned up after the holidays. There would be no Christmas card from Geo, one of the very few I still received. Nor would I return him one, one of the few I still sent. The thought stung and made me ever more thankful to have this letter and the box.

I'm healing, but it has been a very slow process. I cannot put my finger on why Geo's loss hit me so hard, but it has. Perhaps because Geo was my contemporary, his death has caused me to re-evaluate my own mortality, and that alone has been extraordinarily daunting. Or perhaps because we never became a couple, Geo may subconsciously be my fish that got away. Or maybe it has something to do with the way he called me sweetheart in that tone that always left me feeling loved and adored, knowing that now I will hear it only as a memory. But whatever it was, Geo's loss has been immense. As big as the man himself with his always perfect hair.

****

Two days before Christmas, still feeling blue about Geo's death, a UPS driver pounded on my door to signal he'd left a package. I plodded out to the front porch by way of the carport expecting to see a box from Amazon, finding instead a small parcel wrapped in brown paper from Quincy, Massachusetts. It was my Christmas present from Brian, Pamie and their daughter Beth-Anne.

I brought the package into the house and before slicing through the tape, I gave Pamie a call.

"I just got your package! Can I open it now, or do I have to save it?" I asked Pam, sounding like a kid on Christmas Eve.

Though I normally would have put the box under the tree untouched until Christmas morning, my spirits really needed a lift. Pamie didn't even hesitate, all for allowing me to open the present early, knowing I'd been in a funk and why. More like sisters than distant relatives, we told each other everything.

"Of course, you can open it now! But you need to promise me you'll call me later when Beth-Anne and Brian get home," she agreed, the lilt and tone of her voice telling me the call would also be for dishing out accolades. I suspected she was either pleased with her *To-From*, pleased with her gift selection, or pleased with both.

Now stricken with curiosity, I grabbed the box cutter from my junk drawer as soon as I said goodbye and sat down with the package next to my Christmas tree on the living room rug. I made one long cut through the brown packaging tape and pulled up the four thick flaps. Beneath several sheets of folded white tissue, I found two gifts, both wrapped in holiday paper, oddly shaped, numbered, and wearing tags. It had taken several years for me to bring Pamie around to creating silly gift tags (she insisted for the longest time she wasn't any good at it), but once I'd convinced her to try, she had seen the light and been making them like a savage. I was so proud of her!

Taking up the gift labeled as #1, I saw the tag had too much writing to be boring and generic. Immediately excited, I read the *To-From*:

> TO: Peach Bikini
>
> FROM: The Khaki Shorts Trio

A small snorty giggle escaped after I finished, and I gave Pamie props for the cute, witty tag. As much as I lovingly teased Pam, Brian, and Beth-Anne about their Florida visitors' uniform of khaki shorts and plain t-shirts, they ribbed me about the peach bikini I was wearing when I first met them in 1987. The bikini's top had been strapless, and I had fallen out of it at the beach when Rick had jokingly thrown a twig on my back while I was lying on my stomach sunning. I thought the twig was a wasp and had come up flailing, causing my bikini top to plummet down to my waist, unintentionally exposing myself to nearby beach goers and my new relatives. The flash had made Brian's entire millennium, never to be forgotten.

Tearing the gift wrap off the oddly shaped package donning the funny tag, I found a can of Spam and a package of alfredo pasta. And not just any alfredo pasta – the exact brand Brian and Pamie brought down from Boston every single year to make for our annual dinner. Any Florida grocery store stocked the identical one, but Brian and Pamie were quintessential creatures of habit. The gift was so authentically them, it tickled me, and made me shake my head and giggle.

Setting the Spam and package of alfredo on the skirt beneath the tree, I drew out the second gift, labeled #2, and read the tag.

To: Sneaky Southern Sister

From: Tired of freezing my tail off

I gently squeezed the contents of the present through the wrapping to venture a guess at what was inside, but I drew a blank. Sneaky Southern Sister? I didn't know what that meant.

Unable to stand the suspense, I tore open the gift in the manner of a toddler. A bright red rubber lobster, about the size of my foot, wearing a green and yellow crocheted sweater fell into my lap and scared the beejeebus out of me.

"Orville!" I shouted into the evergreen scented air. "Why do you always have to do me like that?"

Laughing, I turned the creature around in my hand as I checked out his attire. This was some getup he had acquired. One never knew what ole' Orv would get into. Or, where.

Orville, the red rubber lobster, or a version of him, had been in my family since the early 1960's. When I was about three years old, Mom, Dad and I went on a family trip to visit my dad's folks Thelma and Joe in Pompano Beach, Florida. For a joke, Thelma had planted the original Orville, who was made of a wobbly gel that always felt wet, between the sheets of the guest bed and waited with delight for my parents to encounter him.

Having driven in our green Impala straight through from Wisconsin to Florida, a journey that took about 26 hours, Mom and Dad were exhausted when we arrived. While Dad chatted with his folks and I entertained them, Mom went off to take a quick nap. She gratefully crawled between the sheets of my grandparent's guest bed, only to have her bare foot encounter the cool, slippery rubber of Orville's slimy tail. Grandma Thelma's sinister plan had come to fruition.

At the first touch of a toe on Orville, Mom went postal, screaming and bolting out of the bed, hollering for my dad as she stood shivering in the corner. Dad came running, whipped back the covers, and came up with Orville in all his wobbly glory.

Hearing the commotion, Thelma and Joe fell out laughing in the living room, waiting for Mom and Dad to come out and give them kudos for pulling off the prank. Instead, not wanting to give my grandmother the satisfaction, Mom and Dad stayed quiet on the subject, then snuck Orville into Thelma's bed while she was doing dishes after dinner. Shortly after retiring for the evening, Mom and Dad lay in the guest bed snickering like six-year-olds until they heard Grandma Thelma's blood-curdling scream. Revenge was a dish best served up slimy.

Turnabout remained fair play throughout the visit. Thelma and Joe stayed mum about their encounter, then snuck Orville into Dad's suitcase and landed him in Wisconsin. From there a new tradition was born. Orville bounced back and forth between the two households for decades until Sean and I were old enough to survive the trauma of finding him in our beds, luggage, drawers, cars, packages, and handbags. As we branched out across the nation, old Orville saw more of the country than I did and attended three colleges. He majored in covert activities and surprise attacks.

To this day nobody ever owns up to getting punked by ole' Orv, so none of us is ever sure who's got him. If he gets wounded in action, the custodial party is responsible for bandaging him up or providing a suitable replacement when the epoxy will no longer hold.

I began the Orville game with Brian, Pamie and Beth-Anne after they witnessed me go ballistic over a rubber lobster in a gift shop while they were down here one year. I spent the evening telling them of Orville's most infamous capers, like when notorious Orville III was waiting for me in the shower the summer of 2010, while I was on vacation in Wisconsin visiting my dad. I went to take a shower one morning, whipped back the shower curtain, and was met with two little beady lobster eyes. I screamed bloody murder and peed myself, cursing like a sailor.

Orville III was the replacement for Orville II, who came up missing after the Great Gas Cap Caper of 1998. That was a combined effort. During a Florida visit from my dad and stepmother that year, Rick and I found Orville II between our bedsheets and my brother and sister-in-law found him in the crisper drawer of their refrigerator, so the four of us conspired to stuff him around the gas cap of Dad and Jo's SUV before they headed back to Wisconsin. When the two stopped in Georgia to gas up, Orville II sprung from the gas compartment like he was spring-loaded. A little birdie told us it was quite hilarious. Oh, to have been a fly. What happened to him after that remains a mystery.

As for Brian, Pamie, and Beth-Anne's Orville, looking quite stylish in his wee crocheted Green Bay sweater, he will need to wait in my gift drawer until the release of this book. I plan to stash him in a box with a first edition signed copy and ship him back to Beantown. By then they all will have forgotten who possesses him. Shhhhh, no tattling. This will be our little secret!

****

And just like that, New Year's Eve is here, Chariot Year has come to a close, and I have survived to tell its stories.

For the annual fondue celebration at Beth and Sinjin's tonight, I purchased raspberries, marshmallows, and dried apricots to be dipped in Beth's luscious chocolate fondue, for which Phyllis was commissioned to make her famous pound cake. That was all Beth and Sinjin required of us this year, saying they would supply everything else. Phyllis and I are spoiled. There will be filet mignon for cooking on the hibachi, cheese fondue with a myriad of veggies, and their secret melted chocolate recipe laced with top-shelf rum. All will be shared over roars of laughter and the love of good friends. It is always a wonderful way to ring in the new year. Surrounding yourself with good people is the key to a happy life.

After making my rounds to family and friends, I bolted home to dress. New Year's Eve Fondue Night was the one occasion where I didn't mind going all out. This year I had chosen crisply creased black dress pants with a long-sleeved lightweight knit black top under the knee-length, silver sequin encrusted jacket I wore to Dani and Shawn's wedding. And, of course, I wore my matching silver sparkle pumps, just for Beth.

Arriving at Beth and Sinjin's before Phyllis, I was greeted at the wooden double doors of their beautiful home by Sinjin, looking like he stepped off the pages of a workout magazine. He enveloped me in a massive hug, the sleeves of his green t-shirt threatening to rip trying to contain his burgeoning biceps. Hearing our commotion, Beth came out of the kitchen to join us in the foyer, cute as a button in a white, sleeveless seersucker dress, her stylish, fringed sandals barely touching the ground under the feather weight of her petite frame.

"Welcome!" Beth exclaimed, glowing, as always. If she had been fussing all day, it surely didn't show.

The dining room table in the room beyond looked stunning, set with a gorgeous vase of orchids and birds of paradise from Sinjin's garden, pressed antique white embroidered napkins with matching placemats, sparkling crystal wine glasses, and gleaming white porcelain china. Beth was the master of effortless presentation.

"So glad you didn't fuss," I chided, giving my little friend a big hug.

Beth laughed and waved off the compliment with the flick of a bedazzled hand.

"Did you see what we did for you?" she asked, giving Sinjin a conspiratorial wink.

Following their gaze, I walked around the huge spray of fresh flowers in the foyer to see what they were talking about. There, on the dining room table, they had placed miniature orange cones all around my place setting.

"For when you use the hibachi," laughed Sinjin. "We want to live to see the new year!"

I doubled over with laughter while they fist-bumped each other with delight. Just then Phyllis came through the door and asked what she had missed. Sinjin hugged her with one arm and pointed to the cones on the table with his free hand. Phyllis was so tickled she snorted.

After that, it was on. Phyllis and I kicked off our shoes, unpacked our goodies, and we all got settled with a glass of wine. Chattering away, we dined on our friends' indescribably delicious offerings. We cooked our filet chunks on the hibachi and topped them with butter-sauteed shitake mushrooms marinaded in a hint of thyme and lemon. In a 3-cheese fondue we dipped pieces of green apple, broccoli, cauliflower, pears, and crusty French bread. After a break to let our bellies rest, the chocolate was brought out, and we nibbled sweets until we thought we would bust. It was glorious!

For hours we noshed and laughed, and chided, and joked, and guffawed until our sides hurt. Then we cleared away the dishes and Phyllis pulled out "The Book". The time had come to figure out what the stars predicted for the upcoming year.

"Who wants to go first?" Phyllis cried, looking right at me.

"Why are you looking at me?" I laughed.

"Because you always want to be first!" Phyllis cried in unison with Sinjin, causing us all to crack up.

It was true. I did always want to be first.

"Okay, so when is your birthday again?" Phyllis asked over the top of her glasses. If she ever remembered the date and broke this tradition, I think we'd all be devastated.

Giving her my birthdate in numbers, Phyllis scratched them on a fancy pad of delicate paper Beth had placed at her setting in preparation for the event. The paper was rimmed with flowers that matched the table décor. I would have expected nothing less.

When Phyllis was done with her computation, she looked up from her calculations and declared, "Eight! Eight is the Strength card. You're going to have a Strength Year!"

The rest of us gasped and looked at one another with wide eyes and dramatic expressions.

"Awesome!" I cried. "What's a Strength Year?" This was my annual response and yet another of our timeless traditions.

While Phyllis flipped to the table of contents in her signed copy of *Tarot Constellations; patterns of personal destiny* by Mary K. Greer, a.k.a. "The Book", I grew a little terrified of what might come next. Would I be receiving strength or needing it? Would the year be fraught with turmoil, or would the Universe cut me a break? Strength could be good or bad. It had better be good!

"Found it!" Phyllis cried, as we all sat silent and waiting on the edges of our seats. "Oh, boy, wait until you hear this!"

Acknowledgements

First and foremost, I want to express my heartfelt thanks to my readers. In a world where there are few things more valuable than time, I am touched and humbled that you chose to spend so many precious moments with me. In return, I hope I have brought a smile, triggered a fun memory, inspired a conversation, or even motivated you to start a *To-From* tradition of your own. Mimicry is the greatest form of flattery. Flatter away!

As I hope it translated, storytelling through gift tagging has provided a way for me to grow and prosper through life's speed bumps by focusing on humor. The focus group that reviewed my manuscript felt I used comedy as a protective shield, which is for the most part true; however, I don't wish that to be wrongly interpreted. Humor is not my deflector; humor is my healer. I hit rock bottom as much as anyone else, succumbing to sobs of self-pity, but when the waterworks subside, I have learned to look for the tiniest thing funny in the situation, be it only the obnoxious snort of my own sob, for that can be enough to help me breathe and find strength to move forward. Laughter through tears can be staggeringly powerful.

Speaking of tears and gnashing of teeth, I need to give a shout out to some wonderful folks who have supported me through this amazing, demanding adventure and made this publication happen:

Bianca Williams-Griffin, my writing coach extraordinaire, you helped my dream come true. Thanks for the pep talks, the insight, the honesty, the professionalism, and the hundreds of thousands of things you did to help me birth this project. You have been a blessing to me and an inspiration. I hope I have done you proud. WE DID IT!

Unity Ministry Book Club of Wauwatosa, your generous comments and unique perspectives were invaluable in my development. I am a better writer because of you! The time and thoughtful consideration to my writing was impactful and I am unspeakably honored to have had you for my first read. THANK YOU!

Marty and Barbara, thanks for holding my hair out of the soup of life. You are beautiful treasures, forever embedded in my heart. I love you both.

Incredible, fabulous friends and family, how lucky I am for having you with me on this fantastical journey! Thank you for generously allowing me to share our stories and adventures. No wonder I love you all so fiercely!

In conclusion, a non-conclusion, this book did nothing to solve my 34 dilemma. As I write this last page, I am on a flight to North Carolina that just landed, and the captain announced that the current time is 7:34 AM. Of course, it is—Angel 34 is still everywhere, all the time, in all its forms. So, as you may have already guessed, in compliance with the pesky, unrelenting Angel 34, I am going to give this book thing another try for my Strength Year. Heaven knows what we're in for but come along if you dare while I venture forth into *"Tag the Present: My Strength Year"*!

www.ingramcontent.com/pod-product-compliance
Lightning Source LLC
Chambersburg PA
CBHW050102170426
43198CB00014B/2433